全国职业技能英语系列教材

餐饮英语

English for Food and Beverages

主　编　赵　丽

副主编　刘爱服　杨　昆

编　者　国　伟　胡嫣茹　梁宝恒

北京大学出版社
PEKING UNIVERSITY PRESS

图书在版编目(CIP)数据

餐饮英语/赵丽主编. —北京:北京大学出版社,2009.6
(全国职业技能英语系列教材)
ISBN 978-7-301-13740-6

Ⅰ. 餐… Ⅱ. 赵… Ⅲ. 饮食业－英语－高等学校:技术学校－教材 Ⅳ. H31

中国版本图书馆CIP数据核字(2008)第 062723 号

书　　　　名:	餐饮英语
著作责任者:	赵　丽　主编
责 任 编 辑:	刘　爽
标 准 书 号:	ISBN 978-7-301-13740-6/H·1982
出 版 发 行:	北京大学出版社
地　　　　址:	北京市海淀区成府路205号　100871
网　　　　址:	http://www.pup.cn
编辑部邮箱:	pupwaiwen@pup.cn
总编室邮箱:	zpup@pup.cn
电　　　　话:	邮购部 62752015　发行部 62750672　编辑部 62759634　出版部 62754962
印 刷 者:	三河市博文印刷有限公司
经 销 者:	新华书店
	787毫米×1092毫米　16开本　19印张　400千字
	2009年6月第1版　2023年8月第5次印刷
定　　　　价:	55.00元(配有光盘)

未经许可,不得以任何方式复制或抄袭本书之部分或全部内容。
版权所有,侵权必究
举报电话:(010)62752024　电子邮箱:fd@pup.pku.edu.cn

总 序

我国高职高专教育的春天来到了。随着国家对高职高专教育重视程度的加深,职业技能教材体系的建设成为了当务之急。高职高专过去沿用和压缩大学本科教材的时代一去不复返了。

语言学家 Harmer 指出:"如果我们希望学生学到的语言是在真实生活中能够使用的语言,那么在教材编写中接受技能和产出技能的培养也应该像在生活中那样有机地结合在一起。"

教改的关键在教师,教师的关键在教材,教材的关键在理念。我们依据《高职高专教育英语课程教学基本要求》的精神和编者做了大量调查,秉承"实用为主,够用为度,学以致用,触类旁通"的原则,历经两年艰辛,为高职高专学生编写了这套专业技能课和实训课的英语教材。

本套教材的内容贴近工作岗位,突出岗位情景英语,是一套职场英语教材,具有很强的实用性、仿真性、职业性,其特色体现在以下几个方面:

1. 开放性

   本套教材在坚持编写理念、原则及体例的前提下,不断增加新的行业或岗位技能英语分册作为教材的延续。

2. 国际性

   本套教材以国内自编为主,以国外引进为辅,取长补短,浑然一体。目前已从德国引进了某些行业的技能英语教材,还将从德国或他国引进优秀教材经过本土化后奉献给广大师生。

3. 职业性

   本套教材是由高校教师与行业专家针对具体工作岗位、情景过程共同设计编写的,同时注重与行业资格证书相结合。

4. 任务性

   基于完成某岗位工作任务而需要的英语知识和技能是本套教材的由来与初衷。因此,各分册均以任务型练习为主。

5. 实用性

本教材注重基础词汇的复习和专业词汇的补充。适合于在校最后一学期的英语教学，着重培养和训练学生初步具有与其日后职业生涯所必需的英语交际能力。

本教材在编写过程中，参考和引用了国内外作者的相关资料，得到了北京大学出版社外语编辑部的倾力奉献，在此，一并向他们表示敬意和感谢。由于本套教材是一种创新和尝试，书中瑕疵必定不少，敬请指正。

丁国声

教育部高职高专英语类专业教学指导委员会委员

河北省高校外语教学研究会副会长

河北外国语职业学院院长

2008年6月

前　言

目前，我国高等职业教育发展迅速，已进入了优质教育和技能型人才培养模式创新阶段。以工作体系为导向，"实用为主，够用为度"，反映了社会对技能型人才的需求，体现了高等职业教育的特征。

高等职业教育从本质上讲就是就业教育。随着行业对从业人员英语应用能力要求的不断提高，高等职业院校的专业英语教育应紧密结合行业的实际，强调英语实际应用的能力，使学习者能将所学到的知识应用到行业中去，培养社会所需求的有用人才。

为了适应上述需要，我们编写了《餐饮英语》一书，该教材符合高等职业教育办学规律，以先进的教学理念为指导，以技能培养为本位，以就业为导向，遵循专业英语的教学规律，紧密结合行业的实际，引导学习者全面进入餐饮服务行业领域，把语言教学和职业教育融为一体，把英语技能的培养与餐饮服务培训相结合，突显了高等职业教育的特点，体现了学以致用的教学原则。

《餐饮英语》一书，按照高等职业教育英语教学的性质和目标要求，以餐饮行业岗位为背景，围绕餐饮服务工作任务设计教学内容，具有鲜明的针对性。本教材内容全面、新颖独特、实用性强，情景设置与餐饮服务人员的实际工作密切相关，涵盖了餐饮服务的各个环节，突出了餐饮行业的实际操作的特点。本教材遵循功能语言学的教学原理，采用任务型教学模式，注重语言技能与职业知识技能的整合，加大了语言的输出量，体现了"在做中学"的教学理念。本教材适用于餐饮管理专业学生、英语专业学生及有意于从事餐饮行业工作的有识之士。

《餐饮英语》共分 10 个单元，每个单元由 Part A 和 Part B 两部分构成，每个部分围绕一个主题展开，以贴近餐饮服务流程的内容为主线，创设真实的交流情景，以活泼有趣、形式多样、激发创造力的教学活动，为学习者提供了最大限度的交流实践机会，使学习者有充分的时间运用所学的专业英语进行交际。每部分由 Start You Off; Focus on Language; Summarize Key Expressions; Give It a Try 和 Do Extension Activities 五项内容组成。教学重点清晰明确，易于教学，内容组织科学合理，循序渐进，每项内容后均配有相关的练习，并配有详实的答案供学习和教学参考。本教材的编写和设计强调实践性，培养学生自主学习的能力。学生的任务是主动地、创造性地参与学习过程，引导学生发挥主体作用，通过各种课堂活动，运用自己掌握的知识和交际能力，主动地与他人交流所学习的语言，从而达到学以致用的目的。

《餐饮英语》由北京联合大学旅游学院赵丽教授担任主编，刘爱服、杨昆为副主编。参加编写的人员还有国伟、胡嫣茹、梁宝恒。赵丽负责教材内容、结构编排设计、全书统稿及第 1 单元、第 3 单元的编写工作。第 2 单元由国伟编写；第 4 单元由刘爱服编写；第 5、6 单元由胡嫣茹编写；第 7、8 单元由梁宝恒编写；第 9、10 单元由杨昆编写。

由于时间仓促，编者水平有限，书中不当之处在所难免，恳请专家和读者不吝赐教。

编者
2009 年 2 月

CONTENTS

Unit 1 Making and Accepting a Reservation ·········· 1
  Part A Making and Accepting a Reservation ·········· 1
  Part B Offering an Alternative to the Guests When Their Needs Are Not Available ······ 12

Unit 2 Receiving the Guests ·········· 23
  Part A Receiving the Guests with the Reservation ·········· 23
  Part B Receiving the Guests without the Reservation ·········· 31

Unit 3 Ordering Food and Taking Orders I ·········· 41
  Part A Asking and Explaining Dishes ·········· 41
  Part B Recommending Dishes ·········· 53

Unit 4 Ordering Food and Taking Orders II ·········· 63
  Part A Asking What the Guest Prefers ·········· 63
  Part B Room Service ·········· 75

Unit 5 Ordering Dessert ·········· 85
  Part A Asking and Telling If Dessert Is Wanted I ·········· 85
  Part B Asking and Telling If Dessert Is Wanted II ·········· 97

Unit 6 Paying the Bill ·········· 107
  Part A Asking for the Bill and Ways of Paying ·········· 107
  Part B Explaining the Charge and Handling Mistakes on the Bill ·········· 121

Unit 7 Bar Service I ·········· 133
  Part A Asking What the Guest Wants to Drink ·········· 133
  Part B Telling What Is Wanted ·········· 146

Unit 8 Bar Service II ·········· 155
  Part A Asking before Serving and Serving the Guest ·········· 155
  Part B Asking How Much Is Owed and Saying Goodbye ·········· 163

Unit 9 Handling Complaints I 173
Part A Complaining about Drinks 173
Part B Complaining about Meat and Food 182

Unit 10 Handling Complaints II 189
Part A Complaining about Service 189
Part B Showing the Way of Dealing with Complaints 197

Vocabulary 204

Key to Exercises 209

Tapescript 242

附录 293

参考文献 296

Unit 1

Making and Accepting a Reservation

Part A Making and Accepting a Reservation

Teaching hours: 2 hours

Learning Goals:

To be able to
- ask and give restaurant hours
- make a reservation by phone
- take and accept a reservation by phone
- book a table
- ask about the time of a reservation
- find out how many people for the reservation
- ask for a seating request

Vocabulary Assistance

chef *n.* 厨师, 主厨	accept *v.* 接受
receptionist *n.* 前台接待	reserve *v.* 预订
manager *n.* 经理	reservation *n.* 预订
hostess *n.* 迎宾女招待员, 领位	request *v.& n.* 要求
waiter *n.* 男服务员	courtesy *n.* 客气话, 礼貌
waitress *n.* 女服务员	confirm *v.* 确认
operator *n.* 接线员, 电话员	midnight *n.* 午夜
cashier *n.* 出纳员	private *adj.* 个人的, 私人的
restaurant *n.* 餐厅, 餐馆	banquet *n.* 筵席, 宴会

English for Food and Beverages

Start You Off

✚ Activity 1

Do the practice in pairs. Look at the time below and answer questions.
A: What time is it?
B: It's_____.

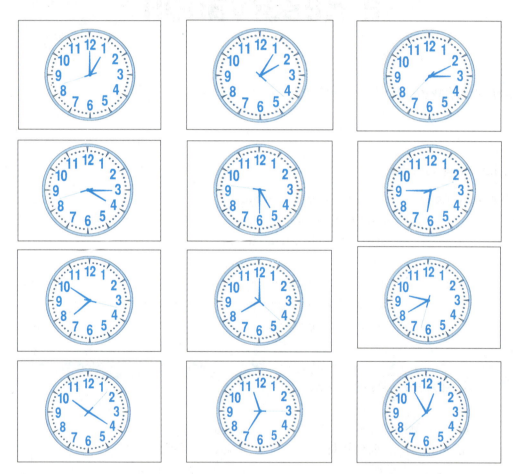

✚ Activity 2

The following pictures show people who work in a hotel in Beijing. Look at the pictures below, try to find out what they do and write down the names of their professions.

Unit 1 Making and Accepting a Reservation

1. ____chef____   2. _____   3. _____   4. _____

5. _____   6. _____   7. _____   8. _____

Now say what these people do, like this:

1 He's a chef who works in the kitchen and cooks food.
2 _____
3 _____
4 _____
5 _____
6 _____
7 _____
8 _____

Focus on Language

 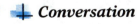 **Conversation**

Reserving a Table through the Telephone

Questions

1. How should you take reservations by phone?
2. What is the telephone courtesy?
3. As a restaurant clerk, how should you clarify the requests of the guests when you are taking reservations from them?
4. How should you get the needed information?
5. How should you confirm guests' requests?

🎧 Listen to the conversation and read after it. Then try to find the answers to the questions.

C=Clerk   G=Guest

C: Good morning! The Four Seasons Restaurant. May I help you?

G: Yes. What time do you open today?

C: We open at 10 a.m., sir, and we close at 2 p.m.

G: Good. I'd like to reserve a table for lunch.

C: What time would you like to have your table?

G: At 11:30.

C: How many are there in your party?

G: Three.

C: All right. May I have your name, please?

G: Mike Jackson.

C: Would you please give me your telephone number?

G: Sure. My phone number is 64907468.

C: Thank you. A table for three at 11:30 for Mr. Mike Jackson. And where would you like to sit?

G: We'd like to sit by the window as we love a bird's eye view of Beijing city.

C: No problem. We'll arrange it for you. Thank you for calling us. We are looking forward to your coming.

➕ Language Tips

1. Opening and closing hours

◆ Could you (please) tell me **when**   the restaurant **opens**?
   Can   **what time**

◇ We **open at 6:00 p.m.**, madam/sir.

◆ Could you (please) tell me **when**   the restaurant **closes**?
   Can   **what time**

◇ We **close at midnight**, madam/sir.

➕ Practice 1

Look at the time table below, follow the way of asking and giving opening and closing hours above and make two-sentence conversations in pairs.

Opening Hour	Closing Hour
5:00 a.m.	5:30 p.m.
5:30 a.m.	6:00 p.m.

Unit 1 Making and Accepting a Reservation

6:00 a.m.	6:30 p.m.
6:30 a.m.	7:00 p.m.
7:00 a.m.	8:00 p.m.
8:30 a.m.	9:00 p.m.
9:00 a.m.	10:00 p.m.
10:00 a.m.	12:00 p.m.

✦ Practice 2

Work in groups and give the names of the restaurants you have been to. Then tell their opening and closing time.

✦ Practice 3

Role-play: calling the places below to find out their opening and closing times. Take turns and do like this:

G=Guest   **C**=Clerk

C: This is the Four Seasons Restaurant. May I help you?
G: Yes. Could you tell me what time you open tonight?
C: We open at 6:00 p.m., madam.
G: And when do you close?
C: We close at midnight.
G: Thank you.

<u>Here is the information you need</u>

Beijing Roast Duck Restaurant	10:00 a.m.—10:00 p.m.
Post Office	9:00 a.m.—6:00 p.m.
Carrefour	9:00 a.m.—10:00 p.m.
Drug Store	8:00 a.m.—6:00 p.m.
National Museum	9:00 a.m.—5:00 p.m.
Bank of China	9:00 a.m.—5:00 p.m.

2. Booking a table

| ◆ I'd like to | **reserve a table** | in your restaurant. |
| | **book a table** | |

| ◇ **Certainly,** | | sir/madam. |

◆ **When would you like your table, sir/madam?**

What time would you like your table,

◇ **At** 7:00 p.m.

Around

╋ Practice 1

Role-play a scene of "Taking a reservation by phone" by following the model and with the information given below. Take turns being the clerk and the guest:

Names of the Restaurants	Time of Reservation
1. Margarita Restaurant	6:00 p.m.
2. Rose Restaurant	8:15 p.m.
3. Four Seasons Restaurant	11:00 a.m.
4. Flower Garden Restaurant	12:00 a.m.
5. Beijing Roast Duck Restaurant	5:00 p.m.

G=Guest **C**=Clerk

C: The Margarita Restaurant. May I help you?
G: I'd like to reserve a table, please.
C: When would you like your table, sir/madam?
G: Around 6:00.

╋ Practice 2

Fill in the blanks with the words that you will hear on the recording.

G=Guest **C**=Clerk

C: Four Seasons Restaurant. _____(1) I help you?
G: What _____(2) do you _____(3) this evening?
C: At 6 p.m., madam. And we _____(4) at 10 p.m.
G: I'd _____(5) to _____(6) a table, please.
C: Sure. For _____(7), _____(8) madam?
G: About 8:00.
C: May I _____(9) your _____(10), please?
G: Sara Black.
C: ...

3. Finding out how many people for the reservation

◆ **How many are there in your party?**

Unit 1 Making and Accepting a Reservation

◆ *For how many people?*

◇ *A party of eight.*

Three.

⊥ Practice 1

Go over the model expressions above and make short conversations in pairs with the information given below.

Reservation for	Party of	Time
1. Ronald Jenkins (Mr.)	2	6:00 p.m.
2. Albert Jones (Mr.)	4	8:15 p.m.
3. John Adams (Mr.)	3	11:00 p.m.
4. Mary Collins (Mrs.)	6	12:00 a.m.
5. Edward Wright (Mr.)	8	5:00 p.m.
6. Nancy Winters (Mrs.)	5	11:30 a.m.

────── Summarize Key Expressions ──────

1. Asking about restaurant hours
   a. When do you open?
   b. How long do you stay open?
   c. How late do you open till?
   d. When do you close?
2. Giving restaurant hours
   a. We open at 6:00 and we close at midnight.
   b. We're open until midnight.
   c. We're open round the clock.
   d. We open 24 hours.
   e. We're open from 10:00 a.m. until midnight.
   f. We open at 6:00 p.m. and we take last orders at 10:30 p.m.
   g. I'm sorry, we're not open on Sundays.
3. Booking a table
   a. I'd like to reserve a table for three.
   b. I'd like to reserve a table near the window for two.
   c. I'd like to book a table for dinner this evening.
   d. I'd like to make a reservation for two for this evening at eight.

4. Asking about the time of a reservation
   a. When would you like your table?
   b. When/At what time are you coming in on Monday evening?
   c. When should we expect you, sir?
   d. What time do you like your table?
   e. For what time, please?
   f. What time would that be?
   g. At what time can we expect you?
5. Finding out how many people for the reservation
   a. How many are there in your party?
   b. For how many people?
   c. For how many?
6. Expecting guests
   a. We are looking forward to your coming.
   b. We look forward to seeing you/ welcoming you.
   c. We look forward to having you with us.
   d. We are expecting you.
   e. We'll be expecting you this evening, sir.

Give It a Try

 Task 1

The clerk is taking a reservation by phone. Listen to the recording and write down the proper information in the telephone reservation form according to the conversation.

Reservation Form

Name of the restaurant: _____

Day taken: _____ ☐ Lunch ☐ Dinner

Time of reservation: _____

Name of the person making the reservation: _____

Unit 1 Making and Accepting a Reservation

> Telephone number: _____
> Logged by/in: _____
> No. in party: _____
> Food taken _____

 Task 2

Listen to the recording and complete the following conversation. Then do the conversation in pairs.

G=Guest   C=Clerk

C: Good morning. Flower Garden Restaurant. _____(1)?
G: _____(2) for the dinner on New Year's Day.
C: Certainly, sir. _____(3)?
G: Just for two, my girl friend and I.
C: _____(4)?
G: Around 6:00 p.m.
C: Fine. Where would you like to sit, sir, in the main restaurant _____(5)?
G: A private room, please.
C: All right, sir. We'll have Flower Hall reserved for you. _____(6), please?
G: Certainly. It's _____(7) Johnson and my_____
   _____(8) is 13501236688.
C: Mr. Johnson, 13501236688... thank you. By the way, as that is the peak hour, we only can keep your room for half an hour. That means you should come before 6:30.
G: _____(9).
C: Thank you for calling. _____(10).

Task 3

Role-play according to the following situations. Do it in pairs. Student A will be the guest and student B will be the clerk.

Guest

1. Your name is David Cook.
   You want to know what time the restaurant opens.
   You want a table for four at 8:30 p.m.

English for Food and Beverages

2. Your name is Peter Stewart.

   You want to reserve a table for this evening.

   There will be six of you.

   You want a table for 7:30 p.m.

3. Your name is Roger William.

   You'd like to have lunch at 11:30 a.m.

   You want to reserve a table near the window for two.

Clerk

1. Someone calls the restaurant.

   The restaurant's hours are from 6:00 a.m. to 10:00 p.m.

2. Someone calls the restaurant.

   The restaurant's hours are from 5:30 a.m. to 11:30 p.m.

3. Someone calls the restaurant.

   The restaurant's hours are from 5:00 a.m. to 11:00 p.m.

Task 4

List out the questions of accepting a reservation asked by the reservation clerk:

Questions of Accepting a Reservation	1. What time would you like your table? / ... 2. ... ...

Do Extension Activities

Activity 1

Listen to the banquet reservation and write down the proper information in the reservation form according to the conversation.

Banquet Reservation Form

Name of the restaurant: _____

Day taken: _____ ☐ Lunch ☐ Dinner _____

Unit 1 Making and Accepting a Reservation

Time of reservation: _____

Name of the person making the reservation: _____

Phone number: _____ Fax number: _____

Logged in: _____ No. in party: _____

Food taken: _____ Wine ordered: _____

Charge per person: _____

Activity 2

Read the following statements and make a tick to the "General Rules" for taking and accepting the reservations by telephone.

☐ Greet your callers warmly and appropriately.

☐ Ask carefully for information from your guests and write down the information clearly on a reservation form or on the reservation book.

☐ The name, the time and date, the number of the party, and any special requirements are the information you should obtain from the caller when you take the reservation.

☐ Get the phone number of the guest for reconfirmation and in case there is an unexpected problem.

☐ You should explain to the guest patiently and offer an alternative if the time or date the guest needs is not available.

☐ Hold the guest on the waiting list if he or she insists on a certain time or date.

☐ A "reserved" card made for the guest on the assigned table will be preferable as it will make the guests feel especially important.

☐ A prior arrangement including the time, the menu, the wine and the payment should be made if a large party wants to have a dinner.

Learning Tips

Guidelines for Taking Reservations by Phone

What should the restaurant clerks do when they are taking reservations from the guests by phone? For those that take a reservation, telephone courtesy is a must. Greet your guest warmly, when you are being called. Then, get the necessary information for the proper reservation in an organized manner. That means, you need to make clear the request of the guest, including the name of the guest, the number of the party, the date and time, and any special requirements. After that you should repeat these information to confirm it with the guest.

Part B Offering an Alternative to the Guests When Their Needs Are Not Available

Teaching hours: 2 hours

Learning Goals:

To be able to
- offer help
- ask for the guest's name
- ask for the guest's phone/mobile phone number
- ask for a seating request
- offer an alternative if the time or date the guest needs is not available.
- introduce the service in the restaurant

Vocabulary Assistance

alternative *n.* 可选择的事物
insist (on) *v.* 坚持
guarantee *v.* 保证
availability *n.* 获得
available *adj.* 可获得的
non-smoking *adj.* 无烟的
occupied *adj.* 占用的
alphabetize *v.* 按字母顺序排列
appreciate *v.* 感谢
liquor *n.* 烈性酒
discount *v.* 优惠,打折
log *v.* 记录

recommend *v.* 推荐
spacious *adj.* 宽敞的
compile *v.* 编制
database *n.* 资料库,数据库
dot *n.* 点儿
dupes (=duplicate) *n.* 副本,复制
logbook *n.* 日志
emergency *n.* 突发事件,紧急情况
private room 单间
corkage fee 开瓶费
minimum charge 最低消费
mobile/cell phone 手机

Unit 1 Making and Accepting a Reservation

———— Start You Off ————

Activity 1

Look at the phone numbers or cell phone numbers and do the short conversations in pairs.

A: What's your phone number/cell phone number?
B: My phone number/cell phone number is _____.

64830172	82416653	13501481190
13810926682	84630942	84714401
13691211806	62037762	13301615863
88068436	13518020942	84612846

13

Activity 2

Listen to the conversation. Tick (✓) the names and titles that are correct.

Name	Title
Maria Cannoli	(Ms.)
James Morrison	(Ms.)
Jeanne Hibbard	(Mrs.)
Dave Moore	(Mr.)

 Activity 3

Listen to these people exchanging phone numbers and e-mail addresses. Circle the incorrect information.

Name	Phone number	E-mail address
Lisa	61-3-9657-1234	lah@zip.com.aw
Junko	(06)-478-2150	junko@aol.com
Sam	382-4167	slee@sunrise.com.sg
Mari	(044)-645-7299	mayo@asu.edu

Focus on Language

 Conversation

Would You Mind Changing Your Time

Questions

1. What would you say when you pick up the phone as a reservation clerk?
2. How do you take a reservation if the time or date the guest needs is not available?
3. What do you explain to the guests?
4. Are you going to offer an alternative to the guests?
5. What would you do if the guest insists on a certain time or date?

Unit 1 Making and Accepting a Reservation

  Listen to the conversation and read after it. Then try to find the answers to the questions.

C=Clerk   **G**=Guest

C: Good morning. The Garden Restaurant. May I help you?

G: Yes, I'd like to make a reservation for two for this evening at 8:00.

C: Just a moment, please. Let me check if there is any availability... I'm sorry, sir. There aren't any tables left for 8:00, but we can book one for you at 9:00.

G: Well, I am afraid that's too late.

C: I'm terribly sorry, sir.

G: How about tomorrow evening?

C: We've already received many bookings for tomorrow evening. So we cannot guarantee. I hope you'll understand.

G: I do, but I would appreciate it if you could arrange it.

C: I'll try my best. Would you please leave your name and your phone number?

G: Mr. Rodger William. My phone number is 84632266.

C: I'll call you when there is a free table for tomorrow evening at 8:00.

G: Thank you very much. Bye.

C: Bye.

Language Tips

1. Taking a reservation if the guest's time is not available

◆ I'd like to make a reservation for this evening at 8:00.

   a table at 6:30 this evening.

◇ ... I'm sorry, sir. The restaurant is fully booked at that time.

   There aren't any tables left. Would you mind changing your time?

Practice 1

Student A will be the guest and Student B will be the reservation clerk. Do the practice according to the given information.

Student A wants to book a table at:
  —11:30 for lunch
  —7:00 for dinner
  —8:00 for dinner
  —12:00 for lunch
  —7:30 for dinner

Student B refuses politely and offers the availability at:
  —12:30

15

—8:00
—9:00
—1:00
—8:30

Practice 2

Make short conversations in pairs according to the information given below.

Time	Tables Available	Tables Unavailable
6:00		√
7:00	√	
8:00		√
9:00	√	
12:30		√

2. Offering help

◆ **Good morning. Garden Restaurant. May I help you?**

   Four Seasons Restaurant. Can I help you?

◇ Yes, I'd like to book a table for two tonight.

   a table tomorrow evening at 7:00.

Practice 1

Make short conversations between the reservation clerk and the guest by using the information given below.

Student A Reservation Clerk   Student B Guest

Restaurants	Time for the table
Four Seasons Restaurant	A table for two at 6:00
Flower Restaurant	A table for six at 7:00
Rose Garden Restaurant	A table for one at 8:00
Roast Duck Restaurant	A table for three at 6:30
Happy Hour Restaurant	A table for five at 7:30
Pearl Restaurant	A table for four at 8:30

Unit 1 Making and Accepting a Reservation

➕ Practice 2

Make more conversations in the same situation in Practice 1 by thinking of the names of the restaurants you have been to and the time for the table with your partner.

3. Asking for the guest's name

◆ **May I have your name, please?**

  Could I have your name, please?

◇ It's William. Rodger William.

◆ **And how do you spell your last name?**

  first name?

◇ It's W-I-L-L-I-A-M.

  R-O-D-G-E-R.

➕ Practice 1

Do the practice in pairs. Student A will be the reservation clerk. Student B will be the guest. Student A asks the guest's name and let him/her spell it for you.

➕ Practice 2

Do the same with two other classmates.

4. Asking for the guest's phone/cell phone numbers

◆ **Could I have your phone number, please?**

  What's your cell phone number?

◇ It's 631-5897.

  13697516822.

➕ Practice 1

Ask your partner his/her phone/cell phone number. Repeat it and write it down.

➕ Practice 2

Ask other classmates their names and phone/cell phone number. Then make a list.

Names of Your Classmates	Phone/Cell Phone Numbers

Summarize Key Expressions

1. Offering help
   a. May I help you?
   b. Can I help you?
   c. What can I do for you?
2. Asking for the guest's name
   a. May I have your name, please?
   b. Could I have your name, please?
   c. And how do you spell your last/first name?
3. Asking for the guest's phone/cell phone number
   a. Could I have your phone number, please?
   b. What's your cell phone number?
   c. And your phone number, please.
4. Asking for a seating request
   a. Would you like a table by the window?
   b. Where would you like to sit, by the window?
   c. Which would you like better, a table in the hall or in a private room?
   d. Would you like a table in the hall or in a private room?
   e. How about the non-smoking area? It is also very quiet.
5. Taking a reservation if the guest's time, date or seating request is not available
   a. I'm sorry, there aren't any tables left for 8:00, but we can book one for you at 8:30.
   b. I'm sorry, our restaurant is fully booked at that time. Would you mind changing your time?
   c. I'm afraid the tables by the windows are fully reserved/are all occupied. I can't guarantee you a table right now. But we'll try our best.
   d. Sorry, the Lily Room has already been reserved. Shall we reserve another room for you?
   e. Sorry, but there is only one table left that seats six people.
6. Introducing the service in the restaurant to the guests
   a. The reservation will be kept for 30 minutes after the reserved time.
   b. Since we have a long waiting list, we would appreciate receiving your call if you are unable to come.
   c. There is no corkage fee for brought-in liquor.
   d. A 10% discount will be offered to those holding a VIP card issued by our restaurant.
   e. There isn't a minimum charge for a private room from 2 p.m.—3 p.m.

Unit 1 Making and Accepting a Reservation

Give It a Try

Task 1

Do the conversation in pairs and fill in the form given below.

Reservation Form

Name of guest: Mr. /Mrs. /Miss/Ms _____
Telephone number: _____
How many people: _____
Available time for reservation: _____
☐ Lunch   ☐ Dinner
Date: _____
Clerk: _____

C=Clerk   **G**=Guest

C: Rose Garden Restaurant. What can I do for you?
G: I'd like to book a table for this evening.
C: For how many people?
G: Three.
C: What time would you like to come, please?
G: Around 7:30 p.m.
C: I am sorry. There aren't any tables left for 7:30. But we can reserve you one at 8:00.
G: That will be fine.
C: May I have your name, please?
G: Peter Stewart.
C: Would you please spell your last name for me?
G: S-T-E-W-A-R-T.
C: A table for three this evening at 8:00 for Mr. Stewart.
G: That's right.
C: Thank you, sir.
G: Thank you. Good-bye.

Task 2

Listen to the following conversation and complete the form with the information you will hear.

Name	
Phone Number	
Time for Reservation	
Guest Request for Seating	
Suggested Location	
No. in Party	
Table Number	

Task 3

Complete the following conversation with appropriate words.

C=Clerk **G**=Guest

C: Beijing Roast Duck Restaurant. _____(1)?
G: I'd like to book _____(2).
C: For how many people?
G: _____(3).
C: _____(4), please?
G: Around 7:30 p.m.
C: I am sorry. There aren't _____(5). But we can reserve_____(6).
G: That will be fine.
C: _____(7)?
G: George Harrison.
C: _____(8) spell your last name?
G: H-A-R-R-I-S-O-N.
C: A table for _____(9) for Mr. _____(10).
G: That's right.
C: Thank you, sir.
G: Thank you. Good-bye.

Task 4

Do the role-play according to the situation. As a reservation clerk, you will need to tell guests that the table they prefer is not available. Make up your own conversation with your partner including sentences given below.

Waiter/Waitress:

—I am sorry. The tables for 6:30 have been fully booked.

Unit 1 Making and Accepting a Reservation

—But we reserve one for you at 7:30.
—Would you like to make a reservation at that time?
—Then I will recommend the Lily Room. It is quiet and spacious.
  And we offer free fruit after 7:30.
—Very good, sir/madam. A table for... at 7:30 this evening in the Lily Room.
—May I have your name, please?
—Thank you very much, Mr. /Mrs. /Miss/Ms...
—Bye.

Do Extension Activities

Activity 1

Read the statements given below and put them into the right columns.

1. I'm sorry, we're not open on Sundays.
2. What time would you like your table?
3. I'm afraid that table is reserved for 6 p.m.
4. How many people are there in your party?
5. In whose name is the reservation made?
6. We open 24 hours.
7. I'm sorry, there aren't any tables for 11:30, but we can give you a table at 12:30.
8. We look forward to having you with us.
9. We're open from 5:30 p.m. until midnight.
10. I'm afraid all the private rooms are reserved. Would you mind sitting in the main dining room?

Accepting a Reservation	1. What time would you like your table? 2. ... ...
Giving Information about the Restaurant	1. I'm sorry, we're not open on Sundays. 2. ... ...
Refusing a Reservation	1. I'm afraid that table is reserved for 6 p.m. 2. ... ...

✢ *Activity 2*

Listen to the short passage and write down what are needed for taking reservations. The reservation desk should be equipped with the items of:

 Learning Tips

The Reservation Book

Reservations are generally recorded first on a telephone reservation form, or directly into the reservation book. If a telephone reservation form is used, information can be compiled later in the reservation book. Usually the host or hostess will alphabetize the list of names of the guests who have reserved a table—this will allow the host to check off the names as the guests come into the restaurant, and will make for a smoother operation. Copies of the telephone reservation form are generally made and kept with the reservation book at the check-in desk.

Receiving the Guests

Part A Receiving the Guests with the Reservation

Teaching hours: 2 hours

Learning Goals:

To be able to
- request the reservation
- find out the number of the guests in the party
- confirm the table
- ask about preferences
- show the guest to the table
- seat the guests

Vocabulary Assistance

seat *v.* 引座	gently *adv.* 文雅地
preference *n.* 喜好	knee *n.* 膝, 膝盖
check *v.* 核对	examine *v.* 检查
suitable *adj.* 合适的, 适宜的	consideration *n.* 考虑因素
menu *n.* 菜单	qualified *adj.* 合格的
special *n.* 特色菜	appearance *n.* 外貌
aisle *n.* 过道	image *n.* 形象
prefer *v.* 更喜欢	achieve *v.* 达到, 完成
lounge *n.* 休息厅	uniform *n.* 工作服
approval *n.* 赞同	polished *adj.* 擦亮的
vacant *adj.* 空着的, 空的	groom *v.* 使整洁
bamboo *n.* 竹	trim *v.* 修剪
direct *v.* 给……指路	tag *n.* 标签
apology *n.* 道歉	under the name of 以……的名字出现
offer *v.* 提供	look over 浏览
alternative *n.* 替换物	private room 单间

English for Food and Beverages

———— Start You Off ————

Activity 1

Brainstorm what kinds of questions restaurant waiters ask the guest.

Activity 2

Brainstorm what kinds of questions the guests typically ask.

———— Focus on Language ————

 Conversation

Receiving the Guests with the Reservation

Questions

1. How should you receive the guest with the reservation?
2. How should you request the reservation?
3. How should you confirm the table?
4. How should you seat the guest?
5. How should you ask about preferences?

 Listen to the conversation and read after it. Then try to find the answers to the questions above.

C=Captain   **P**=Mr. Porter

C: Good evening, madam and sir. Do you have the reservation?
P: Yes, we've reserved a table for 2 at 6 o'clock under the name of Mr. Porter.
C: Ah, Mr. Porter (*checking the reservation book*). That's right, a table for 2 at 6 o'clock. Ma'am, sir, your table is ready. Please follow me. Will this table be suitable?
P: Yes. This is nice. Thank you.
C: I'll give you a few minutes to look over the menus. Can I get you anything to drink?
P: I'd like a glass of beer, please. My wife would like ice water.

C: Good. I'll be back with your drinks.

C: (*a moment later*) Here you are: ice water for the lady, and you, sir... and here is your beer. Would you like to hear tonight's specials?

P: Sure.

Language Tips

1. Requesting the reservation and confirming the table

◆ ***Do you have*** a reservation?

Have you got

Have you had

Have you booked a table?

◇ Yes, we've ***reserved*** a table for 2 at 6 o'clock.

booked

◆ That's right, a table for 2 at 6 o'clock.

Practice 1

Look at the table below. Work in pairs, follow the way of asking and answering above and make two-sentence conversations.

Number of the guests	Reserved time
3	11:00 a.m.
4	11:30 a.m.
5	12:00 a.m.
6	1:00 p.m.
8	1:30 p.m.
10	6:00 p.m.
12	6:30 p.m.
15	7:00 p.m.

Practice 2

Role-play the waiter or waitress and the guest in pairs according to the information given in the table below. Pay attention to how to request the guest about the reservation and how to answer the question. Take turns and do like this:

G=Guest   W=Waiter/Waitress

W: Good evening, sir. Welcome to the Great Wall Restaurant.

G: Good evening. My name is Max. I've reserved a table for 6 at 7:00 p.m.

W: Oh, yes, Mr. Max. A table for 6 at 7:00 p.m. We've been expecting you. This way, please.

G: Thank you.

Names of the Restaurants	Time of Reservation	Party of	Names of the Guests
1. Margarita Restaurant	6:00 p.m.	3	Mr. Carson
2. Rose Restaurant	8:15 p.m.	5	Mr. Roger
3. Four Seasons Restaurant	11:00 a.m.	8	Ms. Carman
4. Flower Garden Restaurant	12:00 a.m.	2	Mr. Johnson
5. Beijing Roast Duck Restaurant	5:00 p.m.	12	Mrs. Jefferson

2. Asking about the preferences

◆ Will this table be　**all right,**　sir /madam?

　　　　　　　　　　　suitable,

◇ **It's OK.** But we prefer　　**a window table.**

　　　　　　　　　　　　　an aisle table.

　It's too noisy. We prefer　**a quiet corner.**

　　　　　　　　　　　　　a private room.

◆ Where would you like to sit,　sir /madam?

◇ We'd like to sit　**by the window.**

　　　　　　　on a quite corner.

◆ Do you prefer smoking or non-smoking,　sir/madam?

◇ **Non-smoking, please.**

Practice 1

Role-play a scene of "Receiving the guest with a reservation" in pairs with the information given below. Take turns being the waiter or waitress and the guest.

W=Waiter/Waitress　　**G**=Guest

W: Greets the guests and asks them whether the table is fine with them or their preferences.

G: Doesn't like the table prepared by the waiter or waitress, because it's too noisy.

W: Tells the guests the restaurant is busy now. Asks them whether they mind waiting for a while in the lounge.

G: Shows approval.

Practice 2

Fill in the blanks with the word that you hear on the tape.

G=Guest   C=Clerk

Dialogue 1

C: Ma'am, sir, your table is _____(1). Please _____(2)me.

G: Thanks.

C: Will this table be _____(3)?

G: Yes. This is _____(4).

Dialogue 2

C: Good evening, Mr. Johnson. We've been _____(1)you.

G: Good evening. My _____(2)table is ready?

C: Yes. Would you like to _____(3)with me? ... Is this table fine _____(4)you?

G: It's OK. But we _____(5)a table by the window.

C: I'm sorry, but the restaurant is _____ (6)now. Would you care to have a drink in the _____(7)while you are waiting?

G: How long a _____(8)?

C: About 15 minutes.

G: Good. Thank you.

──── Summarize Key Expressions ────

1. Requesting the reservation
    a. Do you have a reservation?
    b. Have you got a reservation?
    c. Have you had a reservation?
    d. Have you booked a table?
2. Confirming the tables
    a. That's right, a table for 6 at 6:00 p.m.
    b. Yes, sir/madam, a table for a party of 12 at 7:00 p.m.
3. Confirming the number of the party
    a. How many are there in your party, please?
    b. How many, please?
    c. Is it only 3 of you?
4. Seating the guests
    a. Would you please come with me?
    b. Would you like to come with me?
    c. Would you please follow me?
    d. Would you come this way, please?
    e. Please step this way.

f. This way, please.

5. Asking about the preferences

   a. Where would you like to sit?

   b. How about this one?

   c. Will this table be all right?

   d. Is this table fine with you?

   e. Would you prefer a window seat?

   f. Would you like to sit by the window?

   g. You can sit where you like.

6. Telling the guests there isn't a vacant table

   a. I'm sorry, but the restaurant is full now.

   b. Would you mind waiting a moment in the lounge?

   c. Would you care to have a drink in the lounge while you are waiting?

7. Bringing the menu

   a. I'll bring you the menu.

   b. Here's the menu.

   c. Your menus.

   d. Would you like to hear tonight's specials?

Give It a Try

Task 1

Listen to the recording and complete the following conversation. Then do the conversation in pairs.

G=Guest   **C**=Clerk

C: Good afternoon, sir. Welcome to the Flower Garden Restaurant. _____(1)?

G: Yes, I reserved a table by phone _____(2).

C: Just a moment, please. Let me have a look at our reservation book. Oh, yes. You reserved a table _____(3) under the name of _____(4).

G: That's right, _____(5)?

C: Yes, Mr. Charles. We've been looking forward to your coming. _____(6)?

G: _____(7).

C: Fine. _____(8). Please follow me.

G: Thank you. _____(9)?

C: Don't worry. We'll direct them to the hall if they arrive.

G: Great. Thanks a lot.

Unit 2 Receiving the Guests

✚ Task 2

Role-play according to the following situations. Do it in pairs. Student A will be the guest and Student B will be the waiter or waitress.

Guest

1. Your name is Martha.
   You've reserved a table for 6:00 pm.
   There are 8 persons in your party.
2. Your name is Alice.
   You've reserved a table for 2 at 7:30 p.m.
   You want a table on a quiet corner.
3. Your name is Clare.
   You'd like to have lunch at 12:00.
   You've reserved a table in a private dining room for two.

Waiter/Waitress

1. Greets the guest.
   Confirms the reservation.
   Tells the guest that the table is ready.
   Shows the guest to the table.
2. Greets the guest.
   Confirms the reservation.
   Apologizes to the guest that the table is not ready yet.
   Asks the guest whether she prefers another table.
3. Greets the guest.
   Confirms the reservation.
   Tells the guest that he just found that there's something wrong with the reserved table. Asks the guest whether he minds sharing the table with other customers and makes an apology.

—————————— Do Extension Activities ——————————

✚ Activity 1

List the steps in the process of seating and serving restaurant guests.

Activity 2

Which of the following statements are regarded as the general rules for receiving the guests with the reservations. Identify each statement with True or False.

- ☐ Greet the guests at the door with a warm smile.
- ☐ Ask carefully for information from your guests and write down the information clearly on a reservation form or on the reservation book.
- ☐ Request the date of the reservation.
- ☐ Confirm the guests with the reservation and the number of the guests to be seated. Show the guests to the prepared table and seat them properly.
- ☐ You should explain to the guest patiently and offer an alternative if the time or date the guest needs is not available.
- ☐ When seating the guests, first help the ladies to take their seats.
- ☐ Pull the chair out, allow the guests to sit and then gently push the chair forward with knees.
- ☐ Examine the table and chair before receiving guests.
- ☐ Note the number of the guests in the party and any special considerations.

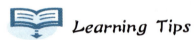 Learning Tips

A Qualified Waiter or Waitress (Ⅰ)

A qualified waiter or waitress has a smart and cheerful appearance while on duty and a positive attitude towards guests. Good appearance can give a good image to the guests, and benefit you as well. To achieve good appearance, you must keep your uniform sparkling clean and fitted with clean, well-pressed shirts and pants, shiny polished shoes. Your hair must be well groomed and neatly trimmed. Long hair of female staff should be tied up neatly. Male staff must be clean shaven. You must keep clean hands and short finger nails. Your name tag should be well placed.

Part B Receiving the Guests without the Reservation

Teaching hours: 2 hours

Learning Goals:

To be able to
- arrange the table for the guests without a reservation
- ask the guests to wait for a while
- apologize for the delay
- seat the guests

Vocabulary Assistance

arrange *v.* 安排
identify *v.* 识别,认出
vacant *adj.* 空着的,空的
sign *n.* 符号,标志
altogether *adv.* 总共
available *adj.* 可获得的,在手边的
delay *v. /n.* 耽搁,推迟
diner *n.* 就餐者
separately *adv.* 分开地,个别地
share *v.* 合用
accommodate *v.* 向……提供
apologize *v.* 道歉
instead *adv.* 反而,却

express *v.* 表达,表示
experience *n.* 经历
dine *v.* 吃饭,就餐
responsibility *n.* 责任,职责
obtain *v.* 获得,得到
consent *v./n.* 同意,赞成
procedure *n.* 程序,步骤
specific *adj.* 具体的,特定的
ensure *v.* 保证
inform *v.* 告知,通知
graphical symbol 图形符号
peak season 高峰期

Start You Off

Activity 1

Try to identify the following public information graphical symbols used on sign and give each one an explanation.

English for Food and Beverages

	Graphical Symbols	Names of the Symbols	Explanation
1	🅿		
2	🅿🚲		
3	←		
4	⬅		
5	➡		
6	🏃🚪		
7	🛗		
8	♿		

Unit 2 Receiving the Guests

续表

	Graphical Symbols	Names of the Symbols	Explanation
9			
10			
11			
12			
13			
14			
15			
16			

English for Food and Beverages

续表

	Graphical Symbols	Names of the Symbols	Explanation
17			
18			
19			
20			

Activity 2

Brainstorm: Have you ever had a meal in a restaurant? For what purpose?

Conversation

Receiving the Guests without the Reservation

Questions

1. How should you receive the guest without the reservation?
2. How should you request the reservation?

Unit 2 Receiving the Guests

3. How should you confirm the number of the party?
4. How should you tell the guests there isn't a vacant table at the moment?
5. How should you ask the guests to wait for a while?
6. How should you seat the guest?

 Listen to the conversation and read after it. Then try to find the answers to the questions above.

C=Captain   H=Mr. Harrison

C: Good evening, sir. How many persons, please?
H: Good evening. Is there a table for 7?
C: Have you made a reservation, sir?
H: No, I'm afraid not.
C: I'm very sorry, sir. All our tables are taken. It's the peak season, you know. But if you'd like to wait, you are more than welcome to do so.
H: How long do you think we'll have to wait?
C: About 15 minutes. Would you mind waiting until it is free? We'll seat your party as soon as possible.
H: Oh... Okay.
C: Would you please tell me your name, sir?
H: Harrison.

   (*After 15 minutes*)

C: Mr. Harrison?
H: Yes. Here.
C: I'm sorry to have kept you waiting. Now we have a table for you.
H: Great!
C: Would you please come with me? (*Leading them to a table in the hall*) Is this table fine with you, Mr. Harrison?
H: It's Okay. But we prefer a table by the window.
C: All right. Please take your seats. Your waiter will be with you in a minute.
H: Thanks a lot.

Language Tips

1. Receive the guest without the reservation

◆ We ***don't have*** a reservation.

   didn't make

◇ I'm sorry, ***but the restaurant is full now.***

   I'm afraid ***we're fully booked at the moment.***

English for Food and Beverages

✤ Practice 1

Role-play a waiter or waitress and a guest in pairs according to the information given in the table below. Pay attention to how to request the guest about the reservation and how to answer the question. Take turns and do like this:

G=Guest   **W**=Waiter/Waitress

W: Good evening, sir. Welcome to Rose Restaurant.

G: Good evening. We have 6 persons altogether, but we don't have a reservation.

W: I'm sorry, sir. We're fully booked at the moment. But if you'd like to wait, you are more than welcome.

Names of the Restaurants	Status of Reservation	Party of	Names of the Guests
1. Margarita Restaurant	none	8	Mr. Adams
2. Great Wall Restaurant	none	3	Mr. Morrison
3. Four Seasons Restaurant	none	2	Ms. Alison
4. Flower Garden Restaurant	none	4	Mr. Sidney
5. Beijing Roast Duck Restaurant	none	5	Mrs. Stewart

✤ Practice 2

The following is a conversation between a guest and a waiter or waitress. Listen carefully and try to fill in the blanks with the word that you hear on the recording.

G=Guest   **W**=Waiter/Waitress

W: Good evening, sir. How many persons, please?

G: Good evening. Is there a_____(1)for 3?

W: Have you made a_____(2)?

G: I'm afraid not. We've just_____(3).

W: I'm sorry, sir. It's the_____(4)season. The restaurant is _____(5)now. I'm afraid we cannot seat you at the _____(6)table. Would you mind sitting_____(7)?

G: No, thanks. We'd_____(8)wait a moment.

2. Asking the guests to wait for a while

◆ Would you mind waiting	*a moment in the lounge*?
	until it is free.

◇ Well... How long	**will**	*we have to wait*?
		it be
		a wait

◆ ***It takes only*** 15 minutes.

Unit 2 Receiving the Guests

About

Around

✤ Practice 1

Role-play a scene of "Asking the guests to wait for a while" in pairs with the information given below. Take turns being the waiter or waitress and the guest.

G=Guest   **W**=Waiter/Waitress

W: Greets the guests and confirms the reservation and the number of the guests.

G: Tells the waiter/waitress the number of the party and you didn't make a reservation.

W: Explains to the guests that the restaurant is full now and there is not a table available.

G: Asks the waiter/waitress how long you have to wait.

✤ Practice 2

Make a short conversation between a guest and a waiter according to the following pictures.

3. Seating the guests who have been kept waiting for a while

◆ We're very sorry   *to have kept you waiting.*

　　　　　　　　　　for the delay.

　I do apologize.

English for Food and Beverages

 Practice 1

Listen to the recording and complete the following conversation. Then do the conversation in pairs.
G=Guest   W=Waiter/Waitress

...

W: Mr. Black?
G: _____(1).
W: _____(2). We can seat your party now.
G: _____(3)!
W: Would you please come with me? ..._____(4)?
G: Nice. _____(5). Thanks a lot.

Practice 2

Discuss first what the host should do for the guests who have to be kept waiting? And then study the following situation and try to make a situational conversation in pairs.

Situation

A group of diners come to your restaurant. They'd like to have a table for 12, but all the tables are taken now because it's a peak season. After a wait of 15 minutes, a table in the hall is ready for them. However, the diners don't like the table. They prefer a table in a private room.

—————— **Summarize Key Expressions** ——————

1. Telling the guests there isn't a vacant table
    a. I'm sorry, but the restaurant is full now.
    b. I'm afraid we're fully booked at the moment.
    c. All our tables are taken.
    d. I'm afraid we cannot seat you at the same table. Would you mind sitting separately?
    e. I'm afraid that table is reserved, sir.
    f. Would you mind sharing a table?
    g. Some other guests wish to join this table.
2. Asking the guests to wait a little while
    a. Would you mind waiting a moment in the lounge?
    b. Would you mind waiting until it is free?
    c. Could you wait in line until a table is free? We can seat you very soon.
    d. Would you care to have a drink in the lounge while you are waiting? We'll accommodate your party as soon as possible.
    e. Could you wait for another 5 minutes, please?
    f. It may take about 15 minutes.
3. Seating the guests who have been kept waiting for a while
    a. I'm sorry to have kept you waiting.

b. We're very sorry for the delay.

c. We can seat your party now. This way, please.

d. Now we have a table for you.

e. I do apologize for the delay. Your table is ready now.

Give It a Try

 Task 1

Role-play according to the following situations. Do it in pairs. Student A will be the guest and Student B will be the waiter or waitress.

Guest

1. Your name is Black.

    You don't make a reservation.

    You want a table for 4.

    You are asked to wait for 15 minutes in line.

2. Your name is Hampton. It's your birthday today.

    You want a table for 8, but you don't have a reservation.

    You are asked to wait for 20 minutes.

    You are asked to sit near the window 20 minutes later.

    You don't like the prepared table. Instead, you want to sit in a private room.

    You are asked to wait another 5 minutes.

3. Your name is Dubois.

    You'd like to have a table for 1.

    You agree to share a table.

Waiter/Waitress

1. Greets the guest.

    Confirms the reservation.

    Explains to the guest that the tables are all taken now.

    Asks the guest to wait in line for about 15 minutes.

    Expresses the apology for the delay.

    Seats the guest.

2. Greets the guest.

    Confirms the reservation.

    Explains to the guest that the restaurant is full now.

    Asks the guest whether he likes to wait for 20 minutes.

    Makes an apology for the delay and seats the guest near the window.

    Asks the guest to wait another 5 minutes.

    Seats the guest in a private room.

3. Greets the guest.

   Confirms the reservation.

   Explains to the guest that the restaurant is busy at the moment.

   Asks the guest whether she'd like to share a table with some other guests.

Do Extension Activities

Activity 1

Describe the best or the worst experience while dining in a restaurant, and discuss the reason why people dine out.

Activity 2

The following statements are general rules for receiving the guests without the reservations. Listen carefully once and try to fill in the blanks.

➤ When there is no_____(1) left and the guests have to_____(2) a table, it is the_____(3) responsibility to obtain the_____(4) of the two parties.

➤ For those guests who_____(5) got reservations, the procedure depends on the_____(6) situation. The identity, number and _____(7) of the guests should also be taken into_____(8).

➤ When keeping the guests waiting _____(9), it is necessary to give_____(10) and apology, and at the same time_____(11) that he or she will be_____(12) as soon as there is a vacant table.

➤ While seating the guests_____(13), the host or hostess should also express the apology for_____(14).

 Learning Tips

A Qualified Waiter or Waitress (Ⅱ)

The first impression received by the incoming guest creates the mood for his entire visit. A courteous and friendly welcome makes the guest feel at home. So whenever you start your encounter with your customers, you should be pleasant, use courtesy phrases, and remember to smile. Avoid using loud voice, clapping hands or snapping fingers to attract attention of others. Never walk with hands in pockets. Train yourself to remember and recognize your guests. This will make them feel comfortable and at home. Do not stand talking in groups; if you need to speak to another member of staff, do it whispering. When talking with guests, never get into an argument, never joke with guests, only smile at their jokes, and never put yourself into a guest's conversation unless you are invited.

Unit 3

Ordering Food and Taking Orders I

Part A Asking and Explaining Dishes

Teaching hours: 2 hours

Learning Goals:

To be able to
- ask the guest if having an aperitif
- ask about dishes
- explain dishes
- offer drinks and food

Vocabulary Assistance

appetizer *n.* 开胃品	toast *n.* 土司,烤面包片
beverage *n.* 饮料	veal *n.* 小牛肉
steak *n.* 牛排	sauté *v.* 嫩炒
ham *n.* 火腿	martini *n.* 马提尼酒
chicken *n.* 鸡肉	caviar *n.* 鱼子酱
mushroom *n.* 蘑菇	entrée *n.* 主菜
salad *n.* 沙拉	lamb *n.* 糕羊肉
cocktail *n.* 凉菜,冷盘,鸡尾酒	spaghetti *n.* 通心粉
melon *n.* 甜瓜,瓜	chicory *n.* 菊苣
omelet *n.* 煎蛋卷(饼)	menu *n.* 菜单
pea *n.* 豌豆	lettuce *n.* 莴苣
aperitif *n.* 开胃酒	à la carte 按菜单点
whisky *n.* 威士忌	table d'hote 套餐的菜
pancake *n.* 薄饼,烙饼	hors d'oeuvre 开胃小吃,开胃冷盘

41

English for Food and Beverages

Start You Off

✚ Activity 1

Look at the pictures below and match them with the right words given below.

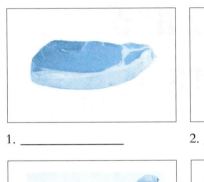

1. _____   2. _____   3. _____

4. _____   5. _____   6. _____

7. _____   8. _____   9. _____

| chicken | soup | fish | tomato | lettuce |
| mushroom | steak | vegetable salad | ham | |

✚ Activity 2

Listen to the guests' orders. Then read the answers below. Listen to the question again, and put a tick (✓) against the right answer.

1. The guest wants

    a. to know the way to room 21.   ☐

    b. a bottle of white wine in the restaurant.   ☐

    c. a bottle of white wine in his room.   ☐

2. The guest wants
   a. a glass of iced water. ☐
   b. a whisky without ice. ☐
   c. a whisky with ice. ☐
3. The guest wants
   a. melon. ☐
   b. soup. ☐
   c. salad. ☐
4. The guest wants
   a. an omelet. ☐
   b. fish. ☐
   c. a steak. ☐
5. The guest wants
   a. a gin and tonic and then rose wine. ☐
   b. just an aperitif. ☐
   c. a gin and tonic and then red wine. ☐

Activity 3

Read the following special terms and explanations. Then match them with an appropriate meaning.

A	B
1. A la carte	a. A liquid for drinking esp. one that is not water or medicine.
2. Table d'hote	b. Order the food in a restaurant according to a list where each dish has its own price.
3. Appetizer	c. A list of dishes in a meal or to be ordered as separate meals in a restaurant.
4. Beverage	d. The main dish of a meal. (Esp. AmE.)
5. Menu	e. Something eaten or drunk before or at the beginning of a meal to increase the desire to eat.
6. Entrée	f. A complete meal of several dishes served at a fixed price in a restaurant.

Focus on Language

Conversation

Questions

1. What would you say when you ask the guests if they would like an aperitif?
2. How do you ask about a dish?
3. How do you explain a dish if the guest asks?
4. What would you say when you offer drinks and food?

English for Food and Beverages

 Listen to the conversation and read after it. Then try to find the answers to the questions.

W=Waiter   **G1**=Guest 1   **G2**=Guest 2

W: Would you like an aperitif before you order?
G1: Yes, we'll all have dry martinis.
W: What would you like to start with?
G1: I'd like the smoked salmon.
G2: That sounds good. I'm going to have the caviar.
W: Here's the menu. What would you like for the entrée?
G1: Now let's see... I'll have the beef chasseur.
G2: I don't like beef very much. What is Noisettes Milanese exactly?
W: That's lamb cooked with herbs and served with spaghetti.
G2: That sounds interesting. I'll try that.
W: Very good, sir. Any vegetables?
G1: I'll have peas and potatoes.
G2: Just chicory for me, please.
W: Thank you very much. I'll be back in a minute.

➕ Language Tips

1. Asking the guest if having an aperitif or an hors d'oeuvre

◆ **Would you like an aperitif before you order?**

   And to start?

◇ We'll all have dry martinis.

   A shrimp cocktail, please.

◇ No, I think we'd like to order straight away.

 ➕ *Practice 1*

Listen to the recording and you'll hear some guests' requests. Number the sentence which meets the guests' needs.

☐ Would you like the Baden dry, sir, or perhaps the Piesporter?
☐ Would you like the Anjou Rose, madam?
☐ Would you like the smoked salmon, madam?
☐ Would you like the soup, madam?
☐ Would you like the Bordeaux Blanc de Blancs, madam, or perhaps the Chablis?

Practice 2

Read the following passage and try to get some information about what the aperitifs are.

Generally speaking, an aperitif can be any drink taken before a meal to stimulate the appetite. But frequently, when many people say "aperitif", they mean not just any drink taken before a meal but specific wines and liquors. Now, in our times, some drinks that contain no or low alcoholic content have become increasingly popular. They may be served "straight up", like the dry Sherries, or "on the rocks", often with a twist of peel or slice of orange, or lemon, etc., as a garnish. The most popular aperitifs around the world are Sherries. The best of these come from Spain. Sherries are categorized roughly, according to sweetness, as rich, medium, or dry. The dry and very dry Sherries are best served well chilled without ice, the medium may be chilled slightly or served at room temperature, and the rich Sherries are full-bodied and are generally not chilled. France produces a number of very popular wines and liqueurs. Among those readily available are: Byrrh, Dubonnet, Lillet, Pernod and St. Raphael. Italy produces Campari, a bitter wine, often served with soda, and Cynar, made from artichokes, and Greece produces ouzo, a strong anise-flavored liqueur. Asia also has some excellent aperitifs, like sake, a Japanese rice usually served warm and raki or arrack, similar to ouzo, from the Middle East.

2. Asking about and explaining a dish

◆ What is the Noisettes Milanese exactly?

◇ It is lamb cooked with herbs and served with spaghetti.

Practice 1

Read the information given below and make short conversations between the waiter and the guest by following the given model.

Student A: What is the Noisettes Milanese exactly?

Student B: It is lamb cooked with herbs and served with spaghetti.

1. gyoza—Gyoza is a kind of dumpling.（日式饺子,类似于我们的"煎饺"）
2. wasabi—Wasabi is a very spicy horse radish sauce.（horse radish 是"辣根", sauce 指"酱", wasabi 是"辣根磨成的辣酱"。）
3. udon and soba noodles—Udon noodles（乌冬面）are thick, and soba noodles（荞麦面）are thin.
4. moussaka—Moussaka（肉和茄子做成的希腊菜）is a Greek dish mainly minced beef /lamb and aubergines（(法)茄子）, onions and tomatoes.
5. mapo tofu—Mapo Tofu is a kind of spicy tofu sautéed with chili sauce.
6. omelette—Omelette is fluffy eggs with ham, cheese or Western.

⊥ Practice 2

Find more food you are familiar with and explain it to your partner.

⊥ Practice 3

Find some food you are not familiar with and ask your partner about it.

3. Offering drink or food

◆ **Would you like something to drink first?**

Would you like the smoked salmon as appetizer?

◇ I'd like a glass of orange juice.

Yes, please.

⊥ Practice 1

A role-play. Make a group of three. Student A will be the waiter offering drink or food. Student B will be Guest 1 and Student C will be Guest 2. Take turns and do like this:

W=Waiter **G1**=Guest 1 **G2**=Guest 2

W: May I take your order now?

G1: We need another minute.

W: Would you like something to drink first?

G1: Yes. I'd like a bottle of beer.

W: And for the lady?

G2: Please bring me a glass of apple juice.

⊥ Practice 2

Make free conversations between a waiter and a customer according to the beverage list given below.

◆ BEVERAGES ◆

Juice······················
small···$0.65 large···$1.25
Orange, Apple, Tomato or Grapefruit
Milk························
small···$0.75 large···$1.45
Pot of Tea············$1.25
Coffee················$1.00

Unit 3 Ordering Food and Taking Orders I

4. Taking the orders for food or drink

◆ **What would you like to order?**

◇ I'd like soup, please.

 Practice 1

Listen to the recording and complete the following conversations.

1. A: What would you like to order?
   B: _____.
2. A: What would you like to order?
   B: _____.
3. A: What would you like to order?
   B: _____.
4. A: What would you like to order?
   B: _____.
5. A: What would you like to order?
   B: _____.
6. A: What would you like to order?
   B: _____.

Practice 2

Do the pair work. Your partner is the waiter and you are the guest. Make a short conversa-tion ordering food and taking the orders according to the Breakfast Menu given below. Then take turns.

GOOD MORNING MENU
Breakfast served from 7:30 to 11:30 A.M.

EGGS & OMELETTES

Eggs (2)··················$3.90
Fried, Scrambled, Poached or Boiled

Omelettes················$4.90
Fluffy 3 eggs omelette-Ham, Cheese or Western
All eggs orders are served with bacon or toast.

OTHER SPECIALTIES

Pancakes··················$4.25
Waffles····················$4.25
French Toast··············$4.50

BEVERAGES

Juice
small········$0.65 large········$1.25
Orange, Apple, Tomato or Grapefruit
Milk····································
small········$0.75 large········$1.45
Pot of Tea···················$1.25
Coffee······················$1.00

Summarize Key Expressions

1. Asking the guest if having an aperitif
   a. Would you like an aperitif before you order?
   b. Would you like a drink before you order?
   c. Would you like to have a drink before you order?
   d. Do you care for a drink before you order?
2. Saying no aperitifs
   a. No, thank you.
   b. No, we'll skip the aperitif.
   c. No, I don't think so. We'll order straight away.
   d. No, I think we'd like to order now.
3. Asking about a dish
   a. What is the Noisettes Milanese exactly?
   b. What's this dish?
   c. What is Mapo Tofu?
4. Explaining a dish
   a. It is lamb cooked with herbs and served with spaghetti.
   b. It is veal breaded and deep fried to golden brown and served with cream gravy.
   c. Mapo Tofu is a kind of spicy tofu sautéed with chili sauce.
5. Offering a drink
   a. Would you like something to drink first?
   b. How about something to drink?
   c. Can I get you something to drink?
   d. Something to drink first?
6. Ordering a drink
   a. Bring me a glass of red wine.
   b. A glass of fruit juice, please.
   c. I'll have a Coke/ a glass of iced tea.
   d. I'd like a glass of apple juice.

Give It a Try

 Task 1

Some guests are ordering lunch. Listen to their orders. Then read the answers in your book and make a tick (√) against the right answer.

1. The guest wants
   ☐ a. a mineral water.　　☐ b. a beer.　　☐ c. a tomato juice.

Unit 3 Ordering Food and Taking Orders

2. The guest wants
   - ☐ a. a dry sherry.
   - ☐ b. a sweet sherry.
   - ☐ c. a medium sherry.
3. The guest wants
   - ☐ a. curried prawns.
   - ☐ b. a prawn cocktail.
   - ☐ c. king prawns.
4. The guest wants
   - ☐ a. pike mousse.
   - ☐ b. pate maison.
   - ☐ c. mussels.
5. The guest wants
   - ☐ a. moussaka.
   - ☐ b. mullet.
   - ☐ c. hare
6. The guest wants
   - ☐ a. chicken chasseur.
   - ☐ b. coq au vin.
   - ☐ c. roast duck.
7. The guest wants
   - ☐ a. spare ribs.
   - ☐ b. Spanish pork.
   - ☐ c. sole.
8. The guest wants
   - ☐ a. goulash.
   - ☐ b. entrecote.
   - ☐ c. veal casserole.

Task 2

Look at the menu below. Listen to the guests ordering their meals and write down the orders.

STARTERS	WINE LIST	
Prawn Cocktail	GERMANY	FRANCE
Soup of the Day	Baden Dry	WHITE
Smoked Salmon	Piesporter Michelsberg	Bordeaux Blanc de Blancs
Fresh Melon	Franken Sylvaner	Chablis, 1983
Pate de Maison	Geisenheimer Schlossgarten	
Salade Nicoise	Niersteiner Domtal	
	Golderner Oktober Riesling	ROSE
MAIN COURSE		Anjou Rosé
Lamb Cutlets		
Fillet Steak		
Sole		RED
Omelette (ham, tomato, mushroom)		Le Piat de Beaujolais
Chicken Kiev		Cotes du Rhone
Salad (ham, beef, chicken)		Mouton Cadet

ORDERS

1. _____
   _____
2. _____
   _____

3. _____

4. _____

5. _____

6. _____

Task 3

Complete the following conversation according to what you will hear.
C=Clerk   G=Guest
C: _____(1), sir?
G: My wife will _____(2), and I'll have _____(3), please.
C: Certainly, sir. A Sherry and a Gin. And _____(4)?
G: Sure. The curried prawns and the clams, please.
C: _____(5).
G: And after that _____(6), and my wife _____(7).
C: And a hare and a roast duck. _____(8).

Task 4

Use the menu given below and make conversations between a waiter and a guest. Try to use the terms or expressions you have learned from this unit while you are making the conversation.

MENU

APERITEFS		MAIN DISHES
Cocktails		Turbot with Crab Sauce
Fruit Juices		Stuffed Fillets of Sole
Gin	Rum	Moussaka
Whisky	Vodka	Hare in Cream Sauce
Sherry	Pastis	Spare Ribs
HORS D'OEUVRES		Roast Duck
Shellfish Cocktail		Italian Veal Casserole
Curried Prawns		Chicken Chasseur
King Prawns		**SWEETS**
Consommé		From the trolley
Clams		

Unit 3 Ordering Food and Taking Orders

─── Do Extension Activities ───

 Activity 1

Listen to the conversation and make a tick (✓) where appropriate.

	Whisky	Brandy	Grape Wine	Distilled from Grain	Distilled from Grapes
Bourbon					
Bordeaux					
Burgundy					
Californian					
Hennessey					
Remy Martin					
Rye					
Scotch					

Activity 2

Role-play a restaurant scene. Take turns being the waiter/waitress and customer. The customer is coming to have lunch. Choose from today's lunch specials.

◆ MENU ◆

TODAY'S LUNCH SPECIALS

CHICKEN FINGERS

Juicy strips of tender white meat deep-fried in crispy batter

CRAB AND ASPARAGUS QUICHE

Made with real crab meat and tender, young asparagus tips

HOT ROAST BEEF SANDWICH

Thick slices of beef, cut fresh from the roast

BREADED FILET OF SOLE

Fresh sole, rolled lightly in bread crumbs, and baked to flaky perfection

All specials come with your choice of:

–Cream of Mushroom Soup or Green Salad

–Potatoes: Baked, Mashed or French Fries

–Vegetable: Buttered or Glazed Carrots

–Dessert: Vanilla Ice Cream or Fresh Fruit

Activity 3

Work in pairs and try to describe the following food or drinks.

1. What is a dry Martini?
2. Could you tell me what paella is?
3. What's blanquette of veal?
4. Could you explain what an Irish coffee is?
5. What's sweet and sour pork?

Learning Tips

Table Service Styles

The three most frequently used service styles are called French, Russian, and American. French service is the most elaborate. The service is from the right with the right hand. Russian service is simpler than French service. The waiter or waitress places plates before the guests from the right side and serves each guest from the left. American service is faster than Russian. The plates are served from the guest's right with the right hand.

Part B Recommending Dishes

Teaching hours: 2 hours

Learning Goals:

To be able to
- ask if the guest is ready to order
- tell we haven't decided what to order
- make a recommendation for the guest
- order the main course
- tell four major cuisines in China

Vocabulary Assistance

toothpick *n.* 牙签
teapot *n.* 茶壶
plate *n.* 盘子
fork *n.* 叉子
spoon *n.* 勺
napkin *n.* 餐巾纸
knife *n.* 刀
glass *n.* 玻璃杯
chopsticks *n.* 筷子
hot *adj.* 辣的,辛辣的
spicy *adj.* 用香料调味的
heavy *adj.* 口味重的
flavor *n.* 味道
fresh *adj.* 新鲜的

light *adj.* 清淡的
stress *v.* 强调
recommend *v.* 推荐
recommendation *n.* 推荐
chili sauce 辣椒酱
spinach *n.* 菠菜
marvelous *adj.* 棒极了
braise *v.* 炖
mince *v.* 切碎,绞肉
shred *v.* 切碎
flambé *v.* 火烧(浇上白兰地等酒后点燃上桌)
broad bean 蚕豆
sea cucumber 海参

English for Food and Beverages

Start You Off

Activity 1

Look at the pictures below and match them with the right words given below.

 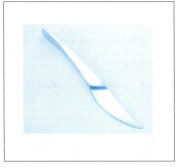 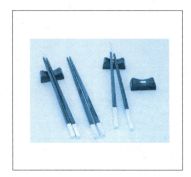

1. _____   2. _____   3. _____

4. _____   5. _____   6. _____

7. _____   8. _____   9. _____

| teapot | plate | fork | spoon | glass |
| toothpick | napkin | knife | chopsticks | |

54

Unit 3 Ordering Food and Taking Orders I

 Activity 2

Listen to the description of the four major cuisines in China and match the cuisines in column A with the features in column B.

A	B
(　) 1. Sichuan Style	a. Fresh and light
(　) 2. Shandong Style	b. Stressing cutting and original flavor
(　) 3. Guangdong Style	c. Hot and spicy
(　) 4. Huaiyang Style	d. Heavy

 Activity 3

Look at the words given below and match the English word with an appropriate word in Chinese.

1. steam   a. 拌
2. stew   b. 炸
3. rinse   c. 烤
4. sauté   d. 烘焙
5. smoke   e. 水煮
6. mix   f. 清蒸
7. fry   g. 煨、炖
8. roast   h. 涮
9. boil   i. 烟熏
10. bake   j. 嫩炒

—— Focus on Language ——

 Conversation

We'd Like to Try Some Chinese Food

Questions

1. What would you say when you are going to take orders?
2. What would you do if the guest has no idea about the food?
3. How do you make a recommendation to the guest?

Listen to the conversation and read after it. Then try to find the answers to the questions.

C=Clerk   G=Guest

C: What would you like to order, sir?
G: I'd like to try some Chinese food.

55

C: Have you had any Chinese food before?

G: No, I haven't.

C: We serve different styles of Chinese food here. But I'm not sure which style you prefer.

G: I have no idea about it.

C: Well, Cantonese food is rather light, Shandong food is heavy, and Sichuan food is usually spicy and hot.

G: Oh, I see. I'd rather have hot food.

C: If so, I suggest you have a taste of Sichuan dishes. Most Sichuan dishes are spicy and hot.

G: Really. So what's your recommendation for me?

C: I think Mapo Tofu, Sichuan style and shredded pork with chili sauce are quite special.

G: All right, I'll have them.

C: Would you like to have rice to go with them?

G: Yes, please.

Language Tips

1. Asking if ready to order

◆ **Are you ready to order, sir?**

Would you like to order now?

◇ Yes. I'd like to try some Chinese food.

◇ Not yet. We're still looking at the menu.

No, we haven't decided yet.

Practice 1

Listen to the recording and make a tick (√) according to the conversation.

	Ready to Order	Not Ready to Order
Guest 1		
Guest 2		
Guest 3		
Guest 4		
Guest 5		

2. Making a recommendation for the guest

◇ What would you recommend for the main course?

Unit 3 Ordering Food and Taking Orders I

◆ **Why don't you try Sichuan dishes? It's very good.**

I would suggest / recommend you have a taste of Shandong cuisine.

Practice 1

These guests cannot decide what vegetables to have. Suggest what they should have, using the pictures given below. First, look at the example.

Making Suggestions

Guest: What's good at the moment in the way of vegetables?

Waiter: I should have the broad beans and the spinach, sir. They're both in season at the moment.

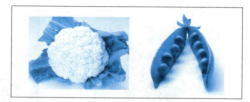

Practice 2

Think of ten Chinese dishes and complete the conversation below in pairs.

Student A: What would you recommend for the main course?

Student B: Why don't you try _____? It's marvelous.

3. Ordering the main course

◆ **What would you like to order, sir/madam?**

What will you have, sir/madam?

◇ **I'll have Sichuan dishes.**

Mapo Tofu, please.

57

English for Food and Beverages

Practice 1

Look at the pictures and make short conversations for ordering the main course in pairs by following the example given below.

Student A: What would you like to order, sir/madam?

Student B: I'll have..., please.

Practice 2

Look at the Menu below and make your order for the main dishes for lunch.

Menu for Lunch

Main Dishes

BRAISED TURTLE WITH GARLIC

STEAMED MINCED PORK BALLS

BIRD'S NEST AND SHREDDED CHICKEN

Summarize Key Expressions

1. Asking if ready to order

   a. Are you ready to order, sir/madam?

   b. Would you like to order now?

   c. Have you decided yet, sir/madam?/Have you decided on something?

   d. Have you chosen what you'd like?

   e. May I take your order now?

   f. What would you like to order, sir/madam?

g. What will you have, sir/madam?
2. Telling we haven't decided yet
   a. No, we're still looking at the menu.
   b. No, we haven't decided yet. What would you recommend for the main course?
   c. Not yet. We are not sure what to order. Maybe you could recommend something to us.
   d. No, we can't read this menu. Maybe you could explain to us.
   e. No, we're not ready yet.
   f. Almost. Could you tell us...?
   g. I'm having trouble deciding. What's your recommendation for me?
3. Recommending dishes
   a. Why don't you try...? It's very good.
   b. I would suggest / recommend you have a taste of...
   c. Perhaps I could recommend...
   d. Perhaps you'd like to have...
   e. Today, our specialty is...
   f. We've got a choice of...
   g. You can choose from...
   h. Shall I make a recommendation?
4. Ordering the main course
   a. I'll have Sichuan dishes.
   b. I think I'll have...
   c. Mapo Tofu, please.

Give It a Try

 Task 1

Listen to the conversation between the guest and the waiter. Tick (✓) the information about what the waiter will recommend and what the guest will take.

Food had, wanted and recommended	Guest	Waiter
Light food		
Braised turtle with garlic		
Steamed minced pork balls		
Soup		
Bird's nest and shredded chicken soup		
Baked pancakes		

English for Food and Beverages

  Task 2

Listen to the following conversation and write down the recommendation made by the waiter.

Recommendation Made by the Waiter

1. _____
2. _____
3. _____
4. _____
5. _____

Task 3

Read the following sentences and decide which parts are spoken by the Guest and which are spoken by the Waiter. Mark the parts with G for Guest and W for Waiter. Then rearrange the order of the conversation and do the conversation with your partner.

W=Waiter **G**=Guest

Ordering Chinese Food

_____ You are welcome.
_____ Is there any difference between them?
_____ How about Braised Sea Cucumber with Spring Onion?
_____ Oh, I like heavy food. What's your specialty for Shandong food?
_____ What would like to order, sir?
_____ Alright, I'll take that. Thank you very much.
_____ Yes, Shandong food is heavy while Guangdong food is light.
_____ I have no idea about Chinese food. What's your recommendation?
_____ Which style do you prefer?
_____ I'd like to try some Chinese food.
_____ We serve Shandong food and Guangdong food here.

―――――――――――― Do Extension Activities ――――――――――――

Activity 1

Read the following passage and fill out the boxes with the right information you will get from your reading.

　　The responsibilities of a restaurant's service staff depend on the size, nature of the restaurant itself, and the type of service dictated by the management. A general organizational scheme for service staff is as follows:

Unit 3 Ordering Food and Taking Orders I

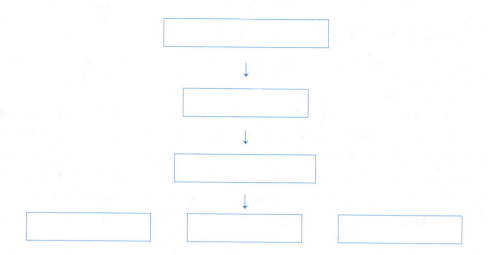

The restaurant manager is in charge of the restaurant and its operation. He is not actually a member of the service staff, but he supervises the captain.

Captain is responsible for all service staff. He welcomes the guests, shows them to their tables, and sometimes takes orders. Captain takes extra care of the customers when carving and flambéing are necessary. He also works as a mediator between service and kitchen staff to maintain good relations and deals with guests' complaints. He controls the positioning of the staff and oversees their performance.

The headwaiter is usually responsible for serving the guests. A restaurant may have more than one headwaiter, with each in charge of two or three tables only. Usually the headwaiter performs the carving and flambéing.

The waiter assists the headwaiter by going back and forth between the kitchen and dining room, bringing out the ordered meals and taking away finished meals.

The wine steward is in charge of all wine-related service in the dining room. He takes orders at the guests' tables and oversees the stocking of the wine cellar.

The bartender is accountable for the mixing and serving of cocktails, aperitifs and liqueurs.

Activity 2

Read the passage again. Choose one of the service staff and complete the following conversation according to the information from the passage. After you finish, change your turns.

A=Student A   B=Student B

A: Hi, _____. How are you doing?

B: Fine. Now I am the captain of Rose Garden Restaurant.

A: Are you in charge of the restaurant?

B: No. That's the job of a restaurant manager, and I'm under the charge of the manager.

A: Then what is your job?

B: My task is to...

61

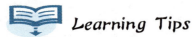 Learning Tips

Chopsticks

Chopsticks originated in China. According to history, the people used chopsticks about 4,000 years ago. Today chopsticks are made of wood, bamboo or plastic. The most expensive are made of ivory or hard green jade. In ancient times, rich people used hard green jade or gold chopsticks to show their wealth. Many kings and emperors used silver ones to test their food. In China chopsticks are related to good luck. On the eve of the Spring Festival many families will put new chopsticks in a long line at dinner as a way of wishing one another good luck.

Unit 4

Ordering Food and Taking Orders II

Part A Asking What the Guest Prefers

Teaching hours: 2 hours

Learning Goals:

To be able to
- order the main course
- ask for special instruction on food
- give special instruction on food
- ask if having anything to go with food
- asking what the guest prefers

Vocabulary Assistance

bean *n.* 菜豆,豆荚
cucumber *n.* 黄瓜
eggplant *n.* 茄子
celery *n.* 芹菜
broccoli *n.* 西兰花,花茎甘蓝
leek *n.* 大葱
carrot *n.* 胡萝卜
cauliflower *n.* 花椰菜,菜花
oatmeal *n.* 燕麦片,燕麦粥

couscous *n.* 肉菜饭
bacon *n.* 培根,咸肉
scramble *v.* 炒(蛋)
chips *n.* 薯条
sausage *n.* 香肠
yoghurt *n.* 酸奶
croissant *n.* 牛角面包
sweet bell pepper 柿子椒
runner bean 红花菜豆

English for Food and Beverages

Start You Off

Activity 1
Look at these vegetables and learn the English words.

Activity 2
Match the words in column A with the appropriate definitions in column B.

A	B
1. bake	a. cook in water or another liquid at 100 degrees centigrade
2. boil	b. cook in water or another liquid at a little less than 100 degrees centigrade
3. fry	c. cook in the water or another liquid at 100 degrees centigrade, slowly and for a long time (e.g. beef)
4. grill	d. cook in steam
5. poach	e. cook in the oven, with very little or no fat (e.g. bread)
6. roast	f. cook in the oven, with fat (e.g. meat)
7. sauté	g. cook under (or over) direct heat (e.g. steak)
8. steam	h. cook in fat or oil
9. stew	i. cook in a little fat, for a short time

Activity 3

The guests want to know how their meals are cooked. Answer their questions, using the information given below, like this:

　　Guest: Is the chicken boiled?（fry）

　　Waiter: No, sir/madam, it's fried.

1. Are the potatoes roasted?（boil）
___

2. Is the steak fried?（grill）
___

3. Are the eggs boiled?（poach）
___

4. Is the trout fried?（bake）
___

5. Does the fruit salad come with ordinary cream?（whip）
___

Focus on Language

 Conversation

How Would You Like Your Steak Cooked

Questions

1. What would you do when you are going to take orders?
2. How do you order the main course?
3. How do you take the orders of the main course?
4. What would you ask the guest for special instruction on food?
5. How do you give special instruction on food as a guest?

　　Listen to the conversation and read after it. Then try to find the answers to the questions.

W=Waiter　　**G1**=Guest 1　　**G2**=Guest 2

W: Are you ready to order, sir?
G1: Yes. I think I'll have the steak.
G2: Steak for me, too, please.
W: How would you like them cooked?
G1: I don't like my steak too underdone. Make mine well-done, please.
G2: Rare for me, please.
W: Fine. What would you like to go with your steaks?
G1: Chips and a green salad, please.
G2: I'll have chips. And peas, if you have them.

65

W: And what would you like to drink? Bottled beer or wine?
G1: We'd like wine better.
W: Would you rather have sweet wine or dry wine?
G1: I prefer sweet wine.
G2: I think dry wine would do nicely.
W: All right, I'll be back soon?

Language Tips

1. Asking and giving special instruction on food

◆ How would you like your steak cooked?

◇ Make mine well-done.

 Practice 1

Model 1
A: Is your steak rare *enough*?
B: I'm afraid it's *too* rare. I can't eat it.

Model 2
A: Is your steak *too* well-done?
B: No, it's not well-done *enough*. I like it *very* well-done.

In a similar way, answer the following questions.

1. Is your wine too dry?   No, ... I like...
2. Is your couscous spicy enough?   I'm afraid... I can't...
3. Is your coffee strong enough?   I'm afraid... I can't...
4. Is your martini too weak?   No, ... I like...

Practice 2
Role-play according to the following situations.
Diner: —You'd like bacon, eggs, toast, and a glass of fresh orange juice.
       —You want your eggs fried, easy over(fried on both sides).
Waiter: —Ask what the diner would like.
        —Ask if he'd like his eggs fried or scrambled.

2. Asking if having anything to go with food

◆ What would you like to go with your steak?

Unit 4 Ordering Food and Taking Orders II

◇ Chips and a green salad, please.

 Practice 1

Look at the list of vegetables given below. Guests can choose which vegetables they want. Listen to the guests ordering their vegetables and write down the ones they want.

SALAD VEGETABLES
Lettuce, cucumber, tomatoes, broad beans, runner beans,
Celery, sweet bell pepper, carrots
VEGETABLES
Cabbage, peas, broad beans, runner beans, spinach,
Eggplant, onions, broccoli, cauliflower, leeks, tomatoes,
Chips, roast potatoes, mushrooms, boiled potatoes

1. Waiter: What would you like with the cold chicken?
   Guest: And with the cold chicken, I'll have _____, _____, _____ and _____, please.
2. Waiter: And what would you like with the roast duck, madam?
   Guest: Let me see, er, roast potatoes, I think, _____ and _____. Yes, that'll do fine, thank you.
3. Waiter: What kind of salad would you like, sir?
   Guest: Celery, I love celery, and let's say _____ and _____. That'll do me nicely.
4. Waiter: And for vegetables, sir?
   Guest: _____, _____, _____ and _____, please.
5. Waiter: Have you decided on your salad, madam?
   Guest: Yes. I'll take the _____, _____ and _____, please.
6. Waiter: What would you like as vegetables, madam?
   Guest: Let me see. Let's say _____, boiled _____ and some _____.
7. Waiter: And as a salad to go with that, madam?
   Guest: Something simple. Just _____ and _____, please.
8. Waiter: And what vegetables would you like with your roast lamb, sir?
   Guest: _____, _____ and, er, what about some _____? Oh, and some _____.
   I'm hungry this evening.

Practice 2

Answer these guests' questions, like this:

Guest: What vegetables come with the steak? (peas, mushrooms, chips and tomatoes)
Waiter: It's served with peas, mushrooms, chips and tomatoes, sir/madam.

1. What do I get in the cold chicken salad? (tomatoes, lettuce, cucumber and celery)
   _____

English for Food and Beverages

2. What vegetables come with the kidneys? (onions, spinach and chips)
   _____

3. What comes with the gammon steak? (chips, broccoli and beans)
   _____

4. What do I get with the roast duck? ((roast) potatoes, carrots, peas and leeks)
   _____

5. What comes with the roast lamb? ((roast) potatoes, broccoli and peas)
   _____

3. Asking what the guest prefers for drinks

◆ **What would you like to drink? Bottled beer or wine?**

Would you rather have sweet wine or dry wine?

◇ We'd like wine better.

I prefer sweet wine.

 Practice 1

Read through the Bar List. Some guests are ordering drinks. Listen to their orders and read the answers in your book. Make a tick (√) against the right order.

BAR LIST

WHISKY	MIXERS & MINERALS
Scotch Proprietary	Baby Juices
Irish	Coke
Rye	Perrier 220ml
Bourbon	Splits
GIN	**APERITIFS**
Proprietary	Willoughbys Sherries
Regular	Tio Pepe
	Croft Original
VODKA	
Proprietary	**VERMOUTHS**
Regular	Dubonnet
Stolichnaya	Martini/Cinzano
COGNAC	**WINE**
Louis Bernard	House per Glass
Martell 3 Star	
Remy Martin 3 Star	**CHAMPAGNE**
Remy Martin VSOP	House per Glass

68

Unit 4 Ordering Food and Taking Orders II

1. The guest has ordered
   - [ ] a. a Dubonnet.
   - [ ] b. a Martini.
   - [ ] c. a Cinzano.
2. The guest has ordered
   - [ ] a. a Proprietary gin.
   - [ ] b. a regular gin and tonic.
   - [ ] c. a regular gin and orange.
3. The guest has ordered
   - [ ] a. a proprietary vodka.
   - [ ] b. a regular vodka.
   - [ ] c. a Stolichnaya.
4. The guest has ordered
   - [ ] a. a rye whisky.
   - [ ] b. a regular scotch.
   - [ ] c. a bourbon.
5. The guest has ordered
   - [ ] a. an ice cream.
   - [ ] b. a lemonade.
   - [ ] c. a Perrier with ice and lemon.
6. The guest has ordered
   - [ ] a. a Martell 3 Star.
   - [ ] b. a Remy Martin 3 Star.
   - [ ] c. a Remy Martin VSOP.
7. The guest has ordered
   - [ ] a. a Croft Original.
   - [ ] b. a Tio Pepe.
   - [ ] c. a Bristol Cream.
8. The guest has ordered
   - [ ] a. rosé wine.
   - [ ] b. red wine.
   - [ ] c. white wine.

Practice 2

Look at the example given below and do the following practice like this:

Example

—I'd like some pate, please.
—Would you rather/prefer the pate de champagne or the pate maison, sir?

Now ask what these guests would prefer. Use the table below.

Would you	prefer rather have	red or white, madam? draught or bottled, sir? the entrecote or the tournedos, madam? cognac or armagnac, sir? mixed vegetable or tomato, madam?

1. I'll have a brandy, please.
   _____

2. Some soup to start with, please?
   _____

3. Could I have a glass of wine?
   _____

4. I'd like a steak as the main course, I think.
   _____

5. A beer, please.
   _____

Practice 3

Look at the wine list and make short conversations in pairs as the model given below.

Model:

A: What would you like to drink?

B: I would rather have/prefer the Baden dry, please.

WINE LIST

GERMANY	FRANCE
Baden Dry	**WHITE**
Piesporter Michelsberg	Bordeaux Blanc de Blancs
Franken Sylvaner	Chablis, 1983
Geisenheimer Schlossgarten	
Niersteiner Domtal	
Golderner Oktober Riesling	**ROSE**
	Anjou Rosé
	RED
	Le Piat de Beaujolais

Summarize Key Expressions

1. Asking for special instruction on food
    a. How would you like your steak cooked?
    b. How do you like your steak done/prepared?
    c. How would you like your steak, medium, rare or well-done?
2. Giving special instruction on food
    a. Make mine well-done.
    b. Rare for me, please.
    c. Not too underdone, please.
3. Asking if having anything to go with food
    a. What would you like to go with your steak?
    b. What would you like to go with your main course?
    c. What vegetable would you like?
    d. What will your vegetable be?
    e. Any vegetables?

Unit 4 Ordering Food and Taking Orders II

4. Asking what the guest prefers for drinks
    a. What would you like to drink? Bottled beer or wine?
    b. Would you rather have sweet wine or dry wine?
    c. Do you prefer red wine or white wine?

———————————— Give It a Try ————————————

  Task 1

Listen to the recording and tick (√) the food or drink ordered by the guests.

Food or Drink Ordered	Conversation 1	Conversation 2	Conversation 3
American breakfast			
Coffee			
Healthy breakfast			
Tomato			
Grapefruit			
Orange			
Danish pastry			
Eggs			
Cheese omelet			
Bacon			
Ham			
Oatmeal			
Sausage			
Yoghurt			
Croissant			

  Task 2

Listen to the conversation and complete it with the information that you will hear.

G=Guest   **W**=waiter

W: Would you care to order now, sir?

G: Yes, please. Well, _____(1) the baked salmon.

W: Good. And _____(2) potatoes _____(3)?

G: _____(4) potatoes.

W: _____(5)?

English for Food and Beverages

G: _____ (6) ... Oh, no. I think _____ (7).
W: The spinach. Yes, sir. _____ (8)?
G: _____ (9), please.
W: _____ (10) it: French, Russian or blue cheese?
G: _____ (11) the French.
W: And _____ (12)? _____ (13)?
G: _____ (14), please.

Task 3

Read the following sentences and decide which parts are spoken by the Guest and which are spoken by the Waiter. Mark the parts with G for Guest and W for Waiter. Then rearrange the order of the conversation and do the conversation with your partner.

W=Waiter **G**=Guest

Ordering Western Food

_____ Nothing right now, thank you.
_____ What would you like to order, madam?
_____ Fine, madam. And what will you have to drink?
_____ I'd like to take the veal cutlet.
_____ I'll have the broccoli.
_____ I'm sorry, madam. But we are all out of the veal cutlet.
_____ Any vegetables?
_____ Baked?
_____ Oh, I see. Bring me the fillet of sole then.
_____ Mashed, boiled, or baked potato?
_____ Very good, madam. Soup or salad?
_____ That sounds good. I'll have the soup.
_____ What's today's soup?
_____ It is French onion.

Do Extension Activities

Activity 1

In the following chart, various foods and drinks are entered in the wrong box. For example, Port appears in Red Wine but it belongs to Dessert Wine. Rearrange the chart so that the food and drinks appear in the correct boxes.

Aperitifs	1 Rioja Chianti Vermouth	8 Hors d'oeuvres

Unit 4 Ordering Food and Taking Orders II

Sparkling Wine	2	Burgundy Vermouth Campari	9 Veal
White Wine	3	Ruby Port Liqueur Brandy Hock Riesling	10 Beef
Rosé Wine	4	Chablis Beaujolais	11 Coffee
Red Wine	5	Champagne Port Beaune	12 Chicken Dessert
Dessert Wine	6	Madeira Rosé d'Anjou Sherry	13 Fish
Liqueurs	7	Cointreau Sherry	14 Lamb

 Activity 2

Listen to the conversation and make a tick (√) against the drinks offered by the bartender.

Drinks	1	2	3	4	5	6
Bourbon						
Cinzano						
Rye						
Malt						
Martini						
Pernod						
Juice						
Tio Pepe						
Sherry						
Louis Bernard						
Mineral water						
Croft Original						
Remy Martin						
Martell						
Bristol Cream						

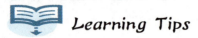 **Learning Tips**

Eating Orders

A tasty meal is composed of a variety of foods, and the foods are eaten in satisfying order—usually one that corresponds to the established custom. The following kinds of food items—for the most part eaten in order—are offered on most menus: appetizers, entrées, vegetables and other side dishes, salads, breads, desserts, and beverages. Hot and cold appetizers, offered to titillate the taste buds, are usually prepared from shellfish, smoked meats and fish, fruits, vegetables, pates, caviar or other exotic and expensive ingredients. The entrée, which is the main dish and comes with at least one vegetable or other side dish, generally falls into these categories: meat, poultry, fish, seafood, eggs, pasta and etc. Desserts are popular menu items which leaves a sweet taste in the guest's mouth. The beverages include coffee, tea, milk, cocoa, soft drinks, bottled water and alcoholic beverages as well as fruit and vegetable juices.

Part B Room Service

Teaching hours: 2 hours

Learning Goals:

To be able to
- offer help
- order room service
- respond to the requirements
- specify wants

Vocabulary Assistance

salt *n.* 盐
sugar *n.* 糖
vinegar *n.* 醋
chili *n.* 辣椒
curry *n.* 咖喱
garlic *n.* 蒜
clove *n.* 丁香
pepper *n.* 胡椒
mustard *n.* 芥末

pastry *n.* 油酥糕点
grapefruit *n.* 葡萄柚, 西柚
poach *v.* 水煮荷包蛋
boil *v.* 水煮
caffeine *n.* 咖啡因
snacks *n.* 点心, 小吃
soy sauce 酱油
oyster sauce 蚝油
fish sauce 鱼露

Start You Off

Activity 1

Look at these ingredients and learn the English words.

salt

sugar

soy sauce

vinegar

English for Food and Beverages

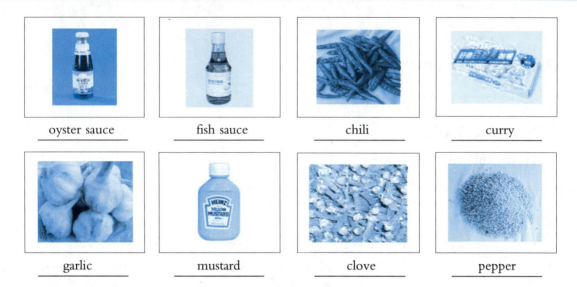

| oyster sauce | fish sauce | chili | curry |
| garlic | mustard | clove | pepper |

Activity 2

Match the English words in column A with the appropriate Chinese definitions in column B.

A	B
1. cubing	a. 捣碎
2. slicing	b. 绞碎
3. mashing	c. 切丁
4. pounding	d. 切片
5. mincing	e. 去渣
6. stirring	f. 捣烂
7. straining	g. 搅拌
8. shelling	h. 去皮
9. skinning	i. 去壳
10. scaling	j. 剁碎
11. chopping into pieces	k. 去鳞

Activity 3

Look at the pictures and try to tell the ways of making eggs in English.

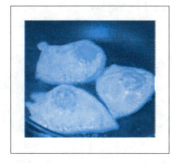
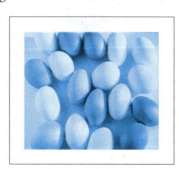

1. _____   2. _____   3. _____

Unit 4 Ordering Food and Taking Orders II

4. _____   5. _____   6. _____

Focus on Language

 Conversation

I Would Like Some Breakfast in My Room

Questions

1. How do the guests order Room Service?
2. How do you take the room service orders?
3. What would you ask when you are taking the guests' orders?
4. How would you ask the guest for special instruction on food?
5. How do you give special instruction on food as a guest?

  Listen to the conversation and read after it. Then try to find the answers to the questions.

W=Waiter   **G**=Guest

W: Room Service. Good morning. Can I help you?
G: Good morning. I'd like some breakfast in my room.
W: May I have your room number, please?
G: Room 201.
W: What would you like to have?
G: I'd like some bacon, two boiled eggs, toast, and a cup of black coffee.
W: How would you like your eggs, sir?
G: Lightly done.
W: Is that all?
G: That's it.
W: All right, I'll bring them to your room right away.
   (A few minutes later.)
W: Room Service, may I come in?
G: Come in, please.

77

W: Mr. Wilson?

G: Yes. Just put them on the table over there.

W: All right. Here are your bacon, boiled eggs, toast and a cup of black coffee. The bacon and toast are 8 *yuan*, the eggs are 3 *yuan* each, and the coffee is 3.50 *yuan*. That comes to 17.50 *yuan*, plus 10% service. So the total is 19.25 *yuan*. Here is the bill.

G: Thank you. Can I have it charged to my account, please?

W: Certainly, sir. Please sign here. Thank you for using room service. Good-bye.

G: Bye.

Language Tips

1. Offering help and ordering room service

◆ **Room Service. May I help you?**

◇ **I'd like some breakfast in my room. It's room 206.**

Practice 1

Some guests are ordering food. Listen to their orders and then complete the following conversations.

1. A: Room Service. May I help you?

   B: I'd like _____, please, the consommé. In Room_____.

2. A: Room Service. Can I help you?

   B: Could you send _____ to Room _____, please?

3. A: Room Service. May I help you?

   B: This is Room _____. Can you _____ as soon as possible, please? I'm in a hurry.

4. A: Room Service. Can I help you?

   B: _____. We'd like _____, please.

5. A: Room Service. May I help you?

   B: May I _____, please? _____.

6. A: Room Service. Can I help you?

   B: _____. We'd like something to eat for the children, please. The _____, for one, and _____.

7. A: Room Service. May I help you?

   B: _____ for my daughter, please, and a minute steak for me. _____.

8. A: Room Service. Can I help you?

   B: This is _____. _____ a tomato soup and a hamburger, please.

Practice 2

Now listen to these guests. They are ordering meals. Write down the orders and the room numbers according to what you will hear.

```
HOTEL
```

1. _____
_____
2. _____
_____
3. _____
_____
4. _____
_____
5. _____
_____
6. _____
_____

2. Specifying wants

◆ What kind of dressing would you like?

◇ **I'll have creamy garlic, please.**

◆ Would you like soup or salad?

◇ **I'd like soup, please.**

Practice 1

What kind of dressing would you like for your salad?

Tick the one you like best.

☐ French dressing
☐ Italian dressing
☐ Blue cheese
☐ Oil and vinegar
☐ Creamy garlic

Practice 2

Do the practice in pairs. Student A will be the waiter/waitress. Student B will be the customer. Make short conversations according to the given cures and examples in "Specifying Wants."

1. soup or salad
2. dressing for your salad

3. potatoes

4. vegetables

5. dessert

...

Practice 3

Role-play a restaurant scene. Take turns being the waiter/waitress specifying wants. Begin like this:

C=Customer   **W**=Waiter/Waitress

C: Excuse me!

W: Yes, sir/madam. What would you like?

...

Summarize Key Expressions

1. Offering help
   a. Can I help you?
   b. May I help you?
   c. What can I do for you?
   d. Could I be of assistance?
   e. Just let me know if there is anything I can do for you?
2. Ordering room service
   a. I'd like some breakfast in my room.
   b. We'd like a snack.
   c. Would you/Could you bring me a salad to my room?
   d. Could I have a vegetable salad, please?
   e. I'll have dinner in my room.
3. Responding to the requirements
   a. Certainly, sir/madam.
   b. Yes, sir/madam.
   c. Immediately, sir/madam.
   d. I'll go and get it right away, sir/madam.
   e. I'll bring them to your room right away/at once, sir/madam.
4. Specifying wants
   a. What kind of dressing would you like?
   b. Would you like soup or salad?
   c. I'll have creamy garlic, please.
   d. I'll take creamy garlic, please.
   e. I'd like soup, please.
5. Asking the way of paying the bill
   a. Can I have it charged to my account, please?

b. Can I have the bill/the check charged to my account, please?

c. Can/Will you please put it on my tab?

Give It a Try

 Task 1

Look at the Breakfast menu. Listen to the recording and put a tick (√) against the right order. Then make conversations of ordering breakfast in pairs.

AMERICAN BREAKFAST
- Fruit juice ················· Tomato, orange or grapefruit
- Two fresh eggs, any style ············· Fried, poached, boiled or scrambled
- ················· With bacon, ham or sausage
- Croissant, toast or Danish pastry
- Coffee or tea

CONTINENTAL BREAKFAST
- Fruit juice ················· Tomato, orange or grapefruit
- Croissant, toast or Danish pastry
- Coffee or tea

HEALTHY BREAKFAST
- Fruit juice ················· Tomato, orange or grapefruit
- Oatmeal or Yoghurt
- Vegetable salad
- Toasted bread
- Coffee, caffeine free coffee or tea

BEVERAGES
- Fresh juice ················· Orange or grapefruit
- Fruit juice ················· Tomato, orange or grapefruit
- Coffee, tea
- Milk, yoghurt
- Hot chocolate

EGGS AND OMELETS
- Two fresh eggs, any style ············· Fried, boiled, scrambled or poached
- Omelets ··············· With bacon, tomato, plain, cheese, mushroom or ham

1. The guest wants
   a. the American breakfast.
   b. the Continental breakfast.
   c. the Healthy breakfast.

2. The guest wants
   a. scrambled eggs with ham.
   b. poached eggs with ham.
   c. scrambled eggs with bacon.

English for Food and Beverages

3. The guest wants
   a. orange juice, oatmeal and tea.
   b. tomato juice, yoghurt and tea.
   c. orange juice, yoghurt and tea.

4. The guest wants
   a. a mushroom omelet.
   b. a ham omelet.
   c. a cheese omelet.

5. The guest wants
   a. fried eggs.
   b. scrambled eggs.
   c. poached eggs.

6. The guest wants
   a. fried eggs and ham.
   b. poached eggs and bacon.
   c. fried eggs and bacon.

7. The guest wants
   a. toast.
   b. a Danish pastry.
   c. a croissant.

8. The guest wants
   a. tomato juice, oatmeal and tea.
   b. tomato juice, oatmeal and coffee.
   c. tomato juice, oatmeal and caffeine free coffee.

Task 2

Listen to the conversation and complete it with the appropriate words you will hear.

G=Guest W=Waiter

W: Good evening. Room Service. _____(1)?

G: _____(2). I'd _____(3) a salad, a T-bone steak and a bottle of red wine. What do you have for _____(4)?

W: We have _____(5) and Chef's salad today.

G: _____(6) the lettuce salad.

W: What kind of _____(7) on your _____(8)?

G: Thousand Islands, please.

W: All right. And one _____(9). What shall I bring you for wine? Sweet or dry?

G: Dry, _____(10).

W: Will there be anything else?

G: No, _____(11).

W: May I have your _____(12) and _____(13), please?

G: Catherine Marks. It's Room 1919.

W: Fine. Room 1919, one _____(14) with _____(15) dressing, one T-bone steak, _____(16) dry red wine.

G: That's it.

W: Thank you for _____(17). I'll send your _____(18) up as soon as possible.

Task 3

Mrs. Julia Marks has ordered the room service and a room service waiter is coming to deliver her orders. Read the following sentences and decide which parts are spoken by the Guest and which are spoken by the Waiter. Mark the parts with G for Guest and W for Waiter. Then rearrange the order of the conversation and do the conversation with your partner.

_____ It's Room Service. May I come in?

Unit 4 Ordering Food and Taking Orders II

_____ Yes, come in, please.

_____ On the table, please.

_____ All right. Would you please sign the bill?

_____ Thank you, madam. I've brought the salad, a T-bone steak and deserts you just ordered. Where should I put them?

_____ Sure. Here you are.

_____ By the way, when could I come back to take away the plates?

_____ I will. Thank you.

_____ Good bye. Have a good night.

_____ After 9:00 tomorrow morning.

_____ Fine, madam. Please enjoy your food. Just call us when you need more orders. We are always at your service.

Do Extension Activities

 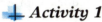

Mr. Robert is staying in a hotel. He finds the mini-bar in his room is nearly empty, so he makes a phone to the Room Service, asking for more replenishment. Listen to the conversation and write down the items for replenishment.

ROOM SERVICE

Name: _____

Room Number: _____

Items for Replenishing the Mini-bar

Snacks:

1. _____
2. _____

Drinks:

1. _____
2. _____
3. _____

Activity 2

Read the following passage and try to get the information about which wine to drink with which food.

WHICH WINE TO DRINK WITH WHICH FOOD

Some customers worry about which wine to drink with which food, and a food service worker may be asked for helpful suggestions. One important point to remember is that wine should not be served with salad because the vinegar in salad dressing destroys the flavor of the

83

wine. A wine list usually groups wines into red, white, rosé, and sparkling. Red wine is usually more full-bodied than white wine and is the standard choice with "butcher's meats"—beef, pork, lamb and veal. White wine, usually lighter in taste, is the usual choice with mild foods such as chicken and egg dishes and most fish. Rosé, an exuberant wine that is usually served chilled, is often the best compromise if the entrées selected by the customers at a particular table range from beef to fish. Rosé is usually thought to "go" with most foods. Sparkling wines, such as champagne, are also considered appropriate for most foods. They, too, are served chilled, and they are the most festive of all wines. Like wine, beer may be served with most meals, although it is most often served with lunches, snacks, and light suppers. Beer may be light and tart or dark and sweet. A food service worker should be able to describe, in general terms, the kinds of beer stocked by the restaurant. This usually includes domestic, imported, premium, and light brands. The server should also know which beers are sold by the bottle or can and which are sold only from a tapped keg—so-called draft beer. Draft beer is usually cheaper than bottled or canned beer.

Activity 3

Ask each other questions in pairs about the information of which wine to drink with which food according to the passage in Activity 2.

Activity 4

Work in groups and try to find out "Wines." Then list them out.

Wines includes:

1. _____
2. _____
3. _____
4. _____

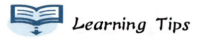 Learning Tips

Room Service

The purpose of room service is to provide guests with a complete service of meals, snacks and beverages in the rooms or suites at all times of the day or night. It is organized from an area adjacent to the kitchens and still room, or from a completely separate area with just the main meals coming from the main kitchen. The key to a successful room service operation is organization. Food must be delivered promptly and at the correct temperature. Guests will become annoyed if their breakfast order arrives an hour late. Incorrect orders also complicate the system, as it takes a great deal of time to return an incorrect order to the kitchen, have it redone, and transport it back to the guests' room.

Unit 5

Ordering Dessert

Part A Asking and Telling If Dessert Is Wanted I

Teaching hours: 2 hours

Learning Goals:

To be able to
- learn some English names for some desserts
- learn some knowledge on dessert
- know how to ask a guest if dessert is wanted
- know how to order dessert
- know how to ask for the dessert menu
- know how to ask for a recommendation
- know how to make a recommendation

Vocabulary Assistance

pudding *n.* 布丁
tart *n.* 蛋挞,果馅饼,小烘饼
blueberry *n.* 蓝莓
mango *n.* 芒果
mousse *n.* 木斯（一种多泡沫含奶油的甜点）
oatmeal *n.* 燕麦片
onion *n.* 洋葱
satisfactory *adj.* 满意的
origin *n.* 起源,由来
preferred *adj.* 首选的
aristocrat *n.* 贵族
emerge *v.* 显现,浮现,形成
cookie *n.* （苏格兰）甜面包,（美国）小甜饼
pumpkin *n.* 南瓜

cherry *n.* 樱桃
pineapple *n.* 菠萝
raisin *n.* 葡萄干
vanilla *n.* 香草
cheese *n.* 奶酪
sundae *n.* 圣代冰淇淋
menu *n.* 菜单
trace *v.* 追踪,回溯
privilege *n.* 特权,特别待遇
luxury *n.* 奢侈,华贵
household *n.* 家庭
haw jelly 山楂糕
pea flour cake 豌豆黄
bean paste cake 绿豆糕

English for Food and Beverages

Start You Off

✚ Activity 1
Discussion

1. What is dessert?
2. How are desserts classified?
3. How many desserts do you know about? Could you name out some popular desserts you know?
4. When is dessert served during a meal? Is it served at the beginning of a meal or in the middle of a meal or at the end of a meal?

✚ Activity 2
Can you name these desserts in English? Try to match the pictures with the words given below.

pudding

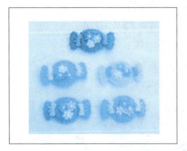

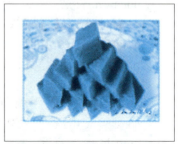

Unit 5 Ordering Dessert

_____   _____   _____

_____   _____

pudding	chocolate	cookie	haw jelly	sweet candy
cake	tart	pea flour cake	bean paste cake	ice cream
pumpkin pie	glutinous rice sesame balls			
Tang Yuan (Glutinous Rice Ball)				
Lǔdagunr (Glutinous Rice Roll Stuffed with Red Bean Paste)				

Now follow the model conversation below and do the questions and answers by replacing the underlined part with the names you have given to the above pictures.

Here is the model conversation:

A: What is it?
B: It's pudding.
A: Do you like it?
B: Yes, I do/No, I don't.

Focus on Language

 Conversation

Ordering Dessert

Questions

1. How should you ask a guest if dessert is wanted?
2. How should you order dessert?
3. How should you ask for a dessert menu?
4. How should you ask for a recommendation?
5. How should you make a recommendation?

Listen to the conversation and try to find the answers to the questions above. Then do the conversation in pairs.

W=Waiter/Waitress   G=Guest

W: Have you found everything satisfactory, madam?
G: Yes, everything is good. Thank you.
W: Would you like some dessert, madam?
G: Yes, I think so. Could I see the dessert menu?
W: Sure, madam. Here you are.
G: What do you recommend? I can't decide.
W: How about apple tarts? They are very popular in our restaurant.
G: Well, thank you. I'd like an apple tart and a strawberry ice cream.
W: Yes, madam. An apple tart and a strawberry ice cream.

Language Tips

1. Asking and telling if dessert is wanted

- *Would you like*   some dessert, sir/madam?

  Would you like to have

- Yes. *I'd like*   an apple tart and a strawberry ice-cream.

  I'd like to have

- Yes, madam/sir. An apple tart and a strawberry ice-cream.

Practice

Pattern Drills.

Practice the expressions "**Would you like some dessert?** *I'd like...*" and "**Would you like to have some dessert?** *I'd like to have...*" by replacing the underlined parts in the model conversations

Unit 5 Ordering Dessert

with the words given in the table. Take turns doing the role-play with your partner. One will be the guest, the other will be the waiter.

Here are the model conversations:

Conversation 1
Waiter: Would you like some dessert?
Guest: Yes. I'd like two apple pies.
Waiter: Yes, sir. Two apple pies.

Conversation 2
Waiter: Would you like to have some dessert, madam?
Guest: Yes. I'd like to have a lemon pie and a sundae ice-cream.
Waiter: Yes, madam. A lemon pie and a sundae ice-cream.

Here are the words you need:

apple pie, strawberry pie, lemon pie, banana pie, cherry pie, blueberry pie, pineapple pie
milk pudding, creamy pudding, fruit pudding, mango pudding, raisin pudding
sponge cake, coffee cake, cream cake, vanilla cream cake, chocolate mousse cake, cheese cake, black forest cake
cookie, fruit cookie, oatmeal cookie, raisin cookie
ice-cream, vanilla ice-cream, strawberry ice-cream, mango ice-cream, sundae ice-cream, coffee ice-cream
tart, apple tart, mango tart, onion tart

2. Asking what the guest would like for dessert

◆ *What would you like* for your dessert?
◇ *I'd like*   some fruit puddings.
   I'd like to have

♦ Practice 1

Find out what kind of dessert your partner would like by doing the role-play according to the following directions. Student A will be the waiter, student B will be the guest.

Student A: (Ask if the guest would like some dessert)?
Student B: Yes, I'd like some.
Student A: (Ask what the guest would like for dessert)?
Student B: (Tell what you would like by choosing the items from the above table).

Practice 2

Tom and his friends are dining in a dessert restaurant. Listen to the conversation and try to find out the dessert they ordered. Fill in the form with what you will hear on the recording.

Guest	Dessert ordered
Tom	
Mary	
Louis	
Darth	

3. Asking for and giving dessert menu

◆ **Could I see** the dessert menu?

   Would you please show me

◇ Sure, sir/madam. Here you are.

Practice

Complete the following conversation with the directions in the brackets. Then take turns doing the role-play with your partner.

W=Waiter/Waitress   G=Guest

W: Have you found everything satisfactory, sir?
G: Yes, everything is good. Thank you.
W: _____(1)? (Ask if dessert is wanted.)
G: Yes, I'd like some. _____(2)? (Ask for the dessert menu)
W: _____(3). (Show the guest the dessert menu.)
G: _____(4).
   (Tell some mango puddings and a chocolate cake are wanted.)
W: Yes, sir. Mango puddings and a chocolate cake.

4. Asking and telling if anything else is wanted

◆ **Would you like anything else,** sir/madam?

◇ Yes, **I'd like to have** some dessert now.

◆ **Would you like anything else? Some dessert?**

◇ Yes. **I'd like some.**

Unit 5 Ordering Dessert

➕ Practice

Make a conversation with your partner according to the following directions.

Waiter: Ask if anything else is wanted.

Guest: Tell that some dessert is wanted.

Waiter: Ask what the guest would like for his/her dessert.

Guest: Choose from the following dessert you prefer.

A. fruit pudding	B. blueberry pie	C. strawberry ice-cream

5. Asking for and giving recommendation

◆ | What | do | you recommend? |
| | would | |
| Would you please recommend some? | | |

◇ | How about | a lemon pie? |
| How about trying | |
| May I recommend | |

➕ Practice 1

Pattern Drills

Practice the expressions "Asking for and giving recommendation" by replacing the underlined parts in the model conversation with the items given below. Take turns doing the role-play with your partner. One will be the guest, the other will be the waiter.

<u>Here is the model conversation:</u>

W=Waiter   **G**=Guest

W: Would you like anything else, sir?

G: Well, I'd like to have some dessert now. What do/would you recommend?

W: How about (trying) <u>some mango puddings</u>? They are very tasty.

G: Then, I'd like to try some. Thank you.

<u>Here are the items you need:</u>

| mango pudding | black forest cake | vanilla ice-cream | apple tart | haw jelly |
| bean paste cake | pea flour cake | | | |

English for Food and Beverages

 Practice 2

Complete the following conversation with what you will hear on the recording. Then take turns doing the role-play with your partner.

W=Waiter/Waitress   **G**=Guest

W: Is everything to your _____(1), sir?
G: Yes, everything is good.
W: _____(2)?
G: Yes. _____(3).
W: _____(4), sir?
G: Would you please _____(5)some?
W: _____(6)haw jellies. They are very _____(7).
G: That will be _____(8)! I'd like to try some. Thank you.

Practice 3

Study the conversation you've completed in **Practice 2** and role-play a scene according to the following situation. One will be the waiter, the other two students will be the guests.

Here is the situation:

Sally and Mary are dining in a restaurant. They have finished the meal and want to try something else. A waiter is serving them...

Waiter:
- You ask the girls if they would like anything else.
- You recommend black forest cake and fruit puddings to the girls since they are very popular among youngsters.
- You take the orders of the guests.

Sally and Mary:
- You tell that you would like some desserts and you ask for recommendation.
- Sally orders black forest cakes and fruit puddings to the waiter's recommendation. Mary orders two coffee ice-creams.

_____ Summarize Key Expressions _____

1. Asking if everything is all right
   a. Is everything all right? b. Have you found everything satisfactory?
   c. How is everything? d. Is everything all right with your meal?
   e. Is everything to your satisfaction? f. How was the food?

Unit 5 Ordering Dessert

2. Telling everything is all right
   a. Yes, everything is good.
   b. Yes, everything is fine.
   c. Yes, I enjoy it very much.
   d. It's very good.
   e. Yes, it's quite fine.
   f. It's delicious.
3. Asking if dessert is wanted
   a. Would you like some dessert?
   b. Would you like to have some dessert?
   c. What would you like for dessert?
   d. Can/Could I bring you some dessert?
   e. Anything for dessert?
   f. Do you care for dessert?
   g. What shall I bring/get you for dessert?
4. Asking for the dessert menu
   a. Could I see the dessert menu?
   b. May I see the dessert menu?
   c. Could you please show me the dessert menu?
   d. Would you please show me the dessert menu?
5. Ordering dessert
   a. I'd like some ice-creams.
   b. I'd like to have some apple pies.
   c. I'd like to try some lemon puddings.
6. Asking if anything else is wanted
   a. Would you like anything else?
   b. Is there anything else?
   c. May I serve you anything else?
7. Asking for recommendation
   a. What do you recommend?
   b. What would you recommend?
   c. What do you suggest?
   d. What would you suggest?
   e. Would you please recommend some?
8. Recommending some dessert
   a. How about some bean paste cakes?
   b. How about trying some strawberry cakes? They are tasty.
   c. I recommend/would recommend you pea flour cakes. It's a kind of traditional snack in Beijing.
   d. Perhaps you'd like some coffee cakes.
   e. May I suggest fruit puddings. They are very delicious.
   f. May I recommend haw jellies. They are very tasty.

──────────────── Give It a Try ────────────────

Task 1

Complete the following conversation with the directions in the brackets. Then take turns doing the role-play with your partner.

G=Guest   **W**=Waiter/Waitress

W: Is everything all right with your meal, sir?
G: Yes, everything is fine.
W: _____(1)? (Ask if anything else is wanted.) Some dessert?

English for Food and Beverages

G: Well. Yes, I'd like some. _____(2)? (Ask for recommendation.)

W: _____(3). (Recommend fruit puddings.) They are very delicious.

G: Okay, I'd like to try some. Thank you.

Task 2

Study the section **Summarize Key Expressions.** Try to use various expressions you've learnt in the section to make conversations according to the following situations. Do the role-play with your partner. One will be the waiter, the other will be the guest.

Situation 1:

Waiter: Ask if everything is all right.

Guest: Tell that everything is all right.

Waiter: Ask if anything else is wanted.

Guest: Tell that he/she wants to have some dessert and ask for dessert menu.

Waiter: Show the dessert menu.

Guest: Order some desserts: black forest cakes and fruit puddings.

Situation 2:

Waiter: Ask if any dessert is wanted.

Guest: Tell he/she would like some and ask for recommendation.

Waiter: Show the guest dessert menu and recommend some dessert.

Guest: Order strawberry pies and a mango ice-cream.

Task 3

Complete the following conversation with what you will hear on the recording, and then do the role-play with your partner. One will be the waiter, the other will be the guest.

G= Guest   W= Waiter

W: _____(1), sir?

G: _____(2), Chinese food is _____(3)!

W: _____(4) to try something else? Some dessert?

G: Yes, _____(5). But _____(6).

W: Well, there are many traditional desserts in Beijing. They are Lúdagunr, _____(7) and etc. I think you can choose from the _____(8). May I bring it over for you, sir?

G: Yes, thank you. That's very kind of you. (1 minute later)

G: What is this?

W: It's called Lúdagunr, that is the _____(9).

G: Is it the local dessert in Beijing?

W: Yes, it is. It's _____(10) among the local people in Beijing.

G: Oh, really? Then I'd like to try some.

W: Yes, sir. I'm sure you will enjoy it.

Unit 5 Ordering Dessert

Do Extension Activities

Activity 1

Follow the way of the above conversation you've completed in **Task 3** and role-play a scene "In a Chinese Restaurant" with your partner according to the following situation.

Situation: In a Chinese Restaurant

Guest:

1. This is the first time you are in Beijing.
2. You are finishing your meal which you find very delicious.
3. You want to try some local desserts.
4. You are asking the waiter to recommend some local desserts to you.
5. In the end, you order a bowl of Tang Yuan and some pea flour cakes.

Waiter:

1. Ask if the guest likes his/her meal.
2. Ask if he/she would like to have some desserts.
3. Tell that there are many local desserts for him/her to try.
4. Show the guest dessert menu.
5. Recommend the guest to try some traditional desserts in Beijing, such as haw jellies, pea flour cakes, bean paste cakes, Tangyuan, Lǜdagunr, glutinous rice sesame balls, and etc.

Activity 2

Fill in the blanks in the following passage with the information you will hear on the recording.

The _____(1)of ice cream can be _____(2)back to at least the _____(3)century B. C. Early _____(4)include the Roman emperor Nero(A.D.37—68) who ordered ice to be brought from the _____(5)and combined with _____(6),and King Tang (A.D.618—907) of Shang, China who had a method of _____(7). It is also said that Alexander the Great _____(8)ice flavored with _____(9)and _____(10)after his meals. This was also _____(11)to his guests after their meals. This _____(12)the _____(13)of desserts even in those days. Over time, _____(14)for ices, sherbets, and milk ices _____(15)and served in the _____(16)Italian and French royal courts.

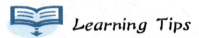 Learning Tips

History of Dessert

The history of desserts can be traced back to many years. Sweet candies were invented around 350 years ago and ice cream origins can be traced back to at least the 4th century B.C. A sweet dish was always preferred at the end of a meal, but before the 19th century sweet was a privilege of the aristocrats and was out of reach of the middle class who considered desserts to be too much expensive and a luxury. In the year 1800 the ice cream industry and other bakery industries emerged, which caused a fall in the prices of desserts. Within a few later years desserts were being enjoyed in every household. After several centuries, the dessert remained popular, but much of its form changed. Even if the origin of dessert is buried in the "sands of time," it doesn't mean that we can't enjoy it. Today a meal is said to be incomplete without desserts.

Unit 5 Ordering Dessert

Part B Asking and Telling If Dessert Is Wanted II

Teaching hours: 2 hours

Learning Goals:

To be able to
- learn some knowledge on dessert
- know what to say and how to do when the dessert ordered is not available
- know how to suggest something else to a guest
- know how to express when dessert is not wanted

Vocabulary Assistance

pastry *n.* 面粉糕饼, 发面饼
toast *n.* 烤面包(片), 吐司面包
derive *v.* 源于, 起源
classify *v.* 分类
specialize *v.* 专门从事
appropriate *adj.* 适当的
enhance *v.* 提高, 增强
expect *v.* 期待, 预期
spicy *adj.* 辛辣的
glutinous *adj.* 粘性的
available *adj.* 可用到的, 可利用的
Spaniard *n.* 西班牙人
Aztec *n.* 阿芝台克人
beverage *n.* 饮料
milkshake *n.* 奶昔
jelly *n.* 果子冻, 一种果冻甜品
consist *v.* 由……组成
incomplete *adj.* 不完善的
prefer *v.* 更喜欢, 宁愿

decoration *n.* 装饰品
separate *adj.* 单独的, 个别的
care *v.* 喜爱
dumpling *n.* 面团布丁, 团子
flour *n.* 面粉
aristocracy *n.* 贵族
constitute *v.* 组成
mechanization *n.* 机械化
colloquial *adj.* 口语的, 通俗的
originate *v.* 起源
be on a diet 节食, 限制饮食
be keen on 对……感兴趣
Quetzalcoatl *n.* 羽蛇神（古代墨西哥阿兹特克人与托尔特克人崇奉的重要神祇）
Debrett *n.* 德布雷特英国贵族年鉴（初版由英国出版家 John Debrett 于 1803 年编纂出版）

Start You Off

＋ Activity 1

Which of the following are desserts? Put a tick to the one which is a dessert and a cross to the one which is not a dessert.

☐ Pastry   ☐ Tea   ☐ Ice Cream   ☐ Coffee   ☐ Milk
☐ Milkshake   ☐ Toast   ☐ Wine   ☐ Cheese   ☐ Cola
☐ Pudding   ☐ Sweet   ☐ Chocolate   ☐ Cookie   ☐ Beer
☐ Apple Pie   ☐ Cake   ☐ Fruit Jelly ☐ Fruit Juice ☐ Tart

＋ Activity 2

The following is a passage about dessert. Read the passage and answer the questions followed.

Dessert derives its name from a French word *desservir*, which means to clear the table. It is a course that typically comes at the end of a dinner, usually consisting of sweets and other strongly flavored dishes. Today desserts have become a standard part of a meal and served in almost all the restaurants. They are classified as frozen dessert, fruit dessert and some varieties of milkshakes also.

In the USA the desserts are quite popular, and every occasion is incomplete without a proper dessert being served. There are several restaurants that specialize in dessert and treat it as a separate meal rather than a course. People prefer to visit these restaurants after their meals. There are many different kinds of desserts, but the most popular are sweet candies, ice creams, puddings and other preparations of chocolates. Desserts are presented at the end of the meal and are often presented in style with appropriate decorations, to enhance the presentation. In major restaurants the customers are given a wide variety of dishes to choose from. Children are often treated with some special desserts, which are prepared specially for them. These consist of a sweet dish, major portion of which consists of chocolates and their favorite cookies.

Questions:

1. Where does the name *dessert* originate from? What does it mean?
   _____

2. Is dessert seved at the beginning of a dinner or at the end of a dinner?
   _____

3. How are desserts classified according to the passage?
   _____

4. How popular are desserts in the U. S.?
   _____

5. Are there any restaurants that serve dessert as a separate meal rather than a course?
   _____

6. What are the most popular desserts?

7. Are desserts often presented with decorations? Why?

Focus on Language

Ordering Dessert

Questions

1. What should you say to a guest when the dessert he/she orders is not available?
2. What and how should you do then?
3. How should you suggest something else to the guest?

Listen to the following conversation and try to find the answers to the questions above. Then do the conversation in pairs.

W=Waiter/Waitress　　**G**=Guest

W: How was the food, madam?
G: Very delicious. Thank you.
W: Would you like anything else, madam?
G: Yes, I'd like to try some dessert. Could you please show me the dessert menu?
W: Yes, madam.
G: I'd like to have some apple tarts and one vanilla ice-cream.
W: Sorry, madam, I'm afraid there are not any apple tarts left. But there are many other desserts you can choose from the menu. Would you please try something else?
G: Well, then make it one chocolate pie.
W: Yes, madam. One chocolate pie and one vanilla ice-cream.

Language Tips

1. Telling dessert is out and suggesting something else

◆ I'd like to have some apple tarts.

◇ *I'm sorry*, sir/madam. *I'm afraid there aren't any* apple tarts *left*.

I'm afraid apple tart *is not available* at the moment.

English for Food and Beverages

◇ | Would you | please try | something else? |
  | | mind trying | |
  | How about | trying | |

✚ Practice 1

Make a conversation with your partner according to the following situation. You will be the waiter, your partner will be the guest.

Here is the situation:

Ask the guest if he would like to have some dessert. The guest asks for the menu and orders some creamy puddings and one chocolate mousse cake. But unfortunately there aren't any chocolate mousse cakes left. Then you suggest the guest to try vanilla cream cakes. In the end the guest orders one vanilla cream cake instead and some creamy puddings.

✚ Practice 2

Complete the following conversation by choosing the appropriate expressions from the choices given below. Then do the role-play with your partner. One will be the guest, the other will be the waiter or waitress.

W=Waiter/Waitress   G=Guest

W: How is the food, sir?
G: _____. Thank you.
W: _____ anything else?
G: Yes, I'd like to have some dessert. Have you got pumpkin pies?
W: I am sorry, sir. _____. _____? They are very tasty.
G: Well, then _____ two cherry pies and one coffee ice-cream.
W: Yes, sir. Two cherry pies and one coffee ice-cream.

Here are the choices:

a. make it
b. How about trying some cherry pies
c. Would you like
d. I'm afraid we haven't got anymore pumpkin pies
e. Very delicious

✚ Practice 3

Look at the table below. The desserts in part A are sold out and the desserts in part B are still available. Make a conversation with your partner according to the following situation.

Here is the situation:

Waiter:

1. Ask the guest if anything else is wanted.

Unit 5 Ordering Dessert

2. Ask what the guest would like for his/her dessert.
3. Feel sorry and tell the guest that the dessert he/she orders is/are not available at the moment and suggest the guest to try something else in part B instead.

Guest:

1. Tell that he/she would like to have some desserts.
2. Ask for the dessert menu and order some desserts in part A.
3. Then order some desserts in part B instead to the waiter's suggestion.

Here is the table:

Part A	Part B
creamy pudding	fruit pudding
black forest cake	vanilla cream cake
cherry pie	blueberry pie
strawberry ice-cream	coffee ice-cream

2. Telling that dessert is not wanted

◆ Would you like any dessert?

◇ *No, thanks. I am on a diet.*

✚ Practice

Role-play the following conversation by replacing the underlined part with the reasons given in the table. Student A will be the waiter, student B will be the guest.

Here is the conversation:

W=Waiter/Waitress   G=Guest

W: Is everything all right with your meal, sir?

G: Yes, it's fine. Thank you.

W: Would you like anything else?

G: No, thank you.

W: Anything for dessert?

G: No, thanks. <u>I'm on a diet</u>. Would you please bring me a cup of black coffee?

W: Yes, sir.

101

English for Food and Beverages

Here are the reasons for refusal:

I have no room for dessert.
I have had enough.
I am not keen on dessert.
I don't feel like dessert.
I don't care for dessert.

Summarize Key Expressions

1. Telling some dessert is out and suggesting something else
   a. I am sorry, there are not any puddings left. Would you mind trying something else?
   b. I am sorry, we haven't got anymore pumpkin pies. How about trying some lemon pies?
   c. I am sorry, raisin tarts are not available. Would you like to try something else?
   d. I am sorry, banana pies are finished. May I suggest cherry pies? They are very popular.
2. Telling dessert is not wanted
   a. No, thanks. I have had enough.
   b. No, thanks. I am not keen on dessert.
   c. No, thanks. I don't care for dessert.
   d. No, thanks. I am on a diet.
   e. No, thanks. I don't feel like dessert. They are fattening.

Give It a Try

Task 1

Try to use expressions you've learnt in the section **Summarize Key Expressions** to make conversations according to the following situations. Do the role-play with your partner. One will be the waiter/waitress, the other will be the guest.

Situation 1

Waiter: Ask if everything is all right.
Guest: Tell everything is fine.
Waiter: Ask if any dessert is wanted.
Guest: Tell that chocolate mousse cake and sundae ice-cream are wanted.
Waiter: Tell that chocolate mousse cake is out and suggest trying something else: cheese cakes, coffee cakes and etc.
Guest: Order two cheese cakes and a sundae ice-cream.

Situation 2

Waiter: Ask if the guest likes the food.
Guest: Tell that the food is delicious but the surrounding is a little bit noisy and some people smoke.
Waiter: Feel sorry about that and ask if any dessert is wanted.
Guest: Tell that dessert is not wanted because he/she is on a diet and he/she thinks that dessert is fattening.

  Task 2

Listen to the conversation and answer the following questions.

Questions:

1. What did the first guest order for his dessert?
   _____

2. What did the second guest order for his dessert at first?
   _____

3. Did the second guest change his order? Why?
   _____

4. What did the second guest order for his dessert then?
   _____

5. Did the third guest order anything for her dessert? Why?
   _____

 Task 3

Part I

Role-play the following conversation with your partner. One will be the guest, the other will be the waiter/waitress.

W=Waiter/Waitress   G=Guest

W: Is everything all right with your meal, sir?
G: Well, the taste is marvelous, but I didn't expect it was so hot.
W: I'm sorry. I should have asked if you care for spicy food.
G: Never mind. I prefer to take it as it is. I'm here to try typical Sichuan food.
W: Thank you, sir. Would you like to try some typical Sichuan desserts?
G: Well. That is a good idea. What do you recommend?
W: How about Sichuan Tang Yuan? It is a kind of stuffed dumplings made of glutinous rice flour served in soup. It's sweet and tasty.
G: Sounds great. I'd like to try some.

Part II

Follow the way of the conversation in Part I and role-play a scene of "Recommending and ordering dessert" according to the following situation. Student A will be the guest and student B will be the waiter.

Here is the situation:

Waiter: Ask if the guest likes the food or not.

Guest: Tell that she enjoys the food very much except for the soup which is a little bit salty.

Waiter: Feel sorry for that and suggest if she would like to have some dessert. Recommend a kind of local dessert in Beijing.

Guest: Be interested in the dessert recommended and would like to have a try.

——— Do Extension Activities ———

 Activity 1

Role-play: *In a Western Restaurant*. Look at the menu below. The items underlined are sold out, and the rest are available. Make a conversation with your partner according to the directions. Do it in pairs. Student A will be the guest and student B will be the waiter.

Directions:

Waiter:

1. Ask if the guest like his meal.
2. Ask if the guest would like to have some dessert.
3. Feel sorry for the unavailability of the desserts ordered by the guest and recommend something else in the dessert menu with the help of the descriptions in italics for each dessert.

Guest:

1. You have finished your meal which you find very delicious.
2. You want to try some special desserts in the restaurant and order some from the menu. But unfortunately the desserts you ordered are not available at the moment.
3. In the end, you order New York Style Cheesecake, Tiramisu and Raspberry Bread Pudding for your dessert.

Here is the dessert menu:

Dessert Menu
New York Style Cheesecake 　　*Rich vanilla cheesecake with your choice of toppings*
Turtle Club Cheesecake 　　*Royal caramel and rich chocolate topped over cheesecake dressed with chopped walnuts*
Tiramisu 　　*An authentic Italian dessert meaning "pick me up," and it will do just that, covered with*

Unit 5 Ordering Dessert

> chocolate sauce
>
> Creme Brulee
>   Classic egg custard served underneath a thin coat of caramelized sugar
>
> Raspberry Bread Pudding
>   Succulent bread pudding laced with raspberries and topped with a whiskey river sauce
>
> Chocolate Flourless Torte
>   Homemade chocolate flourless cake topped with raspberry sauce & whipped cream
>
> Chocolate Brownie
>   Homemade brownie served under hot fudge sauce & ice cream
>
> Chocolate Mousse
>   Velvety mousse laced with dark rich chocolate
>
> Ice Cream Sundae or Sorbet
>   Rich vanilla ice-cream topped with your choice of hot fudge, chocolate or caramel, or sweet raspberry sorbet to cleanse the palate

 Activity 2

Part I Spot Dictation

Fill in the blanks in the following passage with the information you will hear on the recording.

   The word _____(1)is most commonly used for this course in U.S., Canada, Australia, and Ireland, while _____(2)or _____(3)would be more typical terms in the UK and some other Common Wealth countries. According to *Debrett*, _____(4)is the proper term, dessert is only to be used if the course _____(5), and sweet is _____(6).

   Although the custom of eating _____(7)after a meal may be very old, dessert as a standard part of a _____(8)is a relatively recent development. Before the rise of the _____(9) in the _____(10), and the mechanization of the _____(11), sweets were a _____(12) of the aristocracy, or a rare _____(13). As sugar became cheaper and more readily available, the _____(14)of dessert spread accordingly.

Part II True or False Questions

Decide whether the following statements are true or false according to the passage. Write T for true or F for false in front of each statement.

(   ) 1. There are different terms for dessert in different parts of the world.
(   ) 2. After the mechanization of the sugar industry, sweets became a privilege of the aristocracy.
(   ) 3. Earlier before the rise of the middle class in 19th century, dessert has developed into a course to ordinary people.
(   ) 4. With sugar becoming cheaper and more available dessert began to develop and become popular.

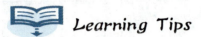 Learning Tips

Dessert

Different cultures have varying ideas on what constitutes a dessert. In China traditional desserts are sometimes made with red beans, sesame, dates or lotus. In Greece honey is a popular medium. Some Spaniards claim that the use of chocolate as a dessert originated with them, but the debate goes back centuries, as the Aztecs felt that their god, Quetzalcoatl, should be credited for the origin of the cocoa bean.

Often, the dessert is seen as a separate meal or snack rather than a course, and may be eaten apart from the meal (usually in less formal settings). Some restaurants specialize in dessert. In colloquial American usage "dessert" has a broader meaning and can refer to anything sweet that follows a meal, including milkshakes and other beverages.

Unit 6

Paying the Bill

Part A Asking for the Bill and Ways of Paying

Teaching hours: 2 hours

Learning Goals:

To be able to
- know how to ask for a bill
- know how to ask the way of payment
- know how to ask and tell if a way of payment is accepted or not
- know how to refuse a way of payment
- know how to tell the amount of a bill
- know how to take the payment in cash
- know how to take the payment by credit card
- know how to take the payment by traveller's cheques
- know how to take separate bills

Vocabulary Assistance

bill *n.* 账单
receipt *n.* 收据
copy *n.* 存根
identification *n.* 身份证明
slang *n.* 俚语
delicate *adj.* 微妙的
intimate *adj.* 亲密的
stingy *adj.* 吝啬的,小气的
change *n.* 找回的零钱
tip *n.* 小费
add *v.* 增加,添加
entertainment *n.* 款待,娱乐
etiquette *n.* 礼节

affluent *adj.* 富裕的
invitee *n.* 被邀请者
service charge 服务费
credit card 信用卡
printed word 印刷体
one bill 合单付账
It's on me. 由我来付账。
Master Card 万事达卡
traveller's cheque 旅游支票
driver's license 驾照
separate bill 分单付账
It's my treat. 我请客。
Go Dutch/Dutch treat AA 制

107

Start You Off

Activity 1

Discuss the following questions with your partner.

1. How should you pay the bill in a restaurant?
2. How many ways of payment do you know in a restaurant?
3. Which way do you prefer to pay the bill in a restaurant?
4. What are the advantages and disadvantages of the different ways of payment?

Activity 2

Look at the two columns below. The left lists the names of some countries and the right lists the terms of some currencies. Match the countries with their currencies.

1. China	A. Dollar
2. United States	B. Franc
3. Britain	C. Mark
4. Japan	D. Yuan
5. Australia	E. Peseta
6. France	F. Crown
7. Germany	G. Yen
8. Canada	H. Pound
9. Sweden	
10. Spain	

Activity 3

How many credit cards do you know? Below is a list of credit cards prevailing in the world. Match the cards with their Chinese counterparts.

1. Visa (Bank Americard)	A. (美国)国际万国卡
2. American Express	B. (美国)运通信用卡
3. Diners Club	C. (美国)维萨卡
4. Master Card	D. (美国)大来信用卡
5. Eurocard	E. (英国)巴克利卡
6. Barclay	F. (日本)信贩卡
7. Carte Blanche	G. (英国)欧洲卡
8. Access	H. (美国)万事达卡
9. Million Card	I. (英国)阿赛斯卡
10. JCB	J. (日本)百万信用卡

Unit 6 Paying the Bill

Focus on Language

Conversation

Paying in Cash

Questions

1. How should you ask for the bill?
2. How should you tell the amount of a bill?
3. How should you show the guest the change and receipt?

Listen to the following conversation and try to find the answers to the questions above. Then do the conversation in pairs.

W=Waiter/Waitress   G=Guest

G: Waiter! The bill, please.

W: Yes, sir. Just a moment, please. (Two minutes later) Here is your bill, sir. It comes to one hundred and sixty eight *yuan* (RMB 168) altogether.

G: Here you are.

W: Thank you. Please wait for a moment, I'll be right back with your change and receipt.
(5 minutes later)

W: Here is your change of thirty two *yuan* and your receipt.

G: Thanks.

W: Have a nice evening.

Language Tips

1. Asking for the bill and showing and telling the amount of the bill / change

◆ **Waiter/Waitress!** **The bill,** please.

   I'd like to settle my bill, please.

   May I have the bill, please?

◇ Just a moment/a second/a minute, please.

   Please wait for a moment/a second/a minute.

◇ **Here is** your bill.

Your bill	comes to	one hundred and sixty eight *yuan* **altogether**.
Your bill	amounts to	one hundred and twenty five *yuan*.
	totals	

◇ Here is your change and receipt.

Here is your change of thirty two *yuan* **and receipt**.

✚ Practice

Study the way of "Asking for the bill and showing and telling the amount of the bill/change" above. Follow the way of the above conversation and make conversations with your partner with the directions and information given below. Use the items in the table one by one to do the role-play.

Here are the directions:

Student A will be the guest: You ask for the bill and pay your bill in cash.
Student B will be waiter/waitress: You show the bill and tell the amount of the bill. You tell the amount of the change and give the change to the guest.

Here is the information you need:

	Amount of the bill	Amount of the change
1	RMB 156	RMB 44
2	RMB 235	RMB 65
3	RMB 368	RMB 32
4	RMB 457	RMB 43
5	RMB 586	RMB 14

2. Giving tips and taking or turning down tips politely

◆ *Don't bother with the change.*

Keep the change, please.

◇ Thank you, sir/madam.

◇ Thank you, sir/madam. But **we don't take tips. Thank you anyway**.

◇ Thank you, sir/madam. A 10% service charge has already been added to your bill. **Thank you all the same**.

Unit 6 Paying the Bill

Practice 1

Situation: The diner has finished his meal and would like to settle the bill. The waiter is helping him. Complete the following conversation with the directions in the brackets. Then do the role-play with your partner.

W=Waiter/Waitress   **G**=Guest

G: _____(1)! _____(2)(Ask for bill.)

W: Yes, sir, _____(3), please. (Ask the guest to wait for a moment.) _____(4)
(Show the bill to the guest and tell the amount of the bill is RMB 108.)

G: Here you are. _____(5)(Tell the waiter to keep the change.)

W: Thank you, sir.

(5 minutes later the waiter is back with the receipt.)

W: _____(6)(Show the guest the receipt.)

G: Thank you.

W: My pleasure. Hope to see you again.

Practice 2

Role-play a scene of "Paying in cash" with the directions given below. Student A will be the waiter, student B will be the guest.

Guest:	Waiter:
1. Ask for the bill;	1. Show the bill to the guest and tell the amount of the bill: RMB 189;
2. Give the waiter RMB 200 and would like him to keep the change;	2. Turn down the tips politely and tell a 5% service charge has already been added to his bill;
3. Show appreciation for the waiter's service.	3. Show the change and the receipt to the guest.

3. Asking the ways of payment and asking and telling if credit card is accepted

◆ How would you like to **pay your bill**?

　　　　　　　　　　settle your bill?

◇ **May I use**　　　credit card?

Will you take/accept

◆ **What kind**　　are you holding?

　　　　　　　have you got?

◇ American Express/Master/Visa…

◆ *That will be fine.*

111

◆ Sorry, *I'm afraid we don't accept that card.*

Asking for signature

◆ Could you **sign** your name here, please?

Could you **sign** here, please?

Practice 1

Look at the table below. The card with a √ is accepted, and the card with a × is not accepted. Follow either of the two conversations below and role-play the scene of accepting or refusing paying by credit card by replacing the underlined part with the cards given in the table.

Here are the cards:

Master Card √	Carte Blanche ×
American Express √	Access √
Diners Club √	Million Card ×
Visa √	JCB √
Eurocard ×	Federal Card ×
Barclay ×	OTB ×

Here are the model conversations:

Accepting:

W=Waiter   **G**=Guest

G: May I have the bill, please?

W: Yes, sir. How would you like to pay your bill, sir?

G: Will you take credit card?

W: What kind are you holding, sir?

G: Master Card.

W: That will be fine.

...

W: Could you sign your name here, please?

G: Certainly.

W: Thank you. Here is your card and your copy.

Refusing:

G: Waitress, will you bring the bill, please.

W: Yes, madam. How would you like to settle your bill?

G: May I use credit card?

W: What kind have you got?

G: Eurocard.

W: I'm sorry, madam. I'm afraid we don't accept that card. Would you mind paying in cash?

G: Okay. How much is the bill?

...

Practice 2

Complete the following conversation with the directions in the brackets. Then do the role-play with your partner.

W=Waiter/Waitress   **G**=Guest

W: Would you like anything else?

G: No, thank you. _____(1). (Ask for bill.)

W: _____(2)? (Ask the way of paying.)

G: _____(3)? (Ask if credit card is accepted.)

W: _____(4)? (Ask what card the guest is holding.)

G: American Express.

W: That will be fine.

G: Here you are.

W: Thank you.

   (2 minutes later)

W: _____(5)? (Ask for signature.)

G: Sure.

W: Thank you. _____(6). (Show the guest the card and the copy.)

Practice 3

Role-play a scene of paying by credit card according to the following situation.

Here is the situation:

A lady is finishing her meal and would like to settle the bill by credit card. The card she is holding is Access. The waiter tells her that the restaurant doesn't accept Access and only take Visa and Master Card and ask if she would pay in cash.

4. Asking and telling if traveller's check is accepted

◆ | *Do you* | *accept* | traveller's cheques?
| | *take* |

| *May I use* | traveller's cheques?

◇ Yes, if you can give us your address and some identification.

Yes, but you'll have to give us your address and some identification.

◆ | *Will* | my driver's license | *be all right*?
| | my passport |

English for Food and Beverages

 **Practice 1**

Paying by Traveller's Checks

Listen to the conversation and read after it. Then do the following conversation in pairs and try to find the answers to the questions given below.

Conversation

W=Waiter/Waitress   **G**=Guest

G: Waitress! May I have the bill, please?
W: Yes, sir.
G: Do you accept traveller's cheques?
W: Yes, if you can give us your address and some identification.
G: Will my driver's license be all right?
W: That's quite all right.
G: Should I put my name and address on the back of the cheque?
W: Yes, please write your name in printed words.
G: Okay, thank you.

Questions

1. How should you pay by traveller's cheques?
2. What should be noticed when signing traveller's cheques?

Practice 2

Role-play a scene of "Paying by traveller's checks" with the key words given in the table.

For the guest	For the waiter
accept, traveller's cheques, passport	address, identification, name, back of the cheque, in printed/block letters

5. Asking and telling if paying separate bills or one bill

◆ **Separate bills or one bill?**

Would you care to have one bill or separate bills?

◇ One bill, please.

Separate bills, please.

114

Practice 1

Do the following conversation in pairs. Student A will be Guest A, Student B will be Guest B, Student C will be the waiter or waitress.

Paying separate bills or one bill

W=Waiter/Waitress   GA=Guest A   GB=Guest B

GA: Waitress! Will you bring us the bill, please?

W: Sure, separate bills or one bill?

GA: It's my treat. One bill, please.

GB: It's on me, this time. You paid last time.

GA: Well, let's go Dutch.

GB: Right, a dutch treat.

W: (To guest A) 48 dollars, please.

GA: Here is 50 dollars. Keep the change, please.

W: Thank you, sir. It's very kind of you.
    (To guest B) Fifty dollars, please.

GB: Here you are.

 ## Practice 2

Fill in the blanks in the following passage with the information you will hear on the recording.

W=Waiter/Waitress   G1=Guest 1   G2=Guest 2

G1: Waiter! _____(1), please?

W: Sure. It comes to _____(2)dollars altogether. Would you _____(3)?

G1: _____(4)this time.

G2: Oh, no._____(5), I insist.

G1: Well, we'd better make it a _____(6).

G2: _____(7).

G1: Here is 130 dollars. _____(8), please.

G2: Here is 130 dollars. _____(9).

W: Thank you, sirs. _____(10).

─────── Summarize Key Expressions ───────

1. Asking for the bill

    a. Waiter, the bill, please.

    b. May/Can I have the bill, please?

    c. I'll take the bill now.

    d. Bring the bill, please. /Will you bring the bill, please.

    e. I would like to settle my bill, please.

2. Telling the amount of the bill/change

    a. Your bill comes to 168 *yuan* altogether.

b. Your bill amounts to 168 *yuan*.

   c. Your bill totals 168 *yuan*.

   d. Here is your change of 32 *yuan*.

3. Telling waiter to keep the change

   a. Don't bother with the change.

   b. Keep the change, please.

4. Turning down the tips politely

   a. Thank you, madam. But we don't take tips. Thank you anyway.

   b. Thank you, sir. A 10% service charge has already been added to your bill. Thank you all the same.

5. Asking the way of payment

   a. How do/would you like to pay your bill?

   b. How do/would you like to settle your bill?

   c. How do/would you like to settle your account, sir? In cash or by credit card?

   d. How do/would you like to make the payment?

   e. Which way do you prefer to paying the bill, please?

   f. Separate bills or one bill?

   g. Would you care to have one check or separate checks?

   h. May I know who is paying, please?

6. Asking if a way of payment is accepted

   a. May I use credit card? /traveller's cheques/ foreign currency?

   b. Will you accept/take/honor traveller's cheques /credit card/ foreign currency?

   c. Do you accept/take/honor foreign currency/traveller's cheques/personal cheques/Visa/Master Card/American Express?

7. Asking which card the guest is holding

   a. Which card do you have?

   b. Which card are you holding?

   c. What kind are you holding?

   d. What kind have you got?

8. Refusing a way of payment

   a. I'm sorry. Our restaurant doesn't accept credit card. We only accept cash.

   b. I'm afraid we do not accept personal cheques here.

   c. I'm afraid we cannot honor traveller's cheques here.

   d. I'm afraid we cannot accept foreign currency as payment here.

9. Asking if some identification is acceptable?

   a. Will my driver's license be all right?

   b. Will my passport be all right?

10. Asking for signature

    a. Could you sign your name here, please?

    b. Could you sign here, please?

11. Asking for signature in printed words
    a. Please write your name in printed words.
    b. Please write your name in block letters.

Task 1

Go over the section **Summarize Key Expressions**. Complete the following conversation with the procedures given below. Then do the role-play with your partner. Student A will be the guest, student B will be the waiter.

Here is the opening part of the conversation:

Waiter: Is everything to your satisfaction, sir?
Guest: Yes, everything is fine.
Waiter: Would you like anything else? Some desserts?
Guest: No, thanks. Just the bill please.
    ...

Here are the procedures:

For the waiter:
1. Show the bill to the guest and tell him the bill amounts to RMB 268.
2. Ask the way of payment.
3. Tell that foreign currency is not accepted in the restaurant.
4. Ask which card the guest has got.
5. Tell the card he holds is accepted.
6. Ask for signature.
7. Show guest the card and the copy.

For the guest:
1. Ask if you can pay in U.S. dollars.
2. Ask if you can pay by credit card.
3. Tell that you are holding Visa.
4. Give the card to the waiter.

Task 2

Listen to the conversation and answer the following questions.

Questions:

1. Did he order anything else?
   _____.

2. How much was the bill?
   _____.

3. How would he like to pay the bill in the first place?
   _____.

4. What kind of credit card was he holding? Could he pay the bill with this card? Why?
   _____.

5. Did he pay his bill by traveller's check? Why?
   _____.

6. How did he pay his bill in the end?
   _____.

7. Did the waitress accept the tip or not? Why?
   _____.

8. How much was the change?
   _____.

Task 3

Role-play a scene of "Paying by traveller's cheques" according to the following situation. Student A will be Grace and student B will be Joe.

Guest:

You are Grace.

You are dining in a restaurant and finishing your meal.

You would like to settle your bill by traveller's cheques.

You ask the waiter if they honor traveller's cheques.

You show your driver license as the identification.

Waiter:

You are Joe.

You are helping the guest settling the bill.

You tell that traveller's cheque is acceptable if some identification can be shown.

You ask the guest to put her name and address on the back of the cheque.

You ask the guest to write her name in printed words.

——— Do Extension Activities ———

 Activity 1

Fill in the blanks with what you will hear on the recording.

In a Chinese Restaurant

G: Waiter! _____(1), please?

Unit 6 Paying the Bill

W: Yes, madam. _____(2)?

G: Do you _____(3)U. S. dollars?

W: Yes, we do. But we only have _____(4). The _____(5)is one hundred U. S. dollar to _____(6)Chinese *yuan*. Besides, there's _____(7)for paying U. S. dollars in cash. Do you _____(8)that?

G: Well, may I use my _____(9)?

W: What kind are you _____(10), madam?

G: _____(11). Do you honor it?

W: Yes, madam.

G: That'll be fine. I'll pay the bill by my credit card. Here you are.

W: Thank you. I'll be right back.

   (2 minutes later)

W: _____(12)?

G: _____(13).

W: Thank you, madam. _____(14).

Activity 2

Role-play a scene of "Paying separate bills" according to the following situation. Student A will be Tom, student B will be Mike, Student C will be the waitress.

Situation:

You are Tom. You and your friend Mike are dining in a restaurant. You are finishing your meal and would like to settle the bill.

Here is the information you need:

Waitress:

1. You tell the amount of the bill is RMB 156.
2. You ask if they care to have one bill or separate bills.
3. You tell them how much they should pay separately.
4. You show appreciation to Tom for the tips.
5. You show Mike the change of RMB 20.

Tom:

1. You would like to pay the bill.
2. Since Mike insists that he should pay the bill you suggest a Dutch treat.
3. You give the waitress RMB 80 and tell her to keep the change.

Mike:

1. You think it should be your treat this time since Tom paid last time.
2. You agree with Tom's suggestion.
3. You give the waitress RMB 100.

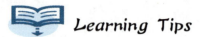 **Learning Tips**

Going Dutch

Going Dutch is a slang term which means that each person eating at a restaurant or paying admission for entertainment pays for himself or herself, rather than one person paying for everyone. It is also called **Dutch Date** and **Dutch Treat**.

There is a delicate etiquette surrounding going Dutch. It may be accepted in some situations, such as between non-intimate friends or less affluent people, but considered stingy in other circumstances, such as on a romantic date or at a business lunch.

The traditional way to handle a bill on a date in the West has been that the one who invited the other takes the bill and the invitee may not even know the actual price of the meal. Some restaurants keep "blind menus" (less commonly known as "ladies' menus"), which do not display prices.

Unit 6 Paying the Bill

Part B Explaining the Charge and Handling Mistakes on the Bill

Teaching hours: 2 hours

Learning Goals:

To be able to
- know how to show disagreement to a bill
- know how to require for an explanation of a charge
- know how to explain a charge
- know how to handle mistakes on a bill
- know how to deal with a wrong change
- know how to make an apology for a mistake

Vocabulary Assistance

extra *adj.* 额外的
towel *n.* 手巾, 毛巾
note *n.* 注释
receipt *n.* 收据
charge *n.* 费用
aware *adj.* 知道的, 明白的, 意识到的

cashier *n.* 出纳员
overcharge *n.* 过多收费
shortchange *v.* 少找钱
check up 核实
break down 列出细目

Start You Off

Activity 1

Discussion

1. What and how should a waiter/waitress do if a guest doesn't understand some charge on his/her bill and ask for an explanation? The following are some choices for your reference. Put a tick before the one/ones which you think is/are appropriate.

☐ Get the manager to deal with the guest.
☐ Insist that the bill doesn't spot a mischarge.
☐ Explain the charge reluctantly.
☐ Explain the charge in a patient way.

2. What and how should a waiter/waitress do if a guest thinks he/she is overcharged? The following are some choices for your reference. Put a tick before the one/ones which you think is/are appropriate.

☐ Get the manager to deal with the problem.

☐ Insist that it is impossible that the guest is overcharged.
☐ Ask the cashier to check it up.
☐ Make an apology if the guest is overcharged.

Activity 2

Follow the model conversations below and do the questions and answers by speaking out the charges in the frames. Do it in pairs.

Model 1
How much is the charge?
It's one hundred and sixty eight *yuan*.

| RMB￥168 | RMB￥217 | RMB￥339 |

Model 2
How much is the charge?
It's one hundred and forty six pounds.

| GB£146 | GB£451 | GB£562 |

Model 3
How much is the charge?
It's one hundred and twenty four dollars.

| US$124 | US$673 | US$985 |

Focus on Language

Conversation

Explaining the Charge

Questions
1. How should you show disagreement to a bill?
2. How and what should a waiter/waitress do when a guest shows disagreement to a bill?
3. How should you require for an explanation of a charge?
4. How should you explain a charge to a guest?

Listen to the conversation and read after it. Then do the conversation in pairs and try to find the answers to the questions above.

W=Waiter/Waitress   **G**=Guest
G: Waitress.
W: Yes, madam.

Unit 6 Paying the Bill

G: There seems to be some mistakes on my bill. What is this extra $ 2 for?
W: May I have a look at your bill, madam?
   (The guest shows the bill to the waitress.)
W: This is the charge for the cold towels.
G: The towels?
W: Yes, the cold towels. (Pointing to the towels on the table)
G: Oh, I see.

Language Tips

1. Requiring for an explanation of a charge

◆ *What is this* extra $ 2 *for*?

◇ *This is the charge for* the cold towels.

Practice

Pattern Drills

Practice the expression "*What is this... for*? *This is the charge for*..." by replacing the underlined parts in the model conversation with the items and prices given in the table. Take turns doing the role-play with your partner. One will be the guest, the other will be the waiter/waitress.

Here is the model conversation:

Guest: What is this <u>thirty yuan</u> for?
Waiter/Waitress: This is the charge for <u>the coffee</u>.

Here is the information you need:

Items	Prices
Coffee	¥ 30
2 Cold towels	¥ 2
Tax	¥ 20
Service charge	¥ 68
Drinks	¥ 55

2. Showing disagreement to a bill and explaining a charge

◆ *I have a question about the bill.*

The bill should come to ¥ 256, *but the bill here is for* ¥ 283.

There seems to be some mistakes on my bill.

◇ *Let me explain that for you, sir/madam.*

We add 5% *tax* and *there's* a 10% *service charge added to each bill*.

English for Food and Beverages

Practice 1

Listen to the conversation and read after it. Then do the conversation in pairs.

G: Excuse me.

W: Yes, madam.

G: I have a question about the bill. I think it should come to four hundred and eighty *yuan* altogether, but the bill here is for five hundred and fifty two *yuan*.

W: Oh, yes. Let me explain that for you, madam. We add 5% tax and there's a 10% service charge added to each bill.

G: Well, I wasn't aware of that.

W: I'm sorry about that. There's a note at the bottom of the menu explaining our policy. I should have explained it to you.

G: I am afraid I haven't enough cash on me. Do you honor credit card?

W: What kind are you holding, madam?

G: Master Card.

W: That'll be fine.

G: Here you are.

W: Thank you, madam. Just a moment, please.

　　(2 minutes later)

W: Could you sign your name here, please?

G: Certainly.

W: Thank you. Here is your card and your copy.

Practice 2

Complete the following conversation with the directions given in the brackets. Then take turns role-playing the conversation with your partner. One will be the guest, the other will be the waiter.

W=Waiter　　　　　G=Guest

G: _____(1)(Ask for bill)

W: Yes, sir. Here it is. _____(2). (Tell the bill amounts to ￥540.)

G: _____ (3)? (Show disagreement to the bill and say the bill should come to ￥450.)

W: _____ (4).(Explain that there is a 10% tax and a 10% service charge added to each bill.)

G: Well, I see.

G: _____(5)? (Ask what item 6 is for.)

W: _____(6). (Explain item 6 is for 2 bowls of rice.)

G: Oh, yes.

G: _____(7)(Ask if you can use credit card, the American Express.)

W: _____(8). (Tell that card is accepted.)

G: Here you are.
W: Thank you, madam.

3. Telling you were overcharged and checking the bill for the guest

◆ ***This costs more than*** we have expected.

I think ***we were overcharged.***

◇ ***I am sorry,*** sir/madam. ***May I check the bill for you, please***?

◇ ***I'll ask the cashier to check it up.***

Practice 1
Pattern Drills

Practice a scene of "A mistake on the bill" by replacing the underlined parts in the model conversation with the items and prices given in the table. Take turns doing the role-play with your partner. One will be the guest, the other will be the waitress.

Here is the model conversation:

G=Guest   **W**=Waitress

G: Waitress. The bill, please.
W: Yes, sir. Here it is.
G: This costs more than I have expected. What this ￥15 for?
W: This is the charge for the lemon pie.
G: But I didn't order lemon pie.
W: I am sorry, sir. I'll ask the cashier to check it up. Excuse me for a moment.
W: I'm awfully sorry, sir. You are right. You didn't order lemon pie. I do apologize for the mistake.
G: That's all right.

Here is the information you need:

Items	Prices
Lemon pie	￥15
Pumpkin pie	￥20
Red wine	￥128
Beer	￥40
Green Tea	￥25
Rice	￥4
Coffee	￥30
Coca-cola	￥18

English for Food and Beverages

Practice 2

Fill in the blanks with what you will hear on the recording. Then do the conversation in pairs.

W=Waitress　　　　**G**=Guest

G: Waitress. _____(1).
W: Yes, sir. Here it is. Your bill _____(2) dollars altogether.
G: The bill _____(3). I think I was _____(4). Can you kindly _____(5) for me?
W: _____ (6). _____ (7) dollars for the food, eighty five dollars for the _____(8) and _____(9) dollars for the beer. Is that right, sir?
G: I'm afraid not. I didn't order any beer.
W: I am sorry, Sir. I'll ask the _____(10). _____(11).
W: _____(12), sir. We put somebody else's _____(13) into your bill. We _____(14).
G: That's all right. (5 minutes later.)
W: Here is your bill. _____(15) dollars.

4. Telling there is a wrong change and making an apology for it

◆ Excuse me, 　I'm afraid you shortchanged me.

　　　　　　　I think you shortchanged me ￥20.

◇ I'm sorry, sir/madam.　　Here is the rest of the change.

　　I'm sorry for the mistake.

Practice 1

Fill in the blanks with what you will hear on the recording. Then do the conversation in pairs.

W=Waitress　　　　**G**=Guest

G: _____(1), waitress.
W: Yes, sir.
G: I'm afraid you _____(2) me. How much is the total of the bill?
W: _____(3).
G: I gave you ￥350. I think _____(4) me ￥40 for the change. But you gave me ￥20 only. You shortchanged me ￥20.
W: I'm sorry sir. _____(5), please? ... Oh, you are right._____(6). I do _____(7). Here is the rest of the_____(8).

Unit 6 Paying the Bill

Practice 2

Role-play a scene of "Giving a guest the wrong change" according to the following situation. Student A will be the waiter and student B will be the guest.

Guest:

1. You pay the bill which totals ¥245.
2. You give the waiter ¥300.
3. You are given ¥45 for the change.
4. You tell the waiter that you are shortchanged.

Waiter:

1. You give the guest ¥45 for his change.
2. You check the bill and find you shortchanged the guest ¥10.
3. You make an apology and give the guest the rest of the change.

Summarize Key Expressions

1. Showing disagreement to a bill
   a. There seems to be some mistakes on my bill.
   b. I have a question about the bill.
   c. I think there is a mistake with my bill.
   d. The bill should come to… , but the bill here is for…
2. Requiring for an explanation of a charge
   a. What is this / this figure for?
   b. What is this item for?
3. Explaining a charge
   a. This is the charge for the cold towels.
   b. This figure here is the charge for…
   c. This amount here is for…
   d. This is the… charge
   e. We add 5% tax and there's a 10% service charge added to each bill.
4. Telling you were overcharged and requiring for a breakdown of the bill
   a. This costs more than I have expected.
   b. I think I was overcharged.
   c. Can you kindly break down the bill for me?
5. Checking the bill for a guest
   a. Excuse me for a moment. I'll ask the cashier to check up your bill.
   b. I am sorry, sir. May I check the bill for you, please?
   c. Excuse me for a moment while I check the details.
   d. Can I check the details for you?
   e. I'll make a double check of the bill for you.

6. Telling there is a wrong change
   a. I'm afraid you shortchanged me.
   b. I think you shortchanged me ¥ 20.
7. Making an apology for a mistake on a bill
   a. I'm awfully sorry for the mistake, sir.
   b. We are terribly sorry, sir. We are terribly busy at this hour. We put somebody else's consumption into your bill.
   c. I do apologize.
   d. I'm sorry, sir. We do apology for the mistake.

———————— Give It a Try ————————

Task 1

How should a waiter/waitress respond to the following situations? Put a tick before the appropriate response.

1. Guest: I think there is a mistake with my bill. I didn't order any dessert. But two apple tarts are added to my bill.
   Waiter: ☐ Are you sure? It couldn't be.
   ☐ I'm sorry. May I check the bill for you, please?

2. Guest: The bill seems a little high to me. Can you check it again?
   Waiter: ☐ I would be happy to.
   ☐ We ran it through the computer, so I'm sure it's fine.

3. Guest: Why didn't anyone tell me about the service charge?
   Waiter: ☐ I'm sorry about that. There is a note at the bottom of the menu explaining our policy. I should have explained that to you.
   ☐ Didn't you notice the message at the bottom of the menu?

4. Guest: The bill charges more than what I have expected.
   Waiter: ☐ Oh, really? I don't believe it.
   ☐ Oh, yes. Let me explain. We add 5% tax and there is a 10% service charge added to each bill.

5. Guest: I think you should have given me ¥ 50 for the change. But you gave me ¥ 40 only.
   Waiter: ☐ Can I check your bill, please? ... Oh, you're absolutely right. I'm so sorry. Here is the rest of your change.
   ☐ Are you sure? Could you please count the change that I gave you again?

Task 2

Complete the following sentences with the words given in the table. Change the form where necessary. Then translate the sentences into Chinese.

receipt	error	overcharge	shortchange	undercharge	service charge

1. There seems to be an _____ on the bill.
2. This costs a little more than we had expected. I think we were _____.
3. I think we were _____. There seems to be an item missing on our bill.
4. There is a 15% _____ added to all meals served after 6 p.m.
5. May I have a look at the _____, please? ... Oh, yes I should have given you $ 25 for your change.
6. I'm afraid you _____ me ￥20. The bill totals ￥360. I gave you ￥400 but you only gave me back ￥20.

Task 3

Use the expressions you've learnt in the section **Summarize Key Expressions** and role-play a scene of "A mistake on the bill" according to the following instructions. Do it in pairs. Student A will be the guest and student B will be the waiter.

Guest:
1. You want the bill.
2. You go over the bill and find an error on your bill.
3. You ask what the ￥85 is for.
4. You tell the waiter you haven't ordered Steamed Perch.
5. You ask if they take a personal cheque.

Waiter:
1. You bring the bill.
2. You explain the charge ￥85 is for the Steamed Perch.
3. You ask the guest to wait for a moment and go to the cashier to check up the details.
4. You find the guest is overcharged.
5. Apologize for the mistake.
6. You don't accept personal cheques. You ask the guest to pay his bill in cash.

——— Do Extension Activities ———

 Activity 1

Listen to the conversation and answer the questions.

Questions:
1. How much do they have to pay according to the waitress?

_____.

2. Does the woman agree with the figure on the bill? Why?
   _____.

3. Is there a mistake on the bill? What is it?
   _____.

4. What is the 63 *yuan* for?
   _____.

5. How much is the food? How much is the red wine?
   _____.

6. How much should be the service charge actually?
   _____.

7. How much should the bill amount to actually?
   _____.

8. How does the mistake arise according to the waitress?
   _____.

9. Who paid the bill in the end? In cash or by credit card?
   _____.

Activity 2

Role-play a scene of "A mistake on the bill" according to the following situation.
Scene: In Four Seasons Restaurant
　　Mr. Henderson is settling his bill and thinks that there seems to be some mistakes on his bill. He is talking to the waiter about this...

Here is the information you need:

Mr. Henderson:

1. You are settling your bill and think you are overcharged.
2. You ask the waiter to break down the items on the bill for you.
3. You find some mistakes in your bill while the waiter is explaining the charge.
4. You tell the waiter that you have ordered only two bottles of beer and haven't ordered prawns.

The Waiter:

1. You break down the bill item by item for the guest in a patient way. (Refer to the bill below to explain the items.)
2. You go to the cashier to check the bill since the guest shows disagreement with the bill.
3. You find that the guest has been overcharged. Two bottles of beer and the prawn should be deducted from the guest's bill.
4. You work out the correct amount of the bill. (Refer to the bill below to work out the correct figure.)
5. You explain to the guest that the cashier is a newcomer and is inexperienced. She made the mistake and put somebody else's consumption into the guest's bill.

6. You make an apology and show the revised bill to the guest and tell him the correct amount of the bill.

Here is the bill for Mr. Henderson:

The part in blue should be corrected.

Four Seasons Restaurant

Roast Duck	￥158
Steamed Mandarin Fish	￥98
Twice Cooked Pork Slices	￥30
Ma Pow Bean Curd	￥25
Lettuce with Oyster Sauce	￥20
Beer ×4	￥40
Prawns	￥88
SUB Total	￥459
10% Service Charge	￥46
TOTAL	￥505

The opening part of their conversation has been written out for you. Complete the conversation with the information given above.

Mr. Henderson: Waiter, may I have the bill, please?

The Waiter: Yes, sir. Just a moment. Here you are, sir. Your bill comes to ￥505 altogether.

Mr. Henderson: There must be some mistakes on my bill. It costs more than I have expected. Can you kindly break it down for me, please?

The Waiter:

Mr. Henderson:

...

...

...

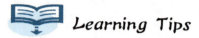 Learning Tips

Feminist Support for and Opposition to Dutch Practice

During the advent of second wave feminism, the late 1960s and 1970s, the women's movement encouraged women to understand aspects of their own personal lives as deeply politicized. Many feminists investigated the framework and assumptions of traditional courtship roles. They subscribed to the idea that there should be equality of the sexes, not just legally, but socially and sexually.

They held that it was mature, empowering and self-respecting for women to pay their own way in romantic dates. They were rejecting traditional gender role assumptions that men should make more money and should pay for affections through dinners and other date costs. In this way, women were making an equal investment in the cost of courtship. It became more common for women to pay their own way or to pay for men's meals. Some women were offended if their male dining partner "grabbed the check."

Since the 1990s, many women have abandoned 1970s feminism's ideals for equality of gender roles and relationships. Many have reverted to adopting "traditional" investment in the courting relationship, and assumptions about men's responsibility to spend money to express affection. The feminist view point is that the other result of this is the creation of a debt or a feeling that female now "owes" the male something, redeemable through the offering of sexual favors. Women began to choose not to put themselves in this position and thus empowered themselves by paying their own way.

Unit 7

Bar Service I

Part A Asking What the Guest Wants to Drink

Teaching hours: 2 hours

Learning Goals:

To be able to
- tell the business hours at the bar
- receive guests appropriately
- show guests to their seats
- ask what guests want to drink
- understand guests' requirement

Vocabulary Assistance

receptionist *n.* 前台接待
waitress *n.* 女服务员
waiter *n.* 男服务员
book *v.* 预订
recommend *v.* 推荐

confirm *v.* 确认
lounge *n.* 酒廊
house specialty 招牌菜
bar manager 酒吧经理
head barman 调酒总管

――――― Start You Off ―――――

Activity 1

Look at the time below and answer the question given below.

Guest: **What time does the bar open and close?**
Waiter: **The bar opens at _____ and closes at _____.**

133

English for Food and Beverages

| 18:00—24:00 | 19:00—23:00 | 18:30—23:30 |

| 19:30—24:00 | 21:00—24:00 | 18:30—24:00 |

Activity 2

The following pictures show people who work in the bars of hotels. Work in pairs and complete the conversation.

Example

Guest: What do you do at the bar?

Clerk: I'm working as a waiter at the bar.

1. ___waiter___   2. _____   3. _____   4. _____

  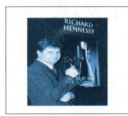 

5. _____   6. _____   7. _____   8. _____

──────── Focus on Language ────────

  Conversation

Booking a Table at the Bar on the Telephone

Questions

1. How would you greet the guest on the phone?
2. What should be told to the guest?

3. How would you make a reservation on the phone?
4. How would you get the needed information?
5. How would you confirm guests' requests?

 Listen to the conversation and read after it. Then try to find the answers to the questions.

C=Reservation Clerk **G**=Guest

C: Good morning. Sunny Day Bar. May I help you?
G: I'd like to reserve a table for a party on Valentine's Day, please.
C: Certainly, sir. For how many people, please?
G: Ten. My old friends are coming to see me then.
C: At what time can we expect you and your friends?
G: Around 20:30.
C: I see. Would you like a table in the lounge or in a private room?
G: A private room is preferred.
C: Certainly sir. We'll have Sunflower Hall reserved for you. Will that be fine? May I have your name and telephone number, please?
G: Sure, it's Larry. My mobile phone number is 13901390139.
C: Mr. Larry, 13901390139... thank you. By the way, we can only keep your room till 22:00.
G: OK. I see.
C: Thank you. We look forward to serving you.

Language Tips

1. Business hours at the bar

◆ Could you (please) tell me **when** the bar **opens**?
Can you tell me **at what time** the bar **opens**?

◆ We **open at 19:00**, madam/sir.
The bar **opens at 19:30** from Monday to Thursday.

◆ Could you (please) tell me **when** the bar **closes**?
Can you tell me **at what time** the bar **closes**?

◆ We **close at midnight**, madam/sir.
The bar **closes at 2:00 a.m.** on Friday and Saturday.

Practice 1

Look at the time-table below and work in pairs to give the opening and closing hours of the bar.

Example

Guest: Could you please tell me when the bar opens and closes?

Clerk: We _____ and _____.

Opening Hour	Closing Hour
6:00 pm	11:30 pm
6:30 pm	11:00 pm
7:00 am	10:30 pm
7:30 am	12:00 pm
6:00 pm	12:00 pm
8:30 am	2:00 am
7:00 am	12:00 pm
8:00 pm	11:30 pm

Practice 2

Work in groups and try to tell the famous bars in Beijing. Please tell the business hours of those bars.

Practice 3

Role-play. Work in pairs and try to find out the business hours at the bars in the form.

Example

G=Guest   **C**=Clerk

C: Good evening. This is the Mayflower Bar. May I help you?

G: Yes. Could you please tell me what time you open tonight?

C: We open at 7:00 p.m., sir.

G: And when do you close then?

C: We close at midnight.

G: Thank you.

C: We look forward to serving you.

Unit 7 Bar Service I

Here is the information you need

Good Friday	10:00 pm—12:00 pm
Sculpture Time	7:00 pm—11:00 pm
Lonely Earth	6:00 pm—11:00 pm
Lijiang Motel	7:00 pm—12:00 pm
Rainman Bar	4:30 pm—11:30 pm
Dragon Bar	6:00 pm—11:30 pm
Irish Bar	7:00 pm—10:30 pm
Landmark Hotel	7:30 pm—12:30 pm

2. Receiving guests appropriately

◆ **Welcome to** Amazon Bar.

◆ **How many persons**, please?

◆ Good evening, sir. **Do you have a reservation**?

◆ Good evening, sir/madam? **May I have your name**, Please?

◆ We are **expecting** you and your friends.

 Practice 1

Listen to the conversation and fill in the blanks with the words that you will hear on the recording.

G=Guest   **C**=Clerk

C: Good evening, sir. _____(1) to Beach Resort Bar. Do you have a _____(2)?
G: Yes. I reserved a table last Sunday.
C: May I have your _____(3), please?
G: _____(4).
C: How many persons, please?
G: A table for _____(5).
C: This way, please. A waiter will come soon to take your order.
G: Thank you.
C: My pleasure.

Practice 2

Role-play. Work in pairs and try to make conversations with the information given below.
G=Guest   **C**=Clerk

C: Good evening, Madam. Welcome to Mayflower Bar. Have you made a reservation?
G: Yes, I have. I've booked a table by the lake.

English for Food and Beverages

C: May I have your name, please?

G: Barbara Lee.

C: How many persons, please?

G: A table for five.

C: This way, please.

Names of bars	Names of guests	Number of persons	Places of tables
Lotus	Howard	4	By the window
Soul	Julie	6	Near the counter
Seven Days	Benson	3	On the roof

3. Showing guests to their seats

◆ *Where would you like to sit?*

◆ *Where would you prefer to sit?*

◆ *I'll show you to your table.*

◆ *How about this table?*

◆ *Is this table fine?*

◆ *We can seat you very soon.*

◆ *Could you wait for another 15 minutes, please?*

 Practice

Go over the model expressions above. Listen to the conversation and do it in pairs.

G=Guest   C=Clerk

C: Good evening, sir. Welcome to Shining-Star Bar. Have you made a reservation, please?

G: Yes, I've booked a table for six.

C: May I have your name, please?

G: MacBeth.

C: Where would you like to sit?

G: We prefer a table on the roof, where we can enjoy the moonlight.

C: I'm afraid the table is not available now. How about one near the pool?

G: OK. It's fine.

C: This way, please. A waitress will come soon to take your order.

G: Thank you.

C: You're welcome.

4. Asking what guests want to drink

◆ *What would you like to have?*

◆ *Would you like to try some French wine?*

◆ *What would you like to drink?*

◆ *Which vintage would you prefer?*

◆ *I would recommend Jin.*

◆ *Would you like to have some snack with your wine?*

  Practice

Listen to the conversation and try to answer the questions given below.

1. What does the clerk recommend to the guest?
2. What does the guest order?
3. What kind of salad does the guest order?
4. What is House Specialty?

C=Clerk   **G**=Guest

C: May I take your order now, sir?

G: Ur... I don't know much about the drinks here. Can you recommend something to us?

C: Certainly. How about Yanjing Beer? It's not too strong and quite popular in Beijing.

G: I'll take it. What goes with the beer?

C: Some snack or salad will be OK. Would you like to have some salad with it?

G: Fine. I'll take the light one.

C: Would you like to try our House Specialty?

G: No, thanks. It's enough for us two.

C: OK. Thank you.

Summarize Key Expressions

1. Asking about the business hours at the bar
   a. When do you open?
   b. At what time does the bar open?
   c. Does the bar open till 1:00 am of the next day?
   d. When do you close?

2. Giving the bar hours
   a. We open at 7:00 pm and close at midnight.
   b. Our bar is open until midnight.
   c. We're open till 11:00 pm.

d. We're open from 10:00 am until midnight.
3. Reserving a table at the bar
   A. I'd like to reserve a table for three at 9:00 pm, this Sunday.
   B. I have reserved a table near the window.
   C. We would like to have a table by the fountain.
   D. I'd like to make a reservation for two at eight.
4. Receiving guests
   A. How many persons in your party?
   B. Do you have a reservation?
   C. May I have your name, please?
   D. Where would you prefer to sit?
   E. I'm afraid the table you reserved is not ready yet.
   F. I'll show you to your table.
   G. Is this table fine with you?
   H. Would you mind waiting until it is free or would you prefer another table?
5. Asking guest to wait for a moment
   A. We can seat you very soon.
   B. Could you wait for 10 minutes, please?
   C. Could you wait in line in the lobby?
   D. I'm sorry to have kept you waiting.
   E. It may take about 15 minutes.
6. Arranging the table
   A. Could you move the chair closer to the table, please?
   B. Would you mind sharing a table with another one?
   C. Would you mind sitting separately?
   D. I'm afraid we cannot seat you by the lake.
   E. Another guest wishes to sit at the counter. Could you move down your chair, please?

 Give It a Try

 Task 1

The clerk is taking a reservation by phone. Listen to the recording and fill in the form according to the conversation.

Reservation Form

Name of the bar: _____

Date taken: _____

Time of reservation: _____

Unit 7 Bar Service I

Name of the person making the reservation: _____

Telephone number: _____

Logged by/in: _____

No. in party: _____

Task 2

Listen to the recording and complete the following conversation.

G=Guest   C=Clerk

C: Good evening, sir. Welcome to _____(1). How many persons, please?

G: A table for _____(2), please?

C: Do you have a _____(3)?

G: No, we don't.

C: Could you please wait a moment? I'll go and see if tables are _____(4) or not. How about this table _____(5), sir?

G: Fine. Thanks.

C: This way, please.

Task 3

Role-play. With the model in Task 2, make conversations with the information given below.

Guest

1. Your name is Mr. Cahill.
   You want to know when the bar opens and closes.
   You want to reserve a table for six at 10:30 pm.

2. Your name is Mary.
   You want to book a table for your birthday party at 7:30 pm Friday evening, March 21.
   There will be seven at the party.
   You want a table outside the lobby.

3. Your name is Juliet.
   You'd like to have a party at the Lily Bar.
   You want to make a reservation on Saturday evening, but tables are not available at that time.
   You change the place of the table and move in the lounge.

Host/Hostess

1. Someone calls the bar.
   You are open from 6:00 pm to midnight.

2. Receiving guests with reservation.
   A guest reserved a table for four by the lake.

3. Arranging seats

A guest has booked a table, but it is not available when he comes. You should arrange them to another table.

Do Extension Activities

✚ Activity 1

Read the following expressions and try to learn them by heart.

1. Would you like to have table d'hote, or a la carte?
2. We offer special menus for different diets.
3. We have a wide range of wines for you to choose.
4. Could you recommend something special to us?
5. Maybe soft drink will suit you.
6. It's very popular with ladies.
7. What is today's special?
8. Which brand of beer would you prefer?
9. If you are in a hurry, I would recommend table d'hote.
10. It will stimulate the appetite.

✚ Activity 2

Read the following tips and try to get some information about the types of bars and service they provide.

1. Pre-Paid Bar

Our Pre-Paid Bar Service is ideal for weddings and other functions. This complete service includes portable bars fully stocked with on-draught beer and all spirits through to wines and soft drinks. Glasses, optics, ice and garnishes etc., together with fully qualified uniformed staff.

2. Pay Bar-Licensed Bar Service

Our "Pay Bar" is similar to the Pre-Paid Bar Service. The only difference is the guests pay for their own drinks. The price quoted for this package includes the necessary "Temporary Events Notice" fee.

3. Mobile Executive Bar

Our stunning mobile bars are versatile, easily placed almost anywhere and can be used at:
- Sporting and Corporate events
- Marquee Weddings, Parties and Functions
- Air Shows and Gymkhanas
- Golf, Cricket, Yacht and Football Clubs
- Leisure Centres/County Show Grounds

Unit 7 Bar Service I

TAKE THE BAR TO THE PEOPLE NOT THE PEOPLE TO THE BAR

Mobile Bar details

↑ Our Executive Mobile Bar Units have 16 metres of under-cover bar area

↑ Includes a Remote Controlled Cooler to ensure that beer stays cool

↑ Bar Pumps for even the thirstiest of guests

↑ Glasses, Optics and Garden Furniture are available

↑ Powered by Mains Electricity or Generator

Mobile Bar Services

This is our signature and what we are famous for. We have eight state of the art Designer Mobile Bars in service, with another four unique and innovative concepts on the way. Our stainless steel bars are designed by ourselves and are able to morph into a whole host of specifications to tastefully suit any space or environment. They have Perspex outers which light up, and for corporate sponsors they have facilities for Light Box Branding. Only Professional Mixologists man our Bars; we also have Flaring Bartenders and awesome Fire Blowers. Another singular aspect of our service are our mind-blowing cocktails. We offer our own electrifying Cocktail Menus and our Cocktail Designers, who have international experience, have their recipes published on a regular basis by Food & Home etc. Look out for the Cocktail of the Month published on this website. Thirst will provide all the respective glasses required for your function.

4. The UFO Bar

The UFO Bar has created quite a stir in the mobile bar industry, being the first circular mobile bar in the country. It has left all *Thirst's* competitors scrambling to come up with something similar. The design however stands alone as a true feat of ingenuity, coupling amazing versatility with functionality and style. The bar consists of four separate segments or lit modules, together with a light box. These can be joined together in a number of formats and sizes, so that the bar can be set up in the most effective way depending on the dynamics of the venue. It can be circular, semi-circular or have a double curve. Packed with all the best and necessary equipment, this bar will add panache to any function, ensuring ample bar space, so there is smooth and accessible service for large numbers of guests.

5. The Light Bar

This state-of-the-art convex shaped bar is called the Light Bar because it creatively uses light to make it stylishly distinctive. It has interchangeable Perspex front panels and interchangeable Perspex bar-tops that light up, so that any color can be displayed, matching with whatever themes are presented at the venue. It also has a panel in the center where there is space available for branding. Needless to say this attractive and elegant bar is fully equipped with ice wells and speed rails, together with glasses and beverage space to serve a high volume of guests.

6. The Cantalever Bar

This bar is unique and completely portable. Manufactured from stainless steel it is fully equipped with ice wells and speed rails, together with glasses and beverage space to serve between fifty and sixty people. It is only one and a half meters long and seventy centimeters deep, folding away into a suitcase-like trunk that can fit through any door. This makes it the perfect back-of-house bar for functions where accessibility or space may be slightly limited, or where something more discreet is required. As with all *Thirst*'s bar units the Cantalever exudes style and has a professional presentation, making it perfect for any client who is keen to impress.

7. Ice Sculptures / Bars

If you want to really impress your guests or your clients, then why not enquire about our ice sculptures/bars. They provide a spectacular and engaging spectacle, are tastefully done, and are tailored to meet your wishes.

8. Coffee & Infused Herbal Tea Bar

Coffee is still one of the world's most popular drinks—who doesn't meet friends for coffee? So why not make more friends and offer some of the superb variations of quality Espresso based coffees we purvey from our unique and stylish Action Coffee Bars. Espresso Solo; Espresso Americano; Espresso Romano; Espresso Macchiato; Cappuccino and Café Latte（拿铁咖啡馆）. Added to that there are other stunning Gourmet Beverage Menu's with a whole host of other drinks to choose from; like Fine International Teas; Liqueur infused Coffees; Ice Blended Espresso based Smoothies and Hot Liqueur Sippers. One of our exclusive concepts is the Herbal Infused Waters or Teas; which is purified water heated and infused with carefully selected fresh fruits, herbs and spices. All ingredients are natural and healthy, there is no caffeine and they are supremely refreshing.

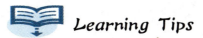 Learning Tips

Wines

The traditional wines are made out of fermented grape juice. The classic wine classification is according to its color. Therefore, the most common wines can be divided into red, white and rose. The grape juice is usually clear and the wine's color comes from the presence of grape skin in its composition. Red wine is commonly made from black or red grapes. White wine doesn't have to be made out of white grapes. On the contrary, white wine can be the product of any color grapes, as long as the skin has been properly removed. Rose wines are in fact white wines made of very dark grapes thus receiving a pink color. Another highly appreciated wine variation is the sparkling wine. Champagne is probably the most renowned sparkling wine and its main characteristic is the incorporation of carbon dioxide.

Part B Telling What Is Wanted

Teaching hours: 2 hours

Learning Goals:

To be able to
- ask if guests have finished their order
- ask guests what else they would like to order
- confirm what guests have already ordered
- ask guests to wait to be served

Vocabulary Assistance

menu *n.* 菜单
recommend *v.* 推荐
alcoholic *adj.* 含酒精的
brew *n.* 酿酒
specialty *n.* 特色菜
appropriately *adv.* 适宜地

brand *n.* 品牌
draught *n.* 扎啤
oyster *n.* 生蚝
snack *n.* 点心,零食
iced water 冰水
soft drink 软饮料

---— Start You Off ———

Activity 1

Look at the picture and read the passage below. Try to learn what is prepared for each option.

Bar Options

Option 1 Open Bar

This package includes standard selections of beer, wine and liquor from our Alcohol Selection Menu. You may request special products not listed on our menu at additional cost. All beverages will be charged the standard pricing from our Alcohol Selection Menu and the total will be billed to the customer at the end of the event. An initial deposit of $ 500 is required for open bar service and will be applied to the final bill.

Option 2 Cash Bar

This package includes standard selections of beer, wine and liquor from our Alcohol Selection Menu. You may request special products not listed on our menu at additional cost. All beverages will be charged the standard pricing from our Alcohol Selection Menu. Special products will be priced according to selection.

Option 3 Combination

This package includes standard selections of beer, wine and liquor from our Alcohol Selection Menu. You may request special products not listed on our menu at additional cost. The customer may open the bar for a predetermined amount of time. All drinks during this time period will be billed to the customer. After the designated time period the bar will revert to cash bar.

Option 4 Champagne Toast

This package includes chilled champagne, plastic glassware and pouring staff. The cost for this package is $3.75 per person. Add $1.00 per person for Glass Champagne Flutes.

All bar packages are subject to an 18% service charge and 8% New Hampshire state sales tax. A copy of Mahalos liquor license and liability insurance is available upon request.

Activity 2

The following form shows a menu at a bar. Look at the forms below and try to tell what service and drinks can be offered there.

BAR SERVICES	75 Guest Minimum	76 to 125 Guest	126 to 175 Guests	176 Plus Guest
Soda & Water Bar	$3.75 pp	$3.75 pp	$3.75 pp	$3.75 pp
Soda, Juice, & Water	$5.00 pp	$5.00 pp	$5.00 pp	$5.00 pp
Value Bar	$10.00 pp	$9.00 pp	$7.50 pp	$7.00 pp
Call Bar	$12.50 pp	$11.50 pp	$10.00 pp	$9.50 pp
Premium Bar	$17.50 pp	$16.50 pp	$15.00 pp	$14.00 pp
Includes	1 Bar	1 Bar	1 Bar	1 Bar
	1 Bartender	1 Bartender	1 Bartender	1 Bartender
	4 hours	4 hours	4 hours	4 hours

Additional Time	$125/Hour	$200/Hour	$250/Hour	$325/Hour
Soda & Water Bar	$50/Hour	$75/Hour	$100/Hour	$125/Hour
Soda, Juice & Water	$75/Hour	$100/Hour	$125/Hour	$150/Hour

* 4 Hours to Include: 1 Hour Setup & 3 Hours Open for Service
* All Prices Per Person Include: 8.25% Tax & 18% Service Charge
* Corkage Fee: Starting at $250

LIQUOR	VALUE BAR	CALL BAR	PREMIUM BAR
Vodka		Smirnoff	Absolut, Skyy
			Stolichnaya
Gin		Barton	Bombay
			Tanqueray
Rum		Ron Rico	Bacardi, Myers
		Malibu	Malibu
Tequila		Suaza	Cuervo Gold
Scotch		Johnnie Walker Red	Johnnie Walker Black
Whiskey		Seagrams 7	Crown Royal
		Jim Beam	Jack Daniels
Brandy		Christian Brothers	Hennessy
Cordials		Baileys	Baileys, Kahlua
		Kahlua	Grand Marnier
Beer	Keg (Choice of Two)	Keg (Choice of Two)	Keg (Choice of Two)
	Bud, Bud Lite	Bud, Bud Lite	Bud, Bud Lite
	MGD, Miller Lite	MGD, Miller Lite	MGD, Miller Lite
Wine	Merlot	Merlot	Merlot
	Chardonnay	Chardonnay	Chardonnay
	White Zinfandel	White Zinfandel	White Zinfandel
Soft Drinks	Coke	Coke	Coke
	Diet Coke	Diet Coke	Diet Coke
	7-UP	7-UP	7-UP
Juice	Orange, Cranberry	Orange, Cranberry	Orange, Cranberry
	Pineapple	Pineapple	Pineapple
Water	Crystal Gyser	Crystal Gyser	Crystal Gyser

Focus on Language

Taking Orders at the Bar

Questions

1. How would you greet guests appropriately?
2. How should you recommend drinks to guests?
3. How should you make clear requests of the guests when you are taking reservations from them?
4. How should you get the needed information?
5. How should you confirm guests' requests?

 Listen to the conversation and read after it. Then try to find the answers to the questions.

Clerk: What may I offer you, ladies and gentlemen?
Bill: I don't know what I want. I'm not really a drinker.
Clerk: An aperitif or some white wine?
Bill: Um... a Sunrise Beer.
Clerk: I don't believe we know that one. How about our special cocktail?
Bill: That sounds good. How about you, Sally?
Sally: I don't drink at all. Do you serve soft drinks?
Clerk: Of course, ma'am. But how about a non-alcoholic cocktail?
Sally: It sounds interesting. I'll take that.
Clerk: What would you like to drink, gentleman?
Tom: Well, none of that stuff they're drinking, eh John?
John: No, Tom. We'll have the usual beer, I suppose?
Tom: Yes, I'm very thirsty.
Clerk: Any special brand, sir?
John: What about your local brew? I hear it's good.
Clerk: It is Five Star Beer. Bottled or draught?
Bill: Let's try the draught.
Clerk: Fine. One special cocktail and one non-alcoholic cocktail for the ladies and two draught Five Star Beer.
John: Could we have some snacks?
Clerk: Certainly, I'll get a fresh supply.

Language Tips

1. Ask if guests have finished their order

◆ Would you like to try some Chinese alcohol?

- *What else would you like to have?*
- *Have you decided what you would like to drink?*
- *Is there anything else I can do for you?*
- *Is that all you have ordered?*

 Practice 1

Listen to the conversation and try to answer the questions given below.

1. What does the guest order at the bar?
2. What does the bartender introduce to the guest?
3. How does the guest have his Scotch?

B=Bartender   **G**=Guest

B: Good evening, sir! What can I make for you tonight?

G: I'll have a Scotch.

B: We have Chivas Regal, Old Par, Johny Walker Black and Red Labels, Cutty Sark, Queen Ann. Which would you like?

G: Give me a Chivas Regal.

B: Royal Salute or 12 years?

G: Royal Salute.

B: One Chivas Regal Royal Salute. And How would you like your Scotch, straight or on the rock?

G: With iced water.

B: Here you are, sir. Scotch with iced water.

Practice 2

Work in groups and give the names of the wines you are familiar with. Then try to tell their prices.

Practice 3

Role-play. Work in pairs and try to make conversations with the example given below. Take turns and do like this:

Example

G=Guest   **C**=Clerk

C: May I take your order now?

G: Yes. Could you tell me what the specialty is here?

C: We have a very extensive cellar. Burgundy is our house wine.

G: OK, I'll take.

C: Would you like to try the dry sherry?

G: No, thank you. I would like to have oysters to go with Burgundy.

C: OK, is there anything I can do for you?

G: No, it is quite enough.

C: Thank you. Your wine will be ready soon.

Here is the information you need

Guest	Clerk
Scotch	fish and prawns
Sherry	shrimp
Mao tai	egg custard with chicken
Royal Salute 12 years	oyster
Crown Royal	caviar

2. Ask guests what else they would like to order

◆ *Is there anything I can do for you?*

◆ *What else would you like to have, sir/madam?*

◆ *Is there anything more you want to have for your party?*

◆ *It's very popular with our guests.*

◆ *Would you like to have any other drinks and snack?*

 Practice 1

Listen to the conversation and read the bill to see what the guest has ordered. Then work in pairs to make conversations with the information given below.

Guest	Drinks	Snack/food
1. Mr. Brown	cognac	salad
2. Ms. Cleric	martini	shrimp
3. Mr. Howard	bottled beer	vegetable
4. Ms. Sanders	iced water	nuts
5. Mr. Ricardo	Chinese red wine	seafood

 Practice 2

Fill in the blanks with the words that you will hear on the recording.

G=Guest   C=Clerk

C: Can I take your order now?

English for Food and Beverages

G: What _____(1)do you have for this evening?

C: Our specialty today is iced _____(2).

G: I'll _____(3)it, please.

C: Sure. Would you like to have beer _____(4)?

G: Draught, please.

C: Would you want to try some seafood?

G: No, thanks.

C: Is there anything you want to have to _____(5)beer?

G: No, it's _____(6)for me.

C: OK, your wine will be _____(7)soon.

3. Confirm what guests have already ordered

◆ *How about Champagne?*

◆ *Anything else, sir?*

◆ *No, thanks. That's all for now.*

◆ *OK. Chablis goes with your shrimp.*

Practice 1

Go over the expressions above and try to make short conversations with the information given below.

Guests	Table	People in the party	Drinks	Food
Mr. Collins	by the window	4	Vermouth	mixed salad
Ms. Kelly	by the lake	3	Blush Rose Wine	
Mr. Gary	on the top floor	6	Semi-Dry White Wine	meat salad

——— Summarize Key Expressions ———

1. Asking if guests have finished their order
    A. What else would you like to drink?
    B. What kind of dessert would you like?
    C. Anything else, sir?
    D. That's all for now.
2. Asking guests what else they would like to order
    A. What else would you like to drink?
    B. Is there anything else I can do for you?
    C. Anything else, sir?
    D. That's all for now.
3. Confirming what guests have already ordered
    A. Are you on a special diet?

B. Would you like your beer draught or bottle?

C. This wine is only served by the bottle.

D. With ice or without ice?

4. Asking guests to wait to be served

A. Your drink will be ready soon.

B. Your wine will be served very soon.

C. You will be served soon.

───────── Give It a Try ─────────

  Task 1

The clerk is taking an order. Listen to the recording and write down the proper information in the form.

Form

Name of the person: _____

Place of tables: _____

No. in party: _____

Drinks taken: _____

Food taken _____

Special requirement _____

Task 2

Role-play according to the following situations. Work in pairs and make short conversations.

Guest

1. Your name is Benson.

   You want to have soft drinks and seafood at the bar.

   You also want to try the local specialty.

2. You are a guest at the hotel, having a meeting with your friends.

   You've reserved a table in the private room at the bar.

   There are seven of you.

   You want to have Galliano Liqueur.

3. You've been seated in the lounge close to the pool.

   You'd like to have a party to celebrate your victory.

   You want to order Crystal Palace, Befeater, and Lariors.

Do Extension Activities

➕ Activity 1

Read the following statements and make a tick to the "General Rules" for taking orders at the bar.

☐ Greet your callers warmly and appropriately.
☐ Give the menu to gentlemen first though there are some ladies in this party.
☐ It will be better for the clerks to give the menu to the host/hostess in a large group.
☐ Take order when guests are seated.
☐ You should explain or recommend to the guest some specialty, Today's Specialty or House Specialty.
☐ When taking order, clerks should ask guests about their special requirements.
☐ When having taken order, clerks should confirm what they have ordered.

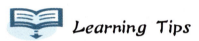 Learning Tips

Pairing Wine and Food Is an Art

Have you ever been in the situation of not knowing exactly which wine on the menu goes best with what you've ordered? Have you ever had trouble selecting wine glasses because you weren't sure about the difference between them? If the answer is "yes" to any of these questions, your wine education needs some improving. At *wineclass. net* you can read professional wine reviews, get information on wine courses and much more.

Drinking wine is supposed to be one of the greater pleasures in life. Knowing how to pair wine and food is essential to enjoying your meal. If a wine is chosen properly, it will enhance the tastefulness of the food and you will appreciate your dining experience more. Simple rules, such as choosing white wine for white meat, are not that difficult to grasp. However, knowing which white wine from that long list you are presented is the most suitable and will give you the maximum pleasure, is an art.

Unit 8

Bar Service II

Part A Asking before Serving and Serving the Guest

Teaching hours: 2 hours

Learning Goals:

To be able to
- ask what guests specially require
- confirm details about beverage
- serve guests
- wish guests enjoy their drink

Vocabulary Assistance

counter *n.* 柜台
feature *n.* 特色
semi-dry *adj.* 半干的
spoil *v.* 破坏,影响

flavor *n.* 味道
delicate *adj.* 香醇
taste *v.* 品尝

―――― Start You Off ――――

Activity 1

Look at the pictures given below. Ask and answer the questions in pairs.

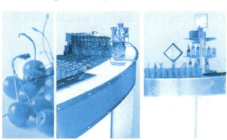

English for Food and Beverages

1. What are these pictures about?
2. What can you learn from the pictures?
3. Where is it?
4. What is the man doing in the picture? What is his job?

 Activity 2

The following pictures show the glasses used at bars. Please try to identify them and tell what they are used for. Write down their English names.

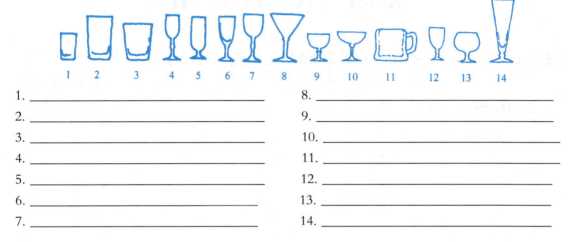

1. _____
2. _____
3. _____
4. _____
5. _____
6. _____
7. _____
8. _____
9. _____
10. _____
11. _____
12. _____
13. _____
14. _____

——————— Focus on Language ———————

 Conversation

Serving the Guests

Questions

1. How should you receive guests at the bar counter?
2. How should you recommend to guests who need help?
3. How should you ask guests what they want to have?
4. How should you get details about guests' order?
5. How should you confirm guests' requests?

Listen to the conversation and read after it. Then try to find the answers to the questions.

B=Bartender　　G=Guest

B: Good evening, sir. What can I make for you tonight?
G: I'll have a Scotch.
B: We have Chivas Regal, Old Par, Johny Walker Black and Red Labels, Cutty Sark, Queen Ann. Which would you like?

G: Give me a Chivas Regal.

B: Royal Salute or 12 years?

G: 12 years.

B: One Chivas Regal 12 years. And how would you like your Scotch, straight or on the rock?

G: Straight.

B: Here you are, sir. Straight Scotch.

G: Thank you.

Language Tips

1. Asking what guests specially require

◆ *Would you like to try something special* in China?

◆ *What would you like to drink*? *How about* champagne?

◆ *Have you decided to try* local brew in Beijing?

◆ *What special drink* would you like to try, sir?

◆ *Which vintage would you prefer*?

Practice 1

Listen to the conversation and fill the blanks with the words you will hear. Then check it in pairs.

G=Guest **C**=Clerk

C: Good evening, sir. Can I help you?

G: Yes, I'd like to try something _____(1) here.

C: What would you like to have, _____(2)?

G: Wine, please. Could you give me any _____(3)?

C: Sure. We have _____(4). We also have some _____(5).

G: How about _____(6)?

C: Yes. How do you like it?

G: _____(7), but not too much.

C: OK. Anything else would you like to have?

G: No, thanks. It's _____(8) for me.

C: Thank you. Your wine will be ready soon.

Practice 2

Work in groups and give the names of the wines you have known. Then tell what flavor and features are.

1. Whisky（威士忌）
2. Rum（兰姆酒）

6. Gin（琴酒/金酒）
7. Sherry（雪利酒）

English for Food and Beverages

3. Vodka（伏特加）
4. Champagne（香槟）
5. Liqueur（利口酒）
8. Brandy（白兰地）
9. Vermouth（苦艾酒/法国威末酒）
10. Cocktail（鸡尾酒）

2. Confirming details about beverages

◆ What would you like to have to **go with** your wine?

◆ The wine is **rather strong**, but never goes to the head.

◆ A Chablis would **go very well with** your oyster.

◆ It's Burgundy **with a rich but delicate body**.

◆ The wine is not **chilled** enough due to the cold weather in Beijing.

◆ Would you like to have **dry or semi-dry**?

Practice 1

Make conversations in pairs with the information given below.

Names of guests	Clerk's Recommendations	Ordered drinks	Requirements	Ways to serve
Mr. Andrew	Whisky and Gin	Whisky	Chilled	
Ms. Yang	Beer, Rum and Liqueur	Beer	Draught	
Mr. Kula	Mao tai and Five-Star Beer	Mao tai	A small glass	

3. Serving guests

◆ *Here is the wine list, sir.*

◆ *I'll put the cork here, sir.*

◆ *How is the taste of the wine, sir?*

◆ *If we add more ice, the taste will be spoiled.*

◆ *Please tell me if it is enough.*

 Practice

Listen to the conversation and try to answer the questions given below.

1. What does the sommelier do in a bar?
2. What does the guest order?
3. How does the sommelier serve the guest?
4. What does he say to the guest when he serves him?

4. Serving during the drink

◆ *This is a little strong. Please be careful.*

◆ *May I serve it to you now?*

◆ *Shall I change it with a smaller one?*

◆ *Shall I serve it now or later?*

Listen and read the conversation and try to tell "dos" and "do nots" during the service.

G=Guest   C=Clerk

C: Your champagne, sir. Please enjoy.

G: Thank you.

C: Excuse me, may I take your glass?

G: Sure, go ahead.

C: Would you like to have anything else?

G: Please give me the menu. I'd like to try some snacks.

C: Here you are.

G: I'd like to have a chocolate pudding.

C: OK. Your pudding will be ready soon.

───── Summarize Key Expressions ─────

1. Asking what guests specially require

    A. What would you like to drink? How about champagne?

    B. Have you decided to try local brew in Beijing?

    C. What special drink would you like to try, sir?

2. Confirming details about beverages

    A. Would you like to have something to go with your wine?

    B. The wine is rather strong, but never goes to the head.

    C. A chablis would go very well with your oyster.

    D. It's burgundy with a rich but delicate body.

    E. The wine is not chilled enough due to the cold weather in Beijing.

3. Serving guests

    A. Here is the wine list, sir.

    B. I'll put the cork here, sir.

    C. How is the taste of the wine, sir?

    D. If we add more ice, the taste will be spoiled.

    E. Please tell me if it is enough.

4. Wishing guests enjoy their drink
   A. Thank you. Please enjoy.
   B. Your salad and wine. Please enjoy.
5. Serving during the drink
   A. This is a little strong. Please be careful.
   B. May I serve it to you now?
   C. Shall I change it with a smaller one?
   D. Shall I serve it now or later?

Give It a Try

Task 1

Role-play according to the following situations. Student A will be the guest and Student B will be the clerk.

Guest

1. You want to know what House Specialty the bar has.
   You want to order some red wine.
   You also want to have some fruits.
2. You want to ask today's specialty.
   You also ask the clerk to give you some recommendation.
   You order chilled bottled beer.
3. You'd like to have vodka, but the bar does not have it.
   You want to try the local brew.
   You order the popular spirit.

Do Extension Activities

Activity 1

Read the passage and try to answer the questions given below.

> **Questions**
>
> 1. How do you define the wine glass?
> 2. How many parts are there in a glass?
> 3. Why is the stem very important for the wine glass?
> 4. What are the features of red wine glasses, white wine glasses and sherry wine glasses?

Wine Glasses

A wine glass is a type of glass stemware which is used to drink and taste wine. It is generally composed of three parts: the bowl, stem, and foot. Selection of a particular wine glass for a wine style is important, as the glass shape can influence its perception.

It is important to note the most obvious, but often most neglected, part of the wine glass—the stem. The proper way to drink from the wine glass, when drinking white or otherwise chilled wine is to grasp it by the stem and drink. The purpose of this is that the temperature of the wine is not affected when holding the glass. This is achieved because the stem is not in direct contact with the wine. It would be more difficult to control the temperature of the wine if one held the glass by the bowl because it is in direct contact with the wine. Also, holding the glass by the bowl will leave fingerprints, which can distort the visual appearance of the wine when examining the clarity and colour of the wine.

Red wine glasses

Glasses for red wine are characterized by their rounder, wider bowl, which gives the wine a chance to breathe. Red wine glasses can have particular styles of their own, such as:

- **Bordeaux glass:** Tall with a wide bowl, and is designed for full bodied red wines like Cabernet and Merlot as it directs wine to the back of the mouth.
- **Burgundy glass:** Larger than the Bordeaux glass, it has a larger bowl to accumulate aromas of more delicate red wines such as Pinot Noir. This style of glass directs wine to the tip of the tongue.

White wine glasses

White wine glasses are generally narrower, although not as narrow as champagne flutes, with somewhat straight or tulip-shaped sides. The narrowness of the white wine glass allows the chilled wine to retain its temperature for two reasons:

1. The reduced surface area of the glass (in comparison to red wine glasses) means less air circulating around the glass and warming the wine.
2. The smaller bowl of the glass means less contact between the hand and the glass, and so body heat does not transfer as easily to the wine.

Champagne flutes are characterised by a long stem with a tall, narrow bowl on top. The shape is designed to keep sparkling wine desirable during its consumption. The glass is designed to be held by the stem to help prevent the heat from the hand from warming the champagne. The bowl itself is designed in a manner to help retain the signature carbonation in the beverage. This is achieved by reducing the surface area at the opening of the bowl.

Champagne flutes are often used at formal engagements, such as award ceremonies and weddings.

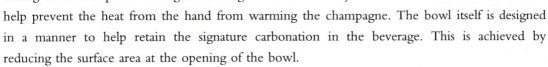

A sherry copita

A sherry glass is drinkware generally used for serving aromatic alcoholic beverages, such as sherry, port, aperitifs and liqueurs, and layered shooters. An ISO-standard sized sherry glass is 120 ml. The *copita*, with its aroma-enhancing.

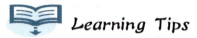 Learning Tips

Wine Glasses

Most people underestimate the importance of correctly choosing their wine glasses. A wine glass can enhance the aroma and offer a beautiful visual presentation. Crystal glasses are considered to be the elite in this area, offering a beautiful light reflection. Wine glasses can be divided into three main categories, according to the type of wine to be served: the red wine glass, the white wine glass and the champagne flute. Red wine glasses are somewhat larger than the other two variations and are characterized by a wide, round bowl. This bowl format allows the wine to breathe and cool quickly after coming in contact with the consumer's hands. Red wine glasses can also be divided into distinctive categories, such as Burgundy glasses or Bordeaux glasses. White wine is usually served in narrower glasses, with tulip-shaped figures. The champagne flute is definitely the narrowest and tallest wine glass. This distinctive design helps the wine retain its sparkling properties during the serving period.

Part B Asking How Much Is Owed and Saying Goodbye

Teaching hours: 2 hours

Learning Goals:

To be able to
- ask guests if they have finished
- tell guests how much is owed
- ask guests to pay the bill
- say good-bye to guests

Vocabulary Assistance

package *n.* 套餐   unfold *v.* 打开
separate *adj.* 各自分开的   change *n.* 零钱
payment *n.* 付款   sneak out 溜走
tip *v.* 给小费   exchange rate 汇率

Start You Off

Activity 1

Read the passage below and try to tell what drinks are offered and the prices of them. Do it in pairs.

Beverage Packages for a Four-Hour Bar

SODA & JUICE BAR

$7 per person includes

Sodas Coke ~ Diet Coke ~ Sprite ~ Ginger Ale ~ Soda Water

Juices Tropicana Cranberry ~ Tropicana Orange

Water Bottled Spring Water (Sparkling & Non-Sparkling)

WINE, BEER, SODA & JUICE BAR

$18 per person includes

House Wines Camelot Cabernet Sauvignon ~ Gallo of Sonoma Reserve Cabernet

Camelot Chardonnay ~ Gallo of Sonoma Reserve Chardonnay
Beers Bass Ale ~ Heineken ~ Amstel Light ~ Budweiser ~ Coors Light
Sodas Coke ~ Diet Coke ~ Sprite ~ Ginger Ale ~ Soda Water
Juices Tropicana Cranberry ~ Tropicana Orange
Water Bottled Spring Water (Sparkling & Non-Sparkling)
FULL BAR
$24 per person includes
Liquor Smirnoff Vodka ~ Dewar's Scotch ~ Beefeater Gin ~ Jack Daniel's ~ Bacardi Rum
House Wines Camelot Cabernet Sauvignon ~ Gallo of Sonoma Reserve Cabernet
Camelot Chardonnay ~ Gallo of Sonoma Reserve Chardonnay
Beers Bass Ale ~ Heineken ~ Amstel Light ~ Budweiser ~ Coors Light
Sodas Coke ~ Diet Coke ~ Sprite ~ Ginger Ale ~ Soda & Tonic Water
Juices & Water Tropicana Cranberry ~ Tropicana Orange
Bottled Spring Water (Sparkling & Non-Sparkling)
CHAMPAGNE Grand Laurent, Blanc De Blanc, Brut NV *$27.50 per bottle*

Focus on Language

 Conversation

Asking the Guests to Pay the Bill

Questions

1. How would you recommend to guests?
2. What does the bartender recommend to the guest?
3. What does the guest require about his drink?
4. How should you tell the guest the price of the drink?
5. How should you ask the guest to pay the bill?

 Listen to the conversation and read after it. Then try to find the answers to the questions.

B=Bartender   **G**=Guest

B: OK. One Chivas Regal Royal Salute. And how would you like your Scotch?

G: With iced water.

B: Here you are, sir. Scotch with iced water.

G: Thank you. Now how much do I owe you?

B: The Chivas Regal Royal Salute is 40 *yuan* plus 10% service charge. So the total is 44 *yuan*. You can hold the payment of the bill until you decide to leave if you like.

G: Really? In American bars you pay drink by drink as you get it.

B: But isn't that too much of trouble?

G: Well, yes, it is. But then it is much safer. You see, American bars can be very crowded and it is very hard to keep an eye on everyone. Besides you can never know what may happen when people drink too much.

B: I see. But we've never met with any experience of a guest sneaking out on us without paying his bill or a situation where the guest is unable to pay his bill or refuses to pay his bill.

G: Well, you've been pushing your luck and you've been lucky so far. That's all. OK, here is 45 *yuan* and you can keep the change.

B: That's very kind of you, sir. But there is no tipping in China. And here is the change.

Language Tips

1. Asking guests if they have finished

◆ *How is the color/bouquet/temperature of* the wine?

◆ *Have you enjoyed* your drinks, sir?

◆ *Is there anything you would like to try,* madam?

◆ *How is your* drink?

◆ *Is everything to your satisfaction*?

Practice 1

Listen and read the conversation. Then work in pairs to practise it by turns.

G=Guest   **C**=Clerk

G: Hi, waiter.

C: Yes, sir. Can I help you?

G: Please give me the menu. I'd like to try something special here.

C: Sure. Here you are.

G: Local brew, Beijing Beer, two bottles, please.

C: OK. You will be served soon.

    ...

C: Excuse me, sir. How is Beijing Beer?

G: Very good. I like it very much. Can I have the bill please?

C: Yes, a moment, please.

Practice 2

Go over the above expressions and make short conversations in groups.

2. Telling guests how much is owed

◆ *Now how much do I owe you*?

OK, here is 45 *yuan*, and you can keep the change.

◆ Mr. Williams, **here is the bill.**

◆ Dry wine and red wine. **The total is** 60 *yuan*.

◆ **Here is the bill,** sir. **Would you like to check it**?

 Practice 1

Listen to the conversation and fill in the blanks.

Name of the guest	Bill of the drink	Monetary unit	Ways of paying	Tips

 Practice 2

Fill in the blanks with the words that you will hear on the recording.

G=Guest   **C**=Clerk

G: Could I have the _____(1), please?

C: Yes, sir. A bill for each or a check for all?

G: A bill for _____(2).

C: Here it is, sir.

G: How much?

C: That amounts to _____(3).

G: _____(4) is that in US dollars?

C: Let me see. It is _____(5).

G: I see. Can I pay by _____(6)?

C: Certainly, sir.

G: Here you are.

C: Thank you. Here are your _____(7), sir. Have a nice day.

G: Thank you.

3. Asking guests to pay the bill

◆ *Shall I explain it to you*?

◆ *How would you like to settle the bill*?

◆ *Would you like to pay in cash/by credit card/traveler's check*?

◆ *Would you like a breakdown of the bill*?

◆ *That's very kind of* you. But there is no tipping in China.

Unit 8 Bar Service II

✦ Practice 1

Listen to the conversation and try to answer the questions given below.

G=Guest   C=Clerk

G: Give me the bill, please.

C: Yes, sir. Just a moment, please. (He unfolds the folder and the guest goes over it.)

G: What's this for?

C: It's for the Semi-Dry Wine and Whisky...

G: I see. And what's this for?

C: That's for the Tsingdao Beer.

G: OK. Here is 100 *yuan*. Give me the receipt, please.

C: Yes, sir. I will. Here're the change and the receipt.

G: Thank you.

C: We look forward to your coming back again.

G: We will.

Questions

1. What did the guest order?
2. How much did he pay for the drink?
3. Did he pay in cash or by credit card?

✦ Practice 2

Make short conversations in pairs with the information given below.

Names of the guests	Drinks ordered	How much owed	Ways of paying
Mr. Howard	Champagne	76 *yuan*	In cash
Ms. Harrison	Beer and Gin	88 *yuan*	Master Card
Mr. Macintosh	Apple juice and Vodka	102 *yuan*	American Express
Ms. Lee	Fruit juice	54 *yuan*	Traveler's check

———— Summarize Key Expressions ————

1. Asking guests if they have finished their drink
   A. Have you enjoyed your drinks, sir?
   B. Is there anything you would like to try, madam?
   C. How is your drink?

D. Is everything to your satisfaction?
2. Telling guests how much is owed

   A. Twenty dollars for the wine and five dollars for salad. The total is 25 dollars.

   B. Mr. Williams, here is the bill.

   C. Dry wine and red wine. The total is 60 *yuan*.

   D. Here is the bill, sir. Would you like to check it?

3. Asking guests to pay the bill

   A. Here is the bill, sir.

   B. One bill or separate bills?

   C. I'm afraid we don't accept traveler's checks.

   D. I'm afraid we don't accept tips. It's against our regulations. Thank you all the same.

   E. You can hold the payment of the bill until you decide to leave if you like.

   F. Would you like a breakdown of the bill?

   G. Shall I explain it to you?

   H. How would you like to settle the bill?

   I. Would you like to pay in cash/by credit card/traveler's check?

4. Saying good-bye to guests

   A. Thank you very much for your coming.

   B. I hope you have enjoyed your drinks with your friends in our bar.

   C. We look forward to your coming again.

Give It a Try

Task 1

Make conversations in pairs with the information given below.

1. The guest asks for the bill. He ordered Sherry and salad. He'd like to pay by Visa Card. The total amount is $500.

3. You call the sommelier for the bill. You're surprised by the amount and ask him to explain some of the items on the bill. There is a 15% service charge. You pay the bill in cash and ask for a receipt.

Task 2

Listen and complete the following conversation.

W=Waiter   **G**=Guest

1. W: Would you like any salad?

   G: No, we're full. I'd like to _____ now.

W: A bill for each or a bill for all?

G: _____. It's my treat.

W: _____?

G: By credit card. Here's it.

W: I'm sorry. But _____. We only accept Visa, American Express and Master.

G: Well, I don't have them with me.

W: Are you staying in the hotel?

G: Yes, my room number is 2305.

W: In that case, you can _____.

G: OK, thanks.

2. G: Waiter, the bill please.

W: _____.

G: What's this for?

W: _____.

G: I see.

W: _____.

G: I'll sign the bill.

W: Please put your room number here.

G: Okay. Thank you.

────────── Do Extension Activities ──────────

 Activity 1

Listen to the conversation and write down the proper information in the form according to the conversation.

No. of guests	Amount	Ways of paying	Accepted cards
G1			
G2			

Activity 2

Work in groups. Read the passage and try to get the information about how to tip a bartender properly.

Tipping—not only appropriately, but well—is a good thing to know how to do it. Many people (including dates, bosses, and coworkers) view how a person tips as a reliable criterion of character. Knowing when and how to do it will ensure good service, show others that you're "socially groomed" (neither a cheapskate nor a showoff), and may cause people to like you more. In general: it's better to tip generously than badly, but there are critical limits on both ends of the spectrum.

1. Assess the crowd. Watch how others are tipping. Use that observation as a "baseline" and do not tip below it, barring overt rudeness on the part of your server, who is extremely busy.

2. Being patient for the first round is the key to an enjoyable evening, whether the bar is visibly "busy" when you walk in or not. Other things outside your purview—shift changes, for instance—may result in slow service of your first drink. A little patience goes a long way in these crucial first moments.

3. Always be ready to pay when you order. Have your money out, or close at hand. Don't wait until the drinks are made and your server has "totaled out" your round before you take your wallet out. Fishing for money not only wastes your server's time, but annoys others waiting for their drink orders to be taken. (Supposedly, you're there to socialize with them; and if you make them wait, you alienate yourself from them.)

4. Tip $1 per drink as a baseline, lacking anything better to go on, even if the only visible drink preparation involved is opening a bottle of beer. This will vary, depending on the kind of bar you're in. This is why crowd assessment matters. A tip of $1 per drink is always an "acceptable" tip. On complicated orders, a bit more is always deeply appreciated. Typically $1 is an acceptable tip for a beer (draft or bottle), but tip $2 for mixed drinks. More if its a complicated mixed drink.

5. Figure that most mixed drinks cost around five dollars: $1 is therefore around 20%.

6. Overt and consistent over-tipping is not only "flashy" and "rude" but in the eyes of bar staff, constitutes an attempt at a bribe to do something that could get them fired and/or land them in jail. Your tip expresses appreciation for services rendered. Nothing more. If your order involves shaking or blending multiple "call" liquors and pouring them into separate chilled glasses, a $2 or even $3 tip per drink is fine. If you're a martini drinker who draws subtle distinctions between a "whisper" and a "breath" of vermouth, you should pay for this difference to find its way into your cocktails. However, over-tipping on simple drinks raises legitimate concerns among staff that you expect "special" treatment in exchange for your exorbitant tip, which will only get you watched like a hawk by employees whose legal certification relies on not over-serving intoxicated patrons who they generally have to assume will be driving home, placing not only themselves but the general public at risk.

7. Remain aware that bar staff have to protect their jobs—tips notwithstanding. Tipping too much, too often raises red flags, and bar staff doesn't want to kill innocent people on the roads, even at the risk of alienating tipping customers. Bar staff would rather alienate customers than go to jail so you can get more wasted than you are.

8. Handle free drinks carefully. Most bartenders expect tips on free rounds. Tipping more is fine, but don't tip the full amount of the drink's cost.

9. When at an "open" bar, always tip generously per drink, but not the full amount the drink would cost you if you were paying for it.

10. Tipping high for your first drink and then not tipping at all is considered "pathetic" and will make bar staff worry about their third party liability the minute you hit the road.

11. Budget the cost of your tips into the cost of your drinks and distribute them more-or-less evenly over the course of your night out. Tipping a bit high early on in the evening is fine, and may expedite service later, but don't "tip out" completely on your first few rounds, unless you want to get thrown out, later.

12. There is almost never a good excuse for not tipping a server. Rude service may deserve a lower tip, but service needs to be considerably bad. Only overtly rude service deserves no tip at all.

13. Servers (including bartenders) usually have to give a percentage of their nightly earnings to bussers, food runners, barbacks, dishwashers, and/or doormen/bouncers. If you leave no tip for a server because you disliked your drink, you're not punishing the owner; you're punishing the server. Not only are you stiffing the server because you didn't like your drink, but he still has to pay out the above mentioned staff whether he gets tipped or not. The "tip out" comes from his sales figure, not his actual tip pool.

In general, tipping "generously" on the side of tipping, but don't "over-tip," if you can possibly avoid it.

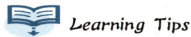

Learning Tips

Two Aspects of Proper Glassware

Proper glassware is essential for both the sales and the enjoyment of wine. Quite often the importance of serving wine in proper glassware is overlooked, but it is the first silent signal your customers receive about how serious your establishment is about wine.

Cleanliness:

Few owners and bartenders realize this but, one of the top reasons that wines are sent back to the bar is because they smell bad. And, while the wine will usually get the blame, most often that bad smell had nothing to do with the wine. If the glass smells bad, so will the wine. The glass should be well cleaned, free of any soap spots or food stains. Soap often leaves a residue that cannot be seen, and when a wine comes in contact with this residue it will negatively affect the taste and smell of the wine. I have been in too many bars where the glass may have started out clean, but, after spending a few hours on an unclean glass mat, bad odor was not far behind. The lesson here is important and should be remembered: Always smell the glasses before you set the room, because if the glass has an odor, so will the wine. The solution? Rinse and rinse again.

Shape:

There are many shapes and sizes of wine glasses and one must be careful not to confuse a good, proper glass with a fashion statement. For Champagne and sparkling wines, the best glass is the tall, tapered flute glass, which is designed to keep the bubbles active. The worst glasses for Champagne and sparkling wines are the small, flat, wide saucer-styled glasses that are often used in catering halls. This type of glass exposes too much of the wine to the air, causing a premature release of the gases needed to sustain the active bubbles that one associates with these wines. The best all-purpose wine glass should be approximately ten to fourteen ounces. The bowl should be of medium size and should taper slightly inward at the top. Tapered glasses are designed to help direct and focus the wine aromas toward the nose. While red wines are usually served in slightly bigger glasses than white wines, this type of glass is acceptable for both.

Unit 9

Handling Complaints I

Part A Complaining about Drinks

Teaching hours: 2 hours

Learning Goals:

To be able to
- tell the different drinks
- tell the most likely problems of drinks
- make complaints in different ways
- say "sorry"
- know the difference of drinking habits

Vocabulary Assistance

complaint *n.* 投诉	apologize *v.* 道歉
refund *n.* 退款	peculiar *adj.* 奇怪的
fault *n.* 错误	ridiculous *adj.* 可笑的
lipstick *n.* 口红	unacceptable *adj.* 无法接受的
stain *n.* 污渍	unreasonable *adj.* 没道理的
handle *v.* 处理	bottled *adj.* 瓶装的
overcharge *v.* 多收（钱）	tidy *adj.* 整洁的
spill *v.* 撒出	messy *adj.* 混乱的
sponge *v.* 用海绵擦	short-handed *adj.* 缺人手的

English for Food and Beverages

─────────── Start You Off ───────────

Activity 1

Look at the drinks menu below.

Drinks Menu

Spirits:	Wines:	Soft Drinks	Hot Drinks
Brandies	Aperitifs	Mineral Water	Coffee
Scotch	White Wine	Coke	Hot Chocolate
Rum	Red Wine	Diet Coke	Milk
Gin	Rose Wine	Juice	Hot Tea
Vodka	Dessert Wine		
Tequila	Liqueurs		
	Sparking Wine		
Bottled Beers and Ciders			
	Cocktails		
	Champagne		

Now ask your partner what he or she wants to drink, like this:

A: What would you like to drink?

B: I'd prefer _____.

Activity 2

Assume you are a customer; please try to figure out as much complaint about the drink served in a restaurant or a bar as you can, like this:

1 Waiter, there is something in my drink.

2 _____

3 _____

4 _____

5 _____

6 _____

7 _____

8 _____

174

Unit 9 Handling Complaints I

Focus on Language

 Conversation

Complaining about Drinks

Questions

1. How to make complaints in a polite way?
2. How to make complaints in a direct way?
3. How to express your anger?
4. What are the main problems of drink?
5. How to make an apology to the guest?

Listen to the conversation and read after it. Then do the conversation in pairs and try to find the answers to the questions above.

Conversation 1

W=Waiter   **G**=Guest

G: Excuse me, waiter.

W: Yes, mum. What can I do for you?

G: I'm sorry to bother you, but I wanted a bottled mineral water, not bottled beer.

W: Sorry, Madam. Let me check the order.

G: Okay, go ahead.

W: I'm terribly sorry about that. It's my fault. Your bottled mineral water will be ready soon.

Language Tips

1. Making complaints in a polite way

◆ I'm sorry to bother you, but I want   *a new cup*.

◇ Okay, madam. I will bring it for you.

◆ Can you help me with this? There is   *something*   in my drink.

◇ Sorry, sir. Let me get you a new one.

◆ Would you mind getting me   *a new wineglass*?

◇ Not at all. It will be ready soon.

175

English for Food and Beverages

 Practice 1

Listen and complete the following conversation.

(A guest is making a complaint to the headwaiter in a restaurant.)

G=Guest   **H**=Headwaiter

G: Excuse me, are you the headwaiter? I want to _____(1).

H: Yes, sir. What can I do for you?

G: _____(2), but my friend and I have been waiting 20 minutes for our drinks.

H: I'm very sorry, sir. Our staff are very busy this evening. _____(3)?

G: One Gin and one Sherry.

H: Don't worry. I will attend to it at once.

Practice 2

Work in pairs and make complaints in a polite way. Make up mini-conversations in the following situations. Try to use different expressions above in each conversation.

1) Your drink is not what you ordered.

2) You are overcharged when you pay the bill.

3) Your wine has a peculiar smell.

4) There is something in your drink.

5) There is lipstick on your glass.

2. Making complaints in a direct way

◆ I want to speak to **the manager, now.**

◇ I'm terribly sorry, madam.

◆ This is **unacceptable.**   I demand a refund.

◇ I'm so sorry, sir.

◆ Why don't you tell me early? **It's your fault**.

◇ I'm so sorry, sir. But, what can I do for you now?

 Practice 1

Listen to the conversation and read after it.

W=Waiter   **M**=Madam

M: Jack, look what that waiter's done! Spilt drink all over my new dress!

W: I'm terribly sorry, madam. Perhaps if I could sponge it with a little warm water...

M: Leave it alone, man. You'll only make it worse.

W: So, what can I do for you now?

M: I want to speak to the manager! You got a big trouble.

176

Practice 2

Read the context for each question, then arrange the words into sentences. Good luck!

1. The bar is not very tidy, you say...
   am I mess! fed with up

   _____

2. A boy complains to his parents because he doesn't want to go to bed early. He says...
   never You up let stay me late!

   _____

3. You get fed up because your colleague is always complaining about things that don't matter. You say...
   complaints! I'm your and tired of sick silly

   _____

4. You want to tell your employees to stop arguing with each other. You say...
   to It's stop! got

   _____

Practice 3

Role-play a scene of "Making complaints" by following the model below. Take a turn being the waiter and the guest:

W=Waiter   **G**=Guest

W: How can I help you, sir?
G: It's about my coffee.
W: What seems to be the problem?
G: It's cold when it is served.
W: For how long has it been served, sir?
G: Oh, dear. Just one minute ago.
W: Who served you?
G: Oh, my God. I forgot. I was reading when it's served.
W: I'm so sorry you've been inconvenienced. Would you like a refund?
G: No, I'd rather have a new hot coffee replaced please.

3. Making apologies

◆ I'm really sorry, **Madam**. I didn't mean to **get you a wrong drink**.

◇ Okay, give me my drink now.

◆ Sorry about the mess. I'll **clear up right away**.

◇ Go ahead.

◆ I'd like to apologize for the way I spoke to you earlier.

◇ Okay, I'd love you say like this.

English for Food and Beverages

 ## Practice 1

Listen to the conversation and read after it.

M=Man **H**=Headwaiter

M: Head waiter, I want to have a word with you.

H: Yes, sir. Is there something wrong, sir?

M: Something wrong? I should think there is something wrong. My wife and I have been kept here waiting nearly an hour for our meal!

H: I'm terribly sorry about that, sir. Our staff has been kept unusually busy this evening. I'll see to it personally myself. Now, if you wouldn't mind just telling me what you ordered.

Practice 2

Work in pairs. Make conversations with the situation: You are the manager in a restaurant. A guest comes to you and makes several complaints. Say "sorry" to him and promise to do something to solve the problem, for example, getting him another one, giving him a refund, or offering him a free drink.

 ## Practice 3

Listen to the recording. Try to find out what the customer is complaining about and how the waiter responds. Then fill out the table below.

	Compliant	Solution
Dialogue 1		
Dialogue 2		
Dialogue 3		
Dialogue 4		
Dialogue 5		

Summarize Key Expressions

1. Asking if the guest likes his/her drinks
    a. Is everything all right with...?
    b. How do you like...?
    c. Are you satisfied with...?
2. Complaining in a polite way
    a. Excuse me, but there's a problem with...
    b. Sorry to bother you, but I think there's something wrong with...
    c. I'm afraid I have to make a complaint.
    d. I'm afraid there's a slight problem with...

e. I'm sorry to bother you, but I want...

   f. I'm sorry to bother you, but I want to see your manager.

   g. Would you mind getting me...

   h. I understand it's not your fault, but...

3. Complaining in a direct way

   a. I want to speak to the manager, now.

   b. This is unacceptable.

   c. It is absolutely ridiculous!

   d. It is really unfair!

   e. It is unreasonable!

   f. I demand a refund.

   g. Why don't you tell me early? It's your fault.

4. Complaining about drinks or service

   a. This glass even got lipstick on it.

   b. This coffee is practically cold.

   c. You got a wrong drink.

   d. There is something wrong with the bill.

   e. This wine's got a most peculiar flavor.

   f. This table-cloth is a disgrace. It's covered with soup stains.

   g. I have been kept here waiting nearly an hour for my meal!

5. Apologizing to the guest

   a. We sincerely apologize for the inconvenience/mess.

   b. I'm extremely sorry about this.

   c. We are terribly/awfully sorry...

   d. We are very sorry...

   e. We are rather sorry...

6. Giving a reason or explanation

   a. We're rather short-handed at present.

   b. You see, the restaurant has just opened.

   c. The fact is we just had an emergency.

   d. A misunderstanding, sir.

   e. There's been a misunderstanding.

7. Promising to take action

   a. We'll attend to it as soon as possible.

   b. Let me get you another one.

   c. Let me get you the refund.

   d. I'll solve the problem for you immediately.

   e. I'll look into the matter immediately.

   f. I'll deal with it myself.

Give It a Try

Role-play according to the following situations. Do it in pairs. Student A will be the guest and Student B will be the clerk.

Guest

1. Your name is Billy.
   You wait at your table for half an hour for being served in a restaurant.
   You can't help making complaints.
2. Your name is Nancy.
   You notice the glass is dirty in a bar.
   You ask for a clean one.
3. Your name is Jack.
   Your beer arrives. You find the glass with the beer is not full.
   You ask for a full one.

Clerk

1. Ask the customer what happened.
2. Say "sorry."
3. Find a best way to cope with the complaints.

Do Extension Activities

Read the following article and find out different drinking habits between China and America. Then have a discussion with the follow-up questions.

Drinking Habits
—by Huang Baoqin

It might be overwhelming for those foreigners who have never been to China to find that Chinese people have to boil drinking water. In the United States, people boil water only when they want to make coffee. But in China people have to boil the water first and then let it cool down to drink due to possible contamination.

Also, Chinese people are not used to putting ice cubes in their drinks, even in summer, which is again different from the situation in the United States. Most Americans have cold drinks when eating regardless of summer or winter. However, in China people are told that it's not good for their stomachs to drink while eating, to say nothing of drinking cold stuff during the meal.

In America one's social class is reflected in the choice of alcoholic drinks. Intellectuals become wine connoisseurs. Upper class people prefer mixed drinks—combinations of liquors and/or wines or other beverages. The most famous of these status-symbol drinks is the Martini, chilled gin mixed with a trace of sweet wine and an olive. Similar drinks have fanciful names: screwdrivers, Bloody Mary, boilermakers, or wallbangers. Working class drinkers prefer straight shots of whiskey or beer. Millions of gallons of beer are consumed in America, almost always extremely cold and carried home in cartons or packs of six cans. Lite beer with limited calories and alcohol content is very popular with weight conscious Americans, and America now has hundreds of mini-breweries located in bars where people congregate to watch sports events on large television screens. These small, automated breweries produce a beer that is not as clear as the canned or bottled beer from the giant corporations, but it has a pleasant, distinctive taste and allows the drinker to feel he has discovered something special unknown to the public at large.

Follow-up questions

1. According to the text, what are the main drinking habits in China?
2. What are the American's drinking habits?
3. Based on the different social class in the US, make a list of the choice of alcoholic drinks.
4. Is there any other drinking habits in China?

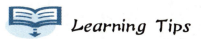

Learning Tips

Guidelines for Making Complaints I

There's an old saying in English: "Manners make the man." It means that having good manners, or being polite to other people, will make you a successful and admirable person. Therefore, no matter how unfair the situation, it's best to phrase your complaint politely. In English, you'll sound more polite if you use indirect language.

However, sometimes you're treated so badly that there's no time for being polite! You can use (some) very direct phrases when a problem is beyond compromise.

Part B Complaining about Meat and Food

Teaching hours: 2 hours

Learning Goals:

To be able to
- tell the different meat and poultry
- tell the taste of food
- tell the main problems of food
- deal with the complaints about food

Vocabulary Assistance

liver *n.* 肝	stewed *adj.* 炖的
tripe *n.* 肚	fried *adj.* 炸的
poultry *n.* 家禽	raw *adj.* 生的
drumsticks *n.* 鸡小腿	frozen *adj.* 冷冻的
gizzards *n.* 鸡胗	tough *adj.* 老的,嚼不动的
trout *n.* 鲑鱼	tender *adj.* 嫩的
lobster *n.* 龙虾	bitter *adj.* 苦的
catfish *n.* 鲶鱼	ground beef 牛肉馅
salmon *n.* 三文鱼	beef rib 牛排骨
mussel *n.* 贻贝	veal cutlet 牛肉片
oyster *n.* 牡蛎	pork chops 猪排
roasted *adj.* 烤的	lamb shank 羊腿肉

―――――― Start You Off ――――――

Activity 1

Look at the pictures below and explain what they are.

Unit 9 Handling Complaints I

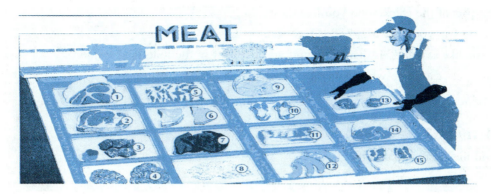

Beef

1. roast beef
2. steak
3. stewing beef
4. ground beef
5. beef ribs
6. veal cutlets
7. liver
8. tripe

Pork

9. ham
10. pork chops
11. bacon
12. sausage

Lamb

13. lamb shanks
14. leg of lamb
15. lamb chops

Poultry

16. chicken
17. turkey
18. duck
19. breasts
20. wings
21. thighs
22. drumsticks
23. gizzards
24. raw chicken
25. cooked chicken

Share your answers with your classmates.

1. Are you a vegetarian, a person who doesn't eat meat?
2. If not, what kind of meat do you eat most often?

183

English for Food and Beverages

3. What part of the chicken do you like most?
4. How do you cook the meat? Fried, roasted or stewed?
5. Do you like seafood? Is there any kind you like best in the following seafood?

    trout   catfish   whole salmon   crab   lobster   shrimp

    oysters   mussels   clams

Activity 2

What do they taste? Match them.

sugar	sour
salt	bitter
vinegar	sweet
pepper	spicy
bitter melon	salty

Then tell your partner what your favorite food is and what it tastes.

1 I like Sichuan food, which is usually spicy and hot.
2 _____
3 _____
4 _____
5 _____

Focus on Language

 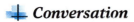 Conversation

Complaining about Meat and Food

Questions

1. How would you express the feeling of dislike?
2. How would you make complaints about the food?
3. How would you make complaints about the service?
4. What are the main problems of food?
5. How would you promise to take action?

Listen to the conversation and read after it. Then do the following conversation in pairs and try to find the answers to the questions above.

W=Waiter   **G**=Guest

G: Waiter! This meal is like old leather! It's enough to break every tooth in your head.
W: Perhaps you'd like to change your order, sir. The steak is very tender.
G: Ok, man. I think I'll have the steak.
W: How would you like your steak cooked?
G: Rare for me, please.

184

Unit 9 Handling Complaints I

Language Tips

1. Complaining about food

◆ Waiter! This meal is like old leather!

◇ Perhaps you'd like to change your order, sir.

◆ The dish tastes too *salty*. I can't take it.

◇ I'm sorry to hear that, sir.

◆ This meat is too *raw*. I can't eat it.

◇ Sorry, sir. How do you like the meat, medium or well-done?

Practice 1

Complete the following conversation.

D=Diner   **W**=Waiter

D: Waiter.

W: _____(1), madam?

D: This _____(2)raw. I _____(3)you I wanted it _____(4).

W: I'm _____(5)sorry, _____(6). Would you _____(7)it _____(8) a little _____(9)?

D: How long will that _____(10)?

W: Just _____(11)minutes. Would _____(12)like a salad, while you're _____(13)?

D: _____(14), thanks, but _____(15)them _____(16)hurry.

W: Yes, madam.

Practice 2

Listen to the conversation and answer the following questions.

1. What compliant has the guest made about her coffee?
2. Does the headwaiter get her another one?
3. What is wrong with the meat?
4. How does the guest feel about it?
5. What does the head waiter promise to do?
6. What does the head waiter offer to give to the guest?
7. Has she accepted it? Why not?
8. What does the head waiter persuade the guest to do?
9. Will she come again?

2. Complaining about service

◆ Waiter. The bill is *wrong*. Can you *explain* it?

◇ Sorry, sir. *We overcharged*.

◆ *How much longer* are we going to have to wait for our dinner?

185

English for Food and Beverages

◇ I'm sorry to have you keep so long.

◆ This is not **what I ordered**, I'm afraid.

◇ Oh, let me see. I'm sorry to trouble you.

Practice 1

Work in pairs and emulate the conversation above once more.

M=Man **W**=Waiter

M: Waiter. I can't quite understand how you manage to get $10 plus $12 plus $65.50 to add up to $150. 50.

W: Just a second, I'll check the bill again. You're quite right, sir. I can't understand how such a mistake could have been made. I do apologize, sir.

M: What a mistake! So, what's the total number?

W: It sums up...

Practice 2

Listen to the conversation carefully and try to fill in the blanks with the missing words.

G=Guest **W**=Waiter

G: Waitress.

W: Yes, madam.

G: You've been _____(1)us since we _____(2).

W: I'm terribly sorry. We _____(3).

G: You've kept us waiting for almost _____(4).
How long are we going to wait for our dinner?

W: Let me _____(5). I'm afraid _____(6)takes quite a while to prepare. Would you like _____(7)while you're waiting?

G: No, thanks.

Practice 3

Role-play on the following situation. Student A is eating in a restaurant. The meat he/she ordered is tough, and the soup is cold. Student A will discuss the problem with the headwaiter of the restaurant and ask him to do something about it. Student B acts as a headwaiter.

Practice 4

Work in groups and tell the worst food or service you have experienced. Then choose a representative from each group to share his/her story with whole class.

──────── Summarize Key Expressions ────────

1. Complaining about food
   a. This meat was recommended but it is not fresh.

b. My steak is tough.

c. My meal is not hot enough. I like it very hot.

d. The coffee isn't strong enough. I like it very strong.

e. The meat is tasteless.

f. The meal is too heavy. I like light food.

g. I don't like frozen fish. I like it fresh.

2. Complaining about service

   a. You've been ignoring us since we were seated.

   b. When I complained to the waiter, he didn't take any notice.

   c. You've kept us waiting for almost half an hour.

   d. How long are we going to wait for our dinner?

   e. This is not what I ordered.

   f. Bill is wrong. Please check it up.

3. Explaining things

   a. I'm sure the waitress didn't mean to be rude to you.

   b. I'm sure he didn't ignore you on purpose.

   c. Perhaps the waiter didn't understand you correctly. He should have changed it.

   d. The problem may be that we've been rather short staffed in the kitchen recently.

4. Apologizing to the guest

   a. I'm sorry to have kept you waiting.

   b. I do apologize for giving you the wrong soup.

   c. Sorry to cause the inconvenience.

   d. We're very sorry for the inconvenience.

5. Promising to take action

   a. I will get you another one.

   b. I'll look into the matter.

   c. I'll have... changed immediately.

   d. I promise it won't happen again.

─────────── Give It a Try ───────────

Task 1

Role-play:

1. Diner: One of the dishes isn't what you ordered. You told the waiter to check the order and change it right now.

   Waiter: The diner complains to you. Apologize to him and promise to get the dish ready soon, as well as ask the diner if he'd like something else.

2. Diner: To your surprise, you can't believe there is a fly in your soup, but it is true. You are so annoyed and want to get compensation.

   Headwaiter: Apologize to the diner and give him a free lunch, but refuse to do something further.

English for Food and Beverages

 Task 2

Listen to the restaurant jokes and complete the answers given by the waiter.
1. I think it's _____(1), sir.
2. That's impossible. A dead fly _____(2).
3. Yes, sir. It's _____(3) that killed them.
4. Yes, sir. We give extra _____(4) on Fridays.
5. Don't worry, sir. There is no _____(5).

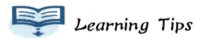 Do Extension Activities

Read the following text and have a discussion about Chinese food and its characteristics.

There is an old saying in English. It says "Bread is everything." China has been well-known for its biggest population in the world. So Chinese people have a better understanding of the importance of the food. This is why Chinese people say, "Have you eaten yet? " when they meet and greet each other. This shows people regard food as their prime need. Chinese cooking has a long history. There are over 8,000 well-known Chinese dishes and 48 basic ways of cooking, including roasting, frying and boiling. There are many schools of Chinese cooking. The most famous are Beijing cooking, Cantonese cooking, Sichuan cooking and Shanghai cooking. Beijing food is heavy and the most typical one is Beijing Roast Duck with a history of over 600 years. People can find Beijing Roast Duck in many restaurants but the best place is Quanjude Restaurant. Cantonese food is light and it is famous for fresh seafood. Sichuan food is spicy and hot. Kung-pao chicken and bean curd with pepper and chili sauce are always the favorites with many foreigners. Shanghai food is oily and sweet. It's always a favorite with people who have a sweet tooth.

Learning Tips

Guidelines for Making Complaints II

Being a customer, you have the right to make complaints, when you find the quality of the food is poor. However, before you take action, be clear in your own mind what you want to happen as a result of making a complaint. Do you want an apology? Do you want a different decision? Do you want the proper service that should have been provided in the first place? Do you want replaced goods? You should mention this to the person you are complaining to and ask for prompt action.

Unit 10

Handling Complaints II

Part A Complaining about Service

Teaching hours: 2 hours

Learning Goals:

To be able to
- tell the main problems of service
- make complaints about service
- express sympathy
- say "no" politely when you cannot help others
- promise to take action

Vocabulary Assistance

appetizer *n.* 开胃菜
brunch *n.* 早午餐
buffet *n.* 自助餐
tip *n.* 小费
sympathy *n.* 同情
inconvenience *n.* 麻烦
compensation *n.* 补偿

ignore *v.* 忽视, 忽略
sympathize *v.* 同情
disturb *v.* 打扰
unapologetic *adj.* 不道歉的
drunk *adj.* (酒) 喝多的
sincerely *adv.* 真诚地
by all means 可以, 同意

Start You Off

Activity 1

Test your vocabulary of restaurant and food. Fill in the blanks with words from the box.

English for Food and Beverages

appetizer	chef	fancy
bar	cook	fast-food
breakfast	dessert	lunch
brunch	dinner	non-smoking
buffet	dishwasher	salad
smoking	tip	waiter
soup		

People Who Work in a Restaurant

The person who serves your food is called a _____. The person who cooks your food is called a _____ if it is a cheap restaurant or a _____ if it is an expensive restaurant. A _____ is somebody who washes dishes. If the food and service is good, people usually leave a _____.

Meals and the Time of Day

Most people eat _____ after they wake up. Around noon people have their midday meal, or _____. And _____ is the meal that people eat in the evening. However, sometimes, especially on Sunday, people like to sleep in, so instead of having breakfast, they eat a meal between breakfast and lunch called _____.

Parts of a Meal

At lunch or dinner sometimes people order a snack before the meal called an _____. A _____ or a _____ is often served alongside the main meal. After dinner, people sometimes treat themselves to _____.

Types of Restaurants

It's nice to eat at a _____ restaurant, but that can be expensive. Sometimes, if you are short on time or short on money, you might go to a _____ restaurant because the food is cheaper and served faster. Some restaurants have a _____, which means you take a plate up to a table loaded with food and you can put as much food as you want on your plate. Other restaurants have a _____ where you can get an alcoholic drink while you are waiting for your table. Most restaurants these days have a _____ and a _____ section.

Activity 2

Work in groups. Have a brainstorm and recall what kind of service you have received in a restaurant or a bar.

1 Booking tables _____
2 Receiving the guest _____
3 _____
4 _____
5 _____

190

6 _____
7 _____
8 _____

Focus on Language

 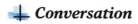 **Conversation**

Complaining about Service

> **Questions**
>
> 1. How would you make complaints about service?
> 2. How would you express sympathy?
> 3. What are the main problems of service?
> 4. How would you say "no" politely when you cannot help others?
> 5. What's the proper attitude towards customers' complaints?

Listen to the conversation and read after it. Then do the conversation in pairs and try to find the answers to the questions above.

H=Hostess   **G**=Guest

H: Good evening, madam.

G: Good evening. My name is Fiona. I have booked a table for two for 7:00.

H: Ah, Ms Fiona. That's right, a table for two. Would you come this way, please? Here is your table.

G: Oh, no. It's not the right table I ordered. I have told you I would like a table by the window. And you promised me one when I made the reservation. Please, check it out.

H: I am sorry, madam. We will check the reservation soon.

G: Ok.

H: I am terribly sorry, madam. It's our fault. We have double booked the table you wanted. And now, it's occupied. Would you like to change a table or wait for the table you booked?

G: Oh, it's ridiculous. I want to see your manager...

Language Tips

1. Making complaints about service

◆ This is not what I ***booked / ordered***. Please check it out.

◇ I'm sorry, sir. We have double booked your table. Could you change a table?

◆ Oh, it's ridiculous. I want to see ***your manager***...

◇ Ok, I will ask him to see you right now.

English for Food and Beverages

Practice 1

Listen to the conversation in the previous part again and answer the questions below.

1. Who is Fiona?
2. Does Fiona have a reservation for the table?
3. What does Fiona book?
4. Is she satisfied with the table? Why not?
5. Whose fault is it in the conversation?
6. What does the hostess say to Fiona?
7. Can the hostess solve the problem herself?
8. Whom does Fiona want to speak to?

Practice 2

Listen to the conversation carefully, then try to fill out the blanks in the conversation.

H=Hostess **G**=Guest

H: Good evening, madam.

G: Good evening. My name is Fiona. I have _____(1) for two for 7:00.

H: Ah, Ms Fiona. That's right, a table for two. Would you come _____(2), please? Here is your table.

G: Oh, no. It's not the right table I ordered. I have told you I'd like a table _____(3). And you _____(4) when I made the reservation. Please, check it out.

H: I am sorry, madam. We will check the reservation soon.

G: Ok.

H: I am terribly sorry, madam. It's our fault. We _____(5) you wanted. And now, _____(6). Would you like to change a table or wait for the table you booked?

G: Oh, it's ridiculous. I want to _____(7)...

2. Saying "no" politely when you cannot do any help

◆ This coffee is too weak.

◇ I'm sorry, madam. I'll get you another one.

◆ This fish was recommended, but it is not fresh.

◇ Oh! Sorry to hear that. This is quite unusual. I'll look into the matter.

◆ It is very kind of you, but I suffered too much here.

◇ Please give us another chance. I'm sure everything will be all right.

Practice 1

Listen to the conversation carefully and answer the questions below.

M=Manager   **G**=Guest

M: Excuse me, madam. I am the manager of the restaurant. I have heard what happened to you.

I am sorry to hear that.

G: What happened to me? I was badly treated. I must complain about the service here.

M: Okay, madam. Would you mind coming with me to my office and telling me what exactly happened there?

G: By all means, I just want to get my table back now...

M: Sit down, please. I sincerely apologize for the inconvenience. However, I have checked your reservation. It says you booked the table for 7 p.m. But it was 7:35 when you arrived here this evening. So...

G: So what? My car broke down on the way here.

M: We only keep the reservation half an hour at dinner time. That is the policy in our restaurant. The receptionist must have told this when you booked the table by phone.

G: Just five minutes late? It is unfair.

M: That is the rule. I am sorry for that. You can take another table and a free drink. Otherwise, I can't do any further.

Practice 2

Listen to the conversation in Practice 1 carefully and answer the questions below.
1. What does the manager say to the guest first?
2. What does the manager want the guest to do?
3. Why does the manager want to talk to the guest in his office?
4. What does the customer insist on?
5. What is the rule in the restaurant?
6. How does the manager explain the rule to the guest?
7. Is the guest satisfied with the manager's explanation?
8. What does the manage say at last?

Practice 3

Work in groups. Have a discussion about: How would you deal with the complaints above
1. if you were a member of the restaurant?
2. if you were the manager in the restaurant?
3. if you were the guest?

Summarize Key Expressions

1. Complaining about service
    a. You've been ignoring us since we were seated.
    b. You've double booked my table.
    c. I am crazy with the noise here. I can't bear it any more.
    d. It is cold here. The air conditioner doesn't work.
    e. This is not what I ordered.

f. I lost my cell phone in your restaurant.
2. Identifying the complaints
   a. Would you mind telling me what exactly happened there?
   b. Would you explain to me what exactly happened?
   c. Perhaps you could tell me what exactly is the matter?
   d. Perhaps you could tell me what the problem is exactly?
   e. Could you explain to me what exactly happened?
   f. What's the problem, exactly?
3. Expressing sympathy
   a. I can certainly understand that you've upset about losing them.
   b. I understand how you feel…
   c. I sympathize with you.
   d. I am sorry to hear that.
   e. That certainly shouldn't have happened.
   f. I can very well understand that you are upset about losing it.
4. Asking for action
   a. I'd like a refund please…
   b. I'd be grateful if you would replace this table cloth immediately.
   c. I would appreciate your sending me a replacement as soon as possible.
   d. Please let me know what you intend to do about this situation.
   e. Please let me talk to your manager right now.
5. Saying "no" politely when you cannot help others
   a. I'm sorry, sir, but I haven't got any record of that.
   b. I'm very sorry. But the fact is we have no table at all.
   c. This is the rule here. I'm afraid I cannot do that.
   d. Sorry. I can't see what we can do any further.
   e. Sorry, we won't be able to guarantee you anything now.
   f. Sorry, we are fully booked for those days.

Give It a Try

Task 1

Role-play:

Guest: You ate at a local restaurant and your chicken was raw in the middle. You sent it back and refused to pay for it. However, the waiter said you had to pay. You asked the manager of the restaurant to solve the problem.

Waiter: A guest complained his chicken was raw in the middle. You replied "cook it a bit more." Finally, you said "no" politely because you cannot help him.

Manager: You asked the guest what happened and expressed sympathy toward the guest. You promised the guest to offer a replacement dish or to deduct the cost of the food from his bill.

Task 2

Choose any situation below to make conversations in pairs. Student A will act as a manager and student B will act as a complainer:

Situation 1

You booked a table in a restaurant for your parents' wedding anniversary. But when you and your family turned up, they'd double booked and said there was no table for you. You claimed compensation.

Situation 2

You and your friend went out for a meal and the service was terrible. You waited an hour for your starter and then another hour for the main course. The waitress was completely unapologetic, so you refused to pay the 15% service charge and make a complaint.

Situation 3

In a bar, you haven't finished your drink, but you were asked to leave the bar because it was the time to close the door.

Situation 4

You were a bit drunk in a bar, and disturbed the other guests. You were asked to behave yourself, otherwise you would be asked to leave the bar.

─── Do Extension Activities ───

Read the customer satisfaction form. Which three of the criteria are most important for you? And explain why?

Steakhouse Restaurant

Thank you for choosing to eat at Steakhouse Restaurant. We are constantly striving to improve the quality of our service and would welcome your comments. Please help us by taking a few moments to complete this form.

	Excellent	Satisfactory	Poor
Location	[ ]	[ ]	[ ]
Atmosphere	[ ]	[ ]	[ ]
Comfort	[ ]	[ ]	[ ]
Cleanliness	[ ]	[ ]	[ ]
Staff friendliness	[ ]	[ ]	[ ]

English for Food and Beverages

Staff attentiveness [ ] [ ] [ ]
Speed of service [ ] [ ] [ ]
Quality of food [ ] [ ] [ ]
Qualify of drink [ ] [ ] [ ]
Value for money [ ] [ ] [ ]

We look forward to your next visit.

Steakhouse Pier 35 Marina, 263-329 Lorimer St.
Port Melbourne Vic 3207 Ph: 9646 0606
Kitchen is open from 11. 45 a.m.—late 7 days

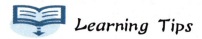 **Learning Tips**

Guidelines for Handling the Complaints

In handling complaints, the restaurant staff should always be polite and helpful. He / she should always be ready to lend an attentive ear to what the guest has to say and always hear the guest out. He / she must not interrupt the guest unless necessary. It is advisable for him/her to jot down what the guest has said. He /she should then make a short apology and express his / her understanding of the guest's situation or sympathy with the guest. After that the staff members should take actions quickly to remove the complaint, either by making polite, patient and detailed explanations, or making swift, effective corrections and remedies, or reporting the complaint to a superior. But whatever he /she intends to do he / she must keep the guest informed of the measures or actions he / she plans to take and when he /she will carry them out.

Part B Showing the Way of Dealing with Complaints

Teaching hours: 2 hours

Learning Goals:

To be able to ▸ identify the complaints
　　　　　　 ▸ solve the problem with the right procedure
　　　　　　 ▸ claim the damage made by the guest
　　　　　　 ▸ express firm requests to the guest
　　　　　　 ▸ ask the guest to pay for the damage

Vocabulary Assistance

damage　*n.* 损失；赔偿金　　　　promotion　*n.* 晋升
request　*n.* 要求　　　　　　　celebration　*n.* 庆祝
lounge　*n.* 大厅　　　　　　　 misunderstand　*v.* 误解
policy　*n.* 规定,制度　　　　　interrupt　*v.* 打断(讲话)
indemnification　*n.* 赔偿　　　replace　*v.* 替代
court　*n.* 法庭　　　　　　　　summarize　*v.* 总结
arbitration　*n.* 仲裁　　　　　private　*adj.* 私人的

────────── Start You Off ──────────

  ### Activity 1

Listen to the following text about how to complain in a restaurant or a bar three times and try to fill in the blanks with the exact words you have just heard.

　　Being a customer, you have the right to make _____(1) and ask for the compensation, if you are _____ (2) with the food, drink or service in a restaurant or a bar. However, before you do so, just calm down and be clear in your own mind what you want to happen as a result of making a complaint. Do you want an _____(3)? Do you want a _____(4)? Do you want the _____(5) that should have been provided in the first place? Do you want _____ (6)? You should mention this to the right _____ (7) or department you are complaining to and ask for prompt action, for instance, the waiter, (or the waitress) the _____(8), the duty manager, even _____(9) department. Finally, if none of them can help you, _____(10) or arbitration services maybe the final choice.

197

English for Food and Beverages

Activity 2

Look at some of the main "rules" for handling complaints:

a. Listen carefully to the complaint

b. Do not interrupt

c. Wait until the person has completely finished

d. Apologize

e. Speak normally

f. Summarize the complaint

g. Explain what action will be taken, and how quickly

h. If the guest is angry, aim to remove the scene to somewhere private

Which of these rules are most important? In groups, decide on the three most important rules.

Focus on Language

Conversation

Complaining about Meat and Food

Questions

1. What is the right procedure to deal with complaint?
2. How would you identify who is responsible for the damage?
3. How would you claim the damage made by the guest?
4. How would you express firm requests to the guest?
5. How would you ask the guest to pay for the damage?

Listen to the conversation and read after it. Then do the conversation in pairs and try to find the answers to the questions above.

W=Waiter   **G**=Guest

G: Waiter.

W: Yes, madam?

G: This coffee is too weak.

W: I'm sorry, madam. I'll get you another one. Is everything all right?

G: No, this fish was recommended, but it is not fresh.

W: Oh! Sorry to hear that. This is quite unusual as we have fresh fish from the market every day.

G: Who knows? It is not fresh and I am not happy about it.

W: I'm terribly sorry, madam. I'll look into the matter. I can give you something replaced, if you'd like a change. That would be our treat, of course.

G: It is very kind of you, but I suffered too much here. All that I need is fresh and healthy food.

I don't want to trouble anyone. No more, thanks.

W: Just feel ease, madam. Please give us another chance. I'm sure everything will be all right again the next time you come.

G: I hope so.

W: Thank you very much, madam.

Language Tips

1. How to deal with the complaints properly

◆ This coffee is too weak.

◇ I'm sorry, madam. I'll get you another one.

◆ This fish was recommended, but it is not fresh.

◇ Oh! Sorry to hear that. This is quite unusual. I'll look into the matter.

◆ It is very kind of you, but I suffered too much here.

◇ Please give us another chance. I'm sure everything will be all right.

Practice 1

Answer the questions below based on the conversation "Complaining about Meat and Food."

1. What complaint has the guest made about her coffee?
2. Does the waiter get her another one?
3. What is wrong with fish?
4. How does the guest feel about it?
5. What does the waiter promise to do?
6. What does the waiter offer to give to the guest?
7. Has she accept it? Why not?
8. What does the waiter persuade the guest to do?
9. Will she come again?

Practice 2

Listen to the following conversation and complete it according to the context.

D=Diner   **W**=Waiter

D: Waiter.

W: _____(1), madam?

D: This _____(2)raw. I _____(3)you I wanted it _____(4).

W: I'm _____(5)sorry, madam. Would you _____(6)it for a little _____(7)?

D: How long will that _____(8)?

W: Just _____(9)minutes. Would you like a _____(10), while you're waiting.

D: _____(11), thanks, but _____(12)them _____(13)hurry.

W: Yes, madam.

2. How to deal with the trouble caused by the guest

◆ Good evening, sir. I'm **the manager** of the restaurant. I'm afraid we've had a complaint about the noise .

◇ Oh, I'm sorry.

◆ As the restaurant policy, I'm afraid that you have to **pay for the damage**.

◇ You don't have the right to do so.

◆ If you think so, we'll call the police to handle this.

◇ Oh, come on. Don't do that.

Practice 1

Listen to the conversation and answer the questions below.
1. What complaint has the manager got?
2. Who makes the complaint?
3. What is the complainer trying to do?
4. Who makes the noise?
5. What does the manager suggest the guest to do?
6. What does the manager say about the damage?
7. Who should pay for the damage?
8. Is the guest willing to pay for the damage?
9. What does the manager say to the guest when he refuses to pay?
10. Does the guest pay at last?

Practice 2

Match the additional sentences below with the "rules" for handling complaints in **Start You Off**. They are not in the same order as the rules.

1. If you repeat the main points of a complaint, you make sure that there is no misunderstanding about the reason for the complaint; and ask the main points calmly so as to cool down the situation.
2. Before saying anything at all, be certain that the guest has completely finished talking and is not just pausing for breath.
3. A short clear apology should be the first thing you offer the guest. This must come before any explanations or reasons.
4. Do not let your voice rise to match the voice of the guest. This will only lead to more argument.
5. Make clear what you will do. Give the guest a definite time so that he understands that his complaint will be attended to.
6. An interruption will cause the guest to carry on louder and louder.

7. It is important to show that you are giving the guest full attention.
8. This could be an office, or an empty lounge. Try to find a place where there is no barrier (table or desk) between you and the guest.

Summarize Key Expressions

1. Explaining the things
   a. Could I have a word with you, sir?
   b. I'm afraid we've had a complaint about the noise from your neighbor.
2. Claiming the damage
   a. There is a lot of damage, isn't there?
   b. The glass is broken.
   c. The chair is damaged beyond repair.
   d. The table cloth is burnt.
3. Expressing firm requests to the guest
   a. I'm sorry to say they are badly damaged.
   b. It's more than a few breakages, I would say.
   c. I don't think you have the right to do so.
   d. Our regulation doesn't permit.
   e. The restaurant has the right to…
   f. I'm afraid we must ask you to leave the hotel.
   g. We'll have to call the police unless…
4. Asking for indemnification
   a. We shall have to ask you for payment towards the replacement of the damaged items.
   b. I'm afraid we have to charge them to your account.
   c. As a restaurant policy, I'm afraid that you have to pay for the damage.
   d. I'm afraid that you have to pay an indemnity. It's our policy.

Give It a Try

Task 1

Role-play:

Student A

You are the headwaiter in a fancy restaurant, you noticed a guest smoking in a non-smoking section. You ask him to go and smoke in the smoking area.

Student B

You are having dinner in a restaurant, and smoking without realizing the sign of non-smoking.

Task 2

Read the following polite sentences that the manager is trying to give to a guest, and identify what the real message is in each of them.

a. I'm sorry sir, but you actually aren't allowed into the dinner-dance unless you're dressed in a suit with a tie...

b. I'm afraid the barman is unable to serve you any further drinks this evening, sir.

c. Sorry, sir. It is time for us to close the door.

d. We'll have to ask you to leave this lounge, sir. We have to consider the other guests, you see...

Now you try to make polite sentences from the following "messages":

—Stop smoking!

—Be quiet!

—We will take you to court if you don't pay!

—You're annoying the other guests! Stop it!

Do Extension Activities

Read the following text and have a discussion about the ways of dealing with complaints.

Dealing with Customer Complaints B. L. A. S. T
by *Albert Barneto*

In a restaurant, handling customer complaints doesn't have to always be a battle, with the right tools and responses you can use complaints to help you build your business. B. L. A. S. T is a great tool that is used to train their employees in the basics of handling customer complaints by companies such as Yum! (Parent company of KFC) Taco Bell, Pizza Hut. The acronym stands for: Believe, Listen, Apologize, Satisfy, Thank.

Believe

This is the cornerstone of handling a customer complaint. It is important to understand that your customer believes that your establishment has wronged them.

Listen

Stop and listen to your customer's complaint. As soon as a customer starts to complain, we start to think of how we will respond to the accusation before we are done listening, and too often the case, already have the response ready to fight back.

Apologize

Always apologize even if you did nothing wrong. From your customers' perspective, they have a legitimate complaint, and they expect an apology. A sincere apology will usually diffuse a lot of frustration that the customer has.

Satisfy

Ask the customer "What can I do to make this right for you?" Be the judge of what is fair of course, but allow them the opportunity to feel empowered over the situation. Many times they may ask for the problem be taken care of on their next visit or maybe that you talk to the person who made the mistakes and correct them.

Thank

With the simple act of complaining, your customer is telling you "I care about your business and your success." They are giving you the opportunity to fix the problem and invite them back so they can give you more of their money.

B. L. A. S. T will help you in dealing with customer complaints.

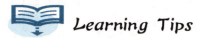

Learning Tips

Guidelines for Identifying the Complaints

People who make complaints and criticism can be friendly and reasonable, while they can also be rude and abusive. No matter how the person behaves, the restaurant staff should always try and be nice to them. An argument with the guest is the most undesirable thing that can happen to a staff member and the restaurant. With good training and a lot of practical experience with guests, everyone can master the art of being nice to guests. Just keep one thing in mind, that is, dissatisfying guest means a loss of potential future business.

Vocabulary

A

à la carte 按菜单点菜	(Unit 3, Part A)
accept *v.* 接受	(Unit 1, Part A)
accommodate *v.* 向……提供	(Unit 2, Part B)
add *v.* 增加,添加	(Unit 6, Part A)
affluent *adj.* 富裕的	(Unit 6, Part A)
aisle *n.* 过道	(Unit 2, Part A)
alcoholic *adj.* 含酒精的	(Unit 7, Part B)
alphabetize *v.* 按字母顺序排列	(Unit 1, Part B)
alternative *adj.* 替换的	(Unit 2, Part A)
alternative *n.* 可选择的事物	(Unit 1, Part B)
altogether *adv.* 总共	(Unit 2, Part A)
aperitif *n.* 开胃酒	(Unit 3, Part A)
apologize *v.* 道歉	(Unit 2, Part B)
apology *v.* 道歉	(Unit 2, Part A)
appetizer *n.* 开胃品	(Unit 3, Part A)
appreciate *v.* 感谢	(Unit 1, Part B)
appropriate *adj.* 适当的	(Unit 5, Part B)
appropriately *adv.* 适宜地	(Unit 7, Part B)
approval *n.* 赞同	(Unit 2, Part A)
arbitration *n.* 仲裁	(Unit 10, Part B)
aristocracy *n.* 贵族	(Unit 5, Part B)
aristocrat *n.* 贵族	(Unit 5, Part A)
arrange *v.* 安排	(Unit 2, Part B)
availability *n.* 获得	(Unit 1, Part B)
available *adj.* 可获得的	(Unit 1, Part B)
aware *adj.* 知道的,明白的,意识到的	(Unit 6, Part B)
Aztec *n.* 阿芝台克人	(Unit 5, Part B)

B

bacon *n.* 培根,咸肉	(Unit 4, Part A)
bamboo *n.* 竹	(Unit 2, Part A)
banquet *n.* 筵席,宴会	(Unit 1, Part A)
bar manager 酒吧经理	(Unit 7, Part A)
bean *n.* 扁豆	(Unit 4, Part A)
bean paste cake 绿豆糕	(Unit 5, Part A)
beef rib 牛排骨	(Unit 9, Part B)
beverage *n.* 饮料	(Unit 3, Part A)
bill *n.* 账单	(Unit 6, Part A)
bitter *adj.* 苦的	(Unit 9, Part B)
blueberry *n.* 蓝莓	(Unit 5, Part A)
boil *v.* 水煮	(Unit 4, Part B)
book *v.* 预订	(Unit 7, Part A)
bottled *adj.* 瓶装的	(Unit 9, Part B)
braise *v.* 炖	(Unit 3, Part B)
brand *n.* 品牌	(Unit 7, Part B)
break down 列出细目	(Unit 6, Part B)
brew *n.* 酿酒	(Unit 7, Part B)
broad bean 蚕豆	(Unit 3, Part B)
broccoli *n.* 西兰花,花茎甘蓝	(Unit 4, Part A)
brunch *n.* 早午餐	(Unit 10, Part A)
buffet *n.* 自助餐	(Unit 10, Part A)

C

caffeine *n.* 咖啡因	(Unit 4, Part B)
care *v.* 喜爱	(Unit 5, Part B)
carrots *n.* 胡萝卜	(Unit 4, Part A)
cashier *n.* 出纳员	(Unit 1, Part A)
catfish *n.* 鲶鱼	(Unit 9, Part B)
cauliflower *n.* 花椰菜,菜花	(Unit 4, Part A)
caviar *n.* 鱼子酱	(Unit 3, Part A)
celebration *n.* 庆祝	(Unit 10, Part B)
celery *n.* 芹菜	(Unit 4, Part A)
change *n.* 找回的零钱	(Unit 6, Part A)
charge *n.* 费用	(Unit 6, Part B)
check up 核实	(Unit 6, Part B)
check *v.* 核对	(Unit 2, Part A)
cheese *n.* 奶酪	(Unit 5, Part B)
chef *n.* 厨师,主厨	(Unit 1, Part A)
cherry *n.* 樱桃	(Unit 5, Part A)
chicken *n.* 鸡肉	(Unit 3, Part A)

Vocabulary

chicory *n.* 菊苣 (Unit 3, Part A)
chili *n.* 辣椒 (Unit 4, Part B)
chili sauce 辣椒酱 (Unit 3, Part B)
chips *n.* 薯条 (Unit 4, Part A)
chopsticks *n.* 筷子 (Unit 3, Part B)
classify *v.* 分类 (Unit 5, Part B)
clove *n.* 丁香 (Unit 4, Part B)
cocktail *n.* 鸡尾酒 (Unit 2, Part A)
colloquial *adj.* 口语的, 通俗的 (Unit 5, Part B)
compensation *n.* 补偿 (Unit 10, Part A)
compile *v.* 编制 (Unit 1, Part B)
complaint *n.* 投诉 (Unit 9, Part A)
confirm *v.* 确认 (Unit 1, Part B)
consent *v./n.* 同意, 赞成 (Unit 2, Part B)
consideration *n.* 考虑因素 (Unit 2, Part A)
consist 由……组成 (Unit 5, Part B)
constitute *v.* 组成 (Unit 5, Part B)
cookie *n.* (苏格兰)甜面包, (美国)小甜饼 (Unit 5, Part A)
copy *n.* 存根 (Unit 6, Part A)
corkage fee 开瓶费 (Unit 1, Part B)
counter *n.* 柜台 (Unit 8, Part A)
court *n.* 法庭 (Unit 10, Part B)
courtesy *n.* 客气话, 礼貌 (Unit 1, Part A)
couscous *n.* 肉菜饭 (Unit 4, Part A)
credit card 信用卡 (Unit 6, Part A)
croissant *n.* 牛角面包 (Unit 4, Part A)
cucumber *n.* 黄瓜 (Unit 4, Part A)
curry *n.* 咖喱 (Unit 4, Part B)

D

damage *n.* 损失; 赔偿金 (Unit 10, Part A)
database *n.* 资料库, 数据库 (Unit 1, Part B)
Debrett *n.* 德布雷特英国贵族年鉴 (Unit 5, Part B)
decoration *n.* 装饰品 (Unit 5, Part B)
delay *v./n.* 耽搁, 推迟 (Unit 2, Part B)
delicate *adj.* 微妙的 (Unit 6, Part A)
derive *v.* 源于, 起源 (Unit 5, Part B)
dine *v.* 吃饭, 就餐 (Unit 2, Part B)
diner *n.* 就餐者 (Unit 2, Part B)
direct *v.* 给……指路 (Unit 2, Part A)
discount *v.* 优惠, 打折 (Unit 1, Part B)
disturb *v.* 打扰 (Unit 10, Part A)
dot *n.* 点儿 (Unit 1, Part B)
draught *n.* 扎啤 (Unit 7, Part B)

driver's license 驾照 (Unit 6, Part A)
drumsticks *n.* 鸡小腿 (Unit 9, Part B)
drunk *adj.* (酒)喝多的 (Unit 10, Part A)
dumpling *n.* 面团布丁, 团子 (Unit 5, Part B)
dupes=duplicate *n.* 副本, 复制 (Unit 1, Part B)

E

eggplant *n.* 茄子 (unit 4, Part A)
emerge *v.* 显现, 浮现, 形成 (Unit 5, Part A)
emergency *n.* 突发事件, 紧急情况 (Unit 1, Part B)
enhance *v.* 提高, 增强 (Unit 5, Part B)
ensure *v.* 保证 (Unit 2, Part B)
entertainment *n.* 款待, 娱乐 (Unit 6, Part A)
entrée *n.* 主菜 (Unit 3, Part A)
etiquette *n.* 礼节 (Unit 6, Part A)
examine *v.* 检查 (Unit 2, Part A)
exchange rate *n.* 汇率 (Unit 8, Part B)
expect *v.* 期待, 预期 (Unit 5, Part A)
experience *n.* 经历 (Unit 2, Part A)
express *v.* 表达, 表示 (Unit 2, Part B)
extra *adj.* 额外的 (Unit 6, Part B)

F

fault *n.* 错误 (Unit 9, Part A)
feature *n.* 特色 (Unit 8, Part A)
fish sauce 鱼露 (Unit 4, Part B)
flambé *v.* 火烧(浇上白兰后点燃上桌) (Unit 3, Part B)
flavor *n.* 味道 (Unit 3, Part B)
flour *n.* 面粉 (Unit 5, Part B)
fork *n.* 叉子 (Unit 3, Part A)
fresh *adj.* 新鲜的 (Unit 3, Part B)
fried *adj.* 炸的 (Unit 9, Part B)
frozen *adj.* 冷冻的 (Unit 9, Part B)

G

garlic *n.* 蒜 (Unit 4, Part B)
gently *adv.* 文雅地 (Unit 2, Part A)
gizzards *n.* 鸡胗 (Unit 9, Part B)
glass *n.* 玻璃杯 (Unit 3, Part B)
glutinous *adj.* 粘性的 (Unit 5, Part B)
Dutch treat AA 制 (Unit 6, Part A)
grapefruit *n.* 葡萄柚, 西柚 (Unit 4, Part B)
graphical symbol 图形符号 (Unit 2, Part B)
ground beef 牛肉陷 (Unit 9, Part B)
guarantee *v.* 保证 (Unit 1, Part B)

205

H

ham *n.* 火腿	(Unit 3, Part A)
handle *v.* 处理	(Unit 9, Part A)
haw jelly 山楂糕	(Unit 5, Part A)
head barman 调酒总管	(Unit 7, Part A)
heavy *adj.* 口味重的	(Unit 3, Part B)
hors d'oeuvre 开胃小吃,开胃冷盘	(Unit 3, Part A)
hostess *n.* 迎宾女招待员,领位	(Unit 1, Part A)
hot *adj.* 辣的,辛辣的	(Unit 3, Part B)
house specialty 招牌菜	(Unit 7, Part A)
household *n.* 家庭	(Unit 5, Part A)

I

iced water 冰水	(Unit 7, Part B)
identification *n.* 身份证明	(Unit 6, Part A)
identify *v.* 识别,认出	(Unit 2, Part A)
ignore *v.* 忽视,忽略	(Unit 10, Part A)
incomplete *adj.* 不完善的	(Unit 5, Part B)
inconvenience *n.* 麻烦	(Unit 10, Part A)
indemnification *n.* 赔偿	(Unit 10, Part B)
inform *v.* 告知,通知	(Unit 2, Part B)
insists (on) *v.* 坚持	(Unit 1, Part B)
instead *adv.* 反而,却	(Unit 2, Part A)
interrupt *v.* 打断(讲话)	(Unit 10, Part B)
intimate *adj.* 亲密的	(Unit 6, Part A)
invitee *n.* 被邀请者	(Unit 6, Part A)
It's my treat. 我请客。	(Unit 6, Part A)
It's on me. 由我付账。	(Unit 6, Part A)

J

Jelly *n.* 果子冻,一种果冻甜品	(Unit 5, Part B)

K

knee *n.* 膝,膝盖	(Unit 2, Part A)
knife *n.* 刀	(Unit 3, Part B)

L

lamb *n.* 羔羊肉	(Unit 3, Part A)
lamb shanks 羊腿肉	(Unit 9, Part B)
leek *n.* 大葱	(Unit 4, Part A)
lettuce *n.* 莴苣	(Unit 3, Part A)
light *adj.* 清淡的	(Unit 3, Part B)
lipstick *n.* 口红	(Unit 9, Part B)
liquor *n.* 烈性酒	(Unit 1, Part B)
liver *n.* 肝	(Unit 9, Part B)
lobster *n.* 龙虾	(Unit 9, Part B)
log *v.* 记录	(Unit 1, Part B)
logbook *n.* 日志	(Unit 1, Part B)
look over 浏览	(Unit 2, Part A)
lounge *n.* 酒廊	(Unit 7, Part A)
lounge *n.* 休息厅	(Unit 2, Part A)
luxury *n.* 奢侈,华贵	(Unit 5, Part A)

M

main restaurant 酒楼大厅	(Unit 2, Part A)
manager *n.* 经理	(Unit 1, Part A)
mango *n.* 芒果	(Unit 5, Part A)
martini *n.* 马提尼酒	(Unit 3, Part A)
marvelous *adj.* 棒极了	(Unit 3, Part B)
Master Card *n.* 万事达卡	(Unit 6, Part A)
mechanization *n.* 机械化	(Unit 5, Part A)
melon *n.* 甜瓜,瓜	(Unit 3, Part A)
menu *n.* 菜单	(Unit 2, Part A)
mess *adj.* 混乱的	(Unit 9, Part A)
midnight *n.* 午夜	(Unit 1, Part B)
milkshake *n.* 奶昔	(Unit 5, Part B)
mince *v.* 切碎,绞肉	(Unit 3, Part A)
minimum charge 最低消费	(Unit 1, Part B)
misunderstand *v.* 误解	(Unit 10, Part B)
mobile/cell phone 手机	(Unit 1, Part B)
mousse *n.* 木斯(一种多泡沫含奶油的甜点) (Unit 5, Part A)	
mushroom *n.* 蘑菇	(Unit 3, Part A)
mussel *n.* 贻贝	(Unit 9, Part B)
mustard *n.* 芥末	(Unit 4, Part B)

N

napkin *n.* 餐巾纸	(Unit 3, Part B)
non-smoking *adj.* 无烟的	(Unit 1, Part B)
note *n.* 注释	(Unit 6, Part B)

O

oatmeal *n.* 燕麦片,燕麦粥	(Unit 4, Part A)
obtain *v.* 获得,得到	(Unit 2, Part B)
occupied *adj.* 占用的	(Unit 1, Part B)
offer *v.* 提供	(Unit 2, Part A)
omelet *n.* 煎蛋卷(饼)	(Unit 3, Part A)
one bill 合单付账	(Unit 6, Part A)

onion *n.* 洋葱	(Unit 5, Part A)	recommend *v.* 推荐	(Unit 1, Part B)
origin *n.* 起源, 由来	(Unit 5, Part A)	recommendation *n.* 推荐	(Unit 3, Part B)
originate *v.* 起源	(Unit 5, Part B)	refund *n.* 退款	(Unit 9, Part A)
overcharge *v.* 多收（钱）	(Unit 9, Part A)	replace *v.* 替代	(Unit 10, Part B)
oyster *n.* 生蚝	(Unit 7, Part B)	request *v.n.* 要求	(Unit 1, Part A)
oyster sauce 蚝油	(Unit 4, Part B)	reservation *n.* 预订	(Unit 1, Part A)
		reserve *v.* 预订	(Unit 1, Part A)
		responsibility *n.* 责任, 职责	(Unit 2, Part B)

P

		restaurant *n.* 餐厅, 餐馆	(Unit 1, Part A)
package *n.* 套餐	(Unit 8, Part B)	ridiculous *adj.* 可笑的	(Unit 9, Part A)
pancake *n.* 薄饼, 烙饼	(Unit 3, Part A)	roasted *adj.* 烤的	(Unit 9, Part B)
pastry *n.* 面粉糕饼, 发面饼	(Unit 5, Part B)	runner bean 红花菜豆	(Unit 4, Part A)
payment *n.* 付款	(Unit 8, Part B)		
pea *n.* 豌豆	(Unit 3, Part A)		

S

pea flour cake 豌豆黄	(Unit 5, Part B)		
peak season 高峰期	(Unit 2, Part B)	salad *n.* 沙拉	(Unit 3, Part A)
peculiar *adj.* 奇怪的	(Unit 9, Part A)	salmon *n.* 三文鱼	(Unit 9, Part B)
pepper *n.* 胡椒	(Unit 4, Part B)	salt *n.* 盐	(Unit 4, Part B)
pineapple *n.* 菠萝	(Unit 5, Part A)	satisfactory *adj.* 满意的	(Unit 5, Part A)
plate *n.* 盘子	(Unit 3, Part B)	sausage *n.* 香肠	(Unit 4, Part A)
poach *v.* 水煮荷包蛋	(Unit 4, Part B)	sauté *v.* 嫩炒	(Unit 3, Part A)
policy *n.* 规定; 制度	(Unit 10, Part B)	scramble *v.* 炒（蛋）	(Unit 4, Part A)
pork chops 猪排	(Unit 9, Part B)	sea cucumber 海参	(Unit 3, Part A)
poultry *n.* 家禽	(Unit 9, Part B)	seat *v.* 引座	(Unit 2, Part A)
prefer *v.* 更喜欢, 宁愿	(Unit 5, Part B)	semi-dry *adj.* 半干的	(Unit 8, Part B)
preference *n.* 喜好	(Unit 2, Part A)	separate *adj.* 单独的, 个别的	(Unit 5, Part A)
preferred *adj.* 首选的	(Unit 5, Part A)	separate bill 分单付账	(Unit 6, Part A)
printed word 印刷体	(Unit 6, Part A)	separately *adv.* 分开的, 个别的	(Unit 2, Part B)
private *adj.* 个人的, 私人的	(Unit 1, Part A)	service charge 服务费	(Unit 6, Part A)
private room 单间	(Unit 1, Part B)	share *v.* 合用	(Unit 2, Part B)
privilege *n.* 特权, 特别待遇	(Unit 5, Part A)	shortchange *v.* 少找钱	(Unit 6, Part A)
procedure *n.* 程序, 步骤	(Unit 2, Part B)	short-handed *adj.* 缺人手的	(Unit 9, Part A)
promotion *n.* 晋升	(Unit 10, Part B)	shred *v.* 切碎	(Unit 3, Part B)
pudding *n.* 布丁	(Unit 5, Part A)	sign *n.* 符号, 标志	(Unit 2, Part B)
pumpkin *n.* 南瓜	(Unit 5, Part A)	sincerely *adv.* 真诚地	(Unit 10, Part B)
		slang *n.* 俚语	(Unit 6, Part A)

Q

		snacks *n.* 点心, 小吃	(Unit 4, Part B)
Quetzalcoatl *n.* 羽蛇神 （古代墨西哥阿兹特克人与托尔特克人崇奉的重要神祇）	(Unit 5, Part B)	sneak out *v.* 溜走	(Unit 8, Part B)
		soft drink 软饮料	(Unit 7, Part B)
		soy sauce 酱油	(Unit 4, Part B)

R

		spacious *adj.* 宽敞的	(Unit 1, Part A)
raisin *n.* 葡萄干	(Unit 5, Part A)	spaghetti *n.* 通心粉	(Unit 3, Part A)
raw *adj.* 生的	(Unit 9, Part B)	Spaniard *n.* 西班牙人	(Unit 5, Part B)
receipt *n.* 收据	(Unit 6, Part A)	special *n.* 特色菜	(Unit 2, Part A)
receptionist *n.* 前台接待	(Unit 1, Part A)	specialize *v.* 专门从事	(Unit 5, Part B)

specialty *n.* 特色菜	(Unit 7, Part B)	toast *n.* 土司,烤面包片	(Unit 3, Part A)
specific *adj.* 具体的,特定的	(Unit 2, Part B)	toothpick *n.* 牙签	(Unit 3, Part B)
spicy *adj.* 辛辣的	(Unit 5, Part B)	tough *adj.* 老的,嚼不动的	(Unit 9, Part B)
spill *v.* 撒出	(Unit 9, Part A)	towel *n.* 手巾,毛巾	(Unit 6, Part B)
spinach *n.* 菠菜	(Unit 3, Part B)	trace *v.* 追踪,回溯	(Unit 5, Part A)
spoil *v.* 破坏,影响	(Unit 8, Part A)	traveller's cheque 旅游支票	(Unit 6, Part A)
sponge *v.* 用海绵擦	(Unit 9, Part A)	tripe *n.* 肚	(Unit 9, Part B)
spoon *n.* 勺	(Unit 3, Part B)	trout *n.* 鲑鱼	(Unit 9, Part B)
stain *n.* 污渍	(Unit 9, Part A)		
steak *n.* 牛排	(Unit 3, Part A)	**U**	
stewed *adj.* 炖的	(Unit 9, Part B)	unacceptable *adj.* 无法接受的	(Unit 9, Part A)
stingy *adj.* 吝啬的,小气的	(Unit 6, Part A)	unapologetic *adj.* 不道歉的	(Unit 10, Part A)
stress *v.* 强调	(Unit 3, Part B)	under the name of 以…的名字出现	(Unit 2, Part A)
sugar *n.* 糖	(Unit 4, Part B)	unfold *v.* 打开	(Unit 8, Part B)
suitable *adj.* 合适的,适宜的	(Unit 2, Part A)	unreasonable *adj.* 没道理的	(Unit 9, Part A)
summarize *v.* 总结	(Unit 10, Part B)		
sundae 圣代冰淇淋	(Unit 5, Part A)	**V**	
sweet bell pepper 柿子椒	(Unit 4, Part A)	vacant *adj.* 空着的,空的	(Unit 2, Part B)
sympathize *v.* 同情	(Unit 10, Part A)	vanilla *n.* 香草	(Unit 5, Part A)
sympathy *n.* 同情	(Unit 10, Part A)	veal *n.* 小牛肉	(Unit 3, Part A)
		veal cutlets 牛肉片	(Unit 9, Part B)
T		vinegar *n.* 醋	(Unit 4, Part B)
table d'hote 套餐的	(Unit 3, Part A)		
tart *n.* 蛋挞,果馅饼,小烘饼	(Unit 5, Part A)	**W**	
taste *v.* 品尝	(Unit 8, Part A)	waiter *n.* 男服务员	(Unit 1, Part A)
teapot *n.* 茶壶	(Unit 3, Part B)	waitress *n.* 女服务员	(Unit 1, Part A)
tender *adj.* 嫩的	(Unit 9, Part B)	whisky *n.* 威士忌	(Unit 3, Part A)
tidy *adj.* 整洁的	(Unit 9, Part A)		
tip *n.* 小费	(Unit 10, Part A)	**Y**	
tip *v.* 给小费	(Unit 8, Part B)	yoghurt *n.* 酸奶	(Unit 4, Part A)

Key to Exercises

Unit 1

Part A

Start You Off

✚ Activity 2

1. chef   2. receptionist   3. waitress   4. operator   5. cashier
6. waiter   7. restaurant manager   8. hostess

1. He's a chef who works in the kitchen and cooks food.
2. She's a restaurant receptionist who takes reservations from guests.
3. She's a waitress who serves customers at their tables in a restaurant.
4. She's an operator who works on the telephone switchboard in a restaurant.
5. She's a cashier who receives and pays out money in a restaurant.
6. He's a waiter who serves customers at their tables in a restaurant.
7. He's a restaurant manager who is in charge of a restaurant and its operation.
8. She's a hostess who greets the customers in a restaurant.

Focus on Language

✚ Language Tips

2. Booking a table

✚ Practice 2

1. May   2. time   3. open   4. close   5. like
6. reserve   7. what   8. time   9. have   10. name

Give It a Try

✚ Task 1

Reservation Form

Name of the restaurant: **Rose Restaurant**
Day taken: **Friday**   ☐ Lunch ☑ Dinner
Time of reservation: **Around 7:00 p.m.**

English for Food and Beverages

Name of the person making the reservation: **Mr. John Smith**
Telephone number: _____
Logged by/in: _____
No. in party: **A party of two**
Food taken: **Western food**

Task 2

1. May I help you
3. For how many people, please
5. or in a private room
7. booked under the name of
9. Okay, I see

2. I'd like to reserve a table
4. At what time can we expect you, sir
6. May I have your name and phone number
8. mobile phone number
10. We'll be expecting you this evening sir. Bye.

Task 4

Questions of Accepting a Reservation

1. What time would you like your table? / For what time? / At what time should we expect you?
2. How many people are there in your party? / For how many?
3. May I have your name, please? / Who's the reservation for? / In whose name is the reservation made?
4. Is there any special requirement? / Any special requirement?
5. Where would you like to sit, by the window? / Would you like a table in the hall or in a private room?

etc.

Do Extension Activities

Activity 1

Banquet Reservation Form

Name of the restaurant: **Flower Garden Restaurant**
Day taken: **The day after tomorrow** ☐ Lunch ☑ Dinner
Time of reservation: **At 7:30 p.m.**
Name of the person making the reservation: **Mr. Li Dan**
Phone number: **13691081196**   Fax number: **64901122**
Logged in: **A private room**   No. In party: **A party of ten**
Food taken: **Chinese food**   Wine ordered: **Martell XO**
Charge per person: **200 yuan**

210

Key to Exercises

Activity 2
T T T T T F T T

Part B

Start You Off

Activity 2

Name	Title	
Maria Cannoli	(Ms.)	✓
James Morrison	(Ms.)	
Jeanne Dubois	(Mrs.)	✓
Dave Moore	(Mr.)	✓

Activity 3

Name	Phone number	E-mail address
Lisa	61-3-9657-1234	lah@zip.com.aw
Junko	(06)-478-2150	junko@aol.com
Sam	382-4167	slee@sunrise.com.sg
Mari	(044)-645-7299	mayo@asu.edu

Focus on Language

Language Tips

1. Taking a reservation if the guest's time is not available

Practice 1
Open answers.

Practice 2
Open answers.

2. Offering Help

Practice 1
Open answers.

211

English for Food and Beverages

Practice 2
Open answers.

3. Asking for the guest's name

Practice 1
Open answers.

Practice 2
Open answers.

Give It a Try

Task 2

Name	John Hampton.
Phone Number	6622-3796
Time for Reservation	6:00
Guest Request for Seating	A table in a private room
Suggested Location	A table in the hall
No. in Party	Two
Table Number	16

Task 3

1. What can I do for you
2. a table for this evening
3. Three
4. What time would you like to come
5. any table left for 7:30
6. you one at 8:00
7. May I have your name, please
8. Would you please
9. three this evening at 8:00
10. Harrison

Do Extension Activities

Activity 1

Accepting a Reservation	1. What time would you like your table? 2. How many people are there in your party? 3. In whose name is the reservation made? 4. We look forward to having you with us.

Key to Exercises

Giving Information about the Restaurant	1. I'm sorry, we're not open on Sundays. 2. We're open from 5:30 p.m. until midnight. 3. We open 24 hours.
Refusing a Reservation	1. I'm afraid that table is reserved for 6 p.m. 2. I'm sorry, there aren't any tables for 11:30, but we can give you a table at 12:30. 3. I'm afraid all the private rooms are reserved. Would you mind sitting in the main dining room?

Activity 2

- a telephone
- a pen or pencil
- a menu
- a wine list
- guest checks

- dupes
- a logbook
- a telephone number file listing employee
- various emergency phone numbers
- a telephone-answering machine

Unit 2

Part A

Start You Off

Activity 1

1. Have you got a reservation, sir/madam?
2. Do you have a reservation?
3. Have you booked a table?
4. How many persons, please?
5. Do you prefer smoking or non-smoking?
6. Where would you like to sit?
7. Will this table be all right?
8. Would you like to sit near the window?
9. Is this table fine with you, sir/madam?
10. Would you mind sitting separately?
11. Would you mind waiting a moment in the lounge?
12. Would you like to hear tonight's specials?

Activity 2

1. Is there a table for 3?
2. Do you have a table for 5?
3. Any chance of getting a table near the window?
4. How long do you think we'll have to wait?
5. How long a wait?
6. How about the rest of our party?
7. Do you have a private room?

Focus on Language

Language Tips

2. Asking about the preferences

Practice 2

Dialogue 1
1. ready   2. follow   3. suitable   4. nice

Dialogue 2
1. expecting   2. reserved   3. come   4. with   5. prefer   6. full   7. lounge   8. wait

Give It a Try

Task 1

1. Have you got a reservation
2. yesterday morning
3. for 12 at 6:30 p.m.
4. Mr. Charles
5. our table is ready now
6. Where would you like to sit
7. We prefer a private dining room
8. We've had Bamboo Hall reserved for you
9. But the rest of our party...

Do Extension Activities

Activity 1

Steps
1. Greeting the guests
2. Requesting the reservation
3. Confirming the table
4. Seating the guest
5. Asking the guests whether they need any drinks
6. Bringing the menu
7. Asking if the guests are ready to order

Key to Exercises

Activity 2

T F F T F T T T F

Part B

Start You Off

Activity 1

	Graphical Symbols	Names of the Symbols	Explanation
1		Parking 停车场	表示供停放机动车的场所
2		Parking for bicycle 自行车停放处	表示供停放自行车的场所
3		Direction 方向	表示方向
4		Way in 入口	表示入口位置或指明进去的通道
5		Way out 出口	表示出口位置或指明出去的通道
6		Emergency exit 紧急出口	表示紧急情况下安全疏散的出口或通道
7		Elevator/lift 电梯	表示公用电梯

续表

	Graphical Symbols	Names of the Symbols	Explanation
8		Facilities for disabled person 残疾人设施	表示供残疾人使用的设施，如轮椅、坡道等
9		Toilet 卫生间	表示卫生间
10		Male 男性	表示专供男性使用的设施，如男厕所、男浴室等
11		Female 女性	表示专供女性使用的设施，如女厕所、女浴室等
12		Rubbish receptacle 废物箱	表示人们扔弃废物的设施
13		Settle accounts 结帐	表示用现金或支票进行结算的场所，如宾馆、酒店的前台结帐处、商场等场所的付款处
14		Restaurant 西餐	表示提供西式餐饮服务的场所，如西餐厅等
15		Chinese restaurant 中餐	表示提供中式餐饮的服务场所，如中餐厅、中餐馆等
16		Snackbar 快餐	表示提供快餐服务的场所

Key to Exercises

续表

	Graphical Symbols	Names of the Symbols	Explanation
17		Bar 酒吧	表示提供饮酒及其他饮料的场所
18		Coffee 咖啡	表示喝咖啡及其他饮料的场所
19		Smoking allowed 允许抽烟	表示允许吸烟的场所
20		No smoking 禁止吸烟	表示禁止吸烟的场所

Focus on Language

Language Tips

1. Receive the guest without the reservation

Practice 2

1. table   2. reservation   3. arrived   4. hot   5. full   6. same   7. separately   8. rather

3. Seating the guests who have been kept waiting for a while

Practice 1

1. Yes. Here   2. We're very sorry for the delay   3. Great

4. Would you like to sit on a quiet corner?   5. We've got something to talk about

Do Extension Activities

Activity 2

1. vacant seats   2. share   3. restaurant's   4. consent
5. haven't   6. specific   7. motivation   8. consideration
9. for free seats   10. explanation   11. ensure   12. informed
13. who have been kept waiting   14. having delayed them for a while

Unit 3

Part A

Start You Off

Activity 1

1. steak 2. ham 3. tomato 4. mushroom 5. chicken
6. vegetable salad 7. fish 8. soup 9. lettuce

Activity 2

1. c 2. c 3. b 4. b 5. a

Activity 3

1. c 2. f 3. e 4. a 5. b 6. d

Focus on Language

Language Tips

1. Asking the guest if having an aperitif or an hors d'oeuvre

Practice 1

> [3] Would you like the Baden dry, sir, or perhaps the Piesporter?
> [5] Would you like the Anjou Rose, madam?
> [2] Would you like the smoked salmon, madam?
> [1] Would you like the soup, madam?
> [4] Would you like the Bordeaux Blanc de Blancs, madam, or perhaps the Chablis?

4. Taking the orders for food or drink

Practice 1

1. I'll have a glass of white wine, please.
2. I'll start with the oysters, please, and then the duck.
3. The mushrooms, followed by the scallops for me.
4. Soup, please.
5. A whisky on the rocks for me, please.
6. I'll have the chicken, with peas, mushrooms and tomatoes.

Key to Exercises

Give It a Try

Task 1
1. b   2. a   3. c   4. a   5. c   6. a   7. a   8. a

Task 2
1. I think I'll have the prawn cocktail to start with, please, and then the beef salad.
2. My wife will have the sole, please, and I'll have the lamb cutlets. And we'd also like a bottle of Anjou Rose.
3. It's one soup, and two smoked salmons. And then one fillet steak, one chicken Kiev and a sole. Also, we'll have a bottle of the Chablis, please.
4. Two Salades Nicoises, one melon and smoked salmon to begin with. And then—what was it? Oh yes, one omelette, one lamb cutlets, one chicken salad and a ham salad. And we'll have a bottle of the Niersteiner Domtal and one of the Cotes du Rhone. That's all, thanks.
5. I'll take the pate to start with, and my husband wants the smoked salmon. He'll have the fillet steak after that, and I'll have the chicken salad. And a bottle of Franken Sylvaner to go with it.
6. Three melons and a pate, followed by one lamb cutlets and three soles. And we'll have the Goldener Oktober to start with, and then the Mouton Cadet to follow. OK? Thanks.

Task 3
1. What would you like to order
2. have a Sherry to start with
3. a Gin
4. will you be having a starter
5. One curried prawns, one clams
6. I'll have the hare
7. would like the roast duck
8. Thank you, sir

Do Extension Activities

Activity 1

	Whisky	Brandy	Grape Wine	Distilled from Grain	Distilled from Grapes
Bourbon	√			√	
Bordeaux			√		
Burgundy			√		
Californian			√		
Hennessey		√			√
Remy Martin		√			√
Rye	√			√	
Scotch	√			√	

Activity 2
Open answers.

219

Activity 3

1. Mix three parts of gin with one part of dry Martini and serve it with an olive.
2. Cook rice and seafood together and serve it in the cooking dish.
3. Cook veal with carrots and onions and serve it in a white sauce with boiled rice.
4. Mix coffee with brown sugar, Irish whiskey, and cream, and serve it as an after-dinner drink.
5. Fried pieces of pork braised in sugar and vinegar sauce.

Part B

Start You Off

Activity 1

1. fork   2. knife   3. chopsticks   4. napkin   5. spoon
6. teapot   7. toothpick   8. plate   9. glass

Activity 2

1−C   2−D   3−A   4−B

Activity 3

1−f   2−g   3−h   4−j   5−i   6−a   7−b   8−c   9−e   10−d

Focus on Language

Language Tips

1. Asking if ready to order

Practice 1

	Ready to Order	Not Ready to Order
Guest 1	✓	
Guest 2		✓
Guest 3	✓	
Guest 4		✓
Guest 5		✓

2. Making a recommendation for the guest

Practice 2

Open answers.

3. Ordering the main course

Practice 2

Open answers.

Key to Exercises

Give It a Try

Task 1

Food had, wanted and recommended	Guest	Waiter
Light food	√	
Braised turtle with garlic		√
Steamed minced pork balls	√	√
Soup	√	
Bird's nest and shredded chicken soup	√	√
Baked pancakes	√	√

Task 2

Recommendation Made by the Waiter

1. Hot pot
2. Mutton
3. Beef
4. Chinese cabbage
5. White gourd

Task 3

Ordering Chinese Food

W: What would like to order, sir?
G: I'd like to try some Chinese food.
W: Which style do you prefer?
G: I have no idea about Chinese food. What's your recommendation?
W: We serve Shandong food and Guangdong food here.
G: Is there any difference between them?
W: Yes, Shandong food is heavy while Guangdong food is light.
G: Oh, I like heavy food. What's your specialty for Shandong food?
W: How about Braised Sea Cucumber with Spring Onion?
G: Alright, I'll take that. Thank you very much.
W: You are welcome.

English for Food and Beverages

Do Extension Activities

✚ Activity 1

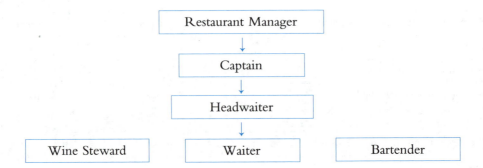

✚ Activity 2
Open answers.

Unit 4

Part A

Start You Off

✚ Activity 2
1-e　2-a　3-h　4-g　5-b　6-f　7-i　8-d　9-c

✚ Activity 3
1. No, sir/madam, they're boiled.
2. No, sir/madam, it's grilled.
3. No, sir/madam, they're poached.
4. No, sir/madam, it's baked.
5. No, sir/madam, it's whipped.

Focus on Language

✚ Language Tips

1. Asking and giving special instruction on food

✚ Practice 1
1. No, it's not dry enough. I like it very dry.
2. I'm afraid it's too spicy. I can't eat it.
3. I'm afraid it's too strong. I can't drink it.
4. No, it's not weak enough. I like them very weak.

222

Key to Exercises

2. Asking if having anything to go with food

Practice 1

1. lettuce, tomatoes, beans and carrots
2. spinach and sweet bell pepper
3. tomatoes and broad beans
4. Mushrooms, chips, peas and tomatoes
5. lettuce, cucumber and carrots
6. leeks, potatoes and cauliflower
7. tomatoes and broad beans
8. Cabbage, chips, broad beans and, broccoli

Practice 2

1. It's served with tomatoes, lettuce, cucumber and celery, sir/madam.
2. They're served with onions, spinach and chips, sir/madam.
3. It's served with chips, broccoli and beans, sir/madam.
4. It's served with (roast) potatoes, carrots, peas and leeks, sir/madam.
5. It's served with (roast) potatoes, broccoli and peas, sir/madam.

3. Asking what the guest prefers for drinks

Practice 1

1. c   2. b   3. c   4. a   5. c   6. c   7. b   8. c

Practice 2

1. Would you rather have/prefer cognac or armagnac, sir?
2. Would you rather have/prefer mixed vegetable or tomato, madam?
3. Would you rather have/prefer red or white, madam?
4. Would you rather have/prefer the entrecote or the tournedos, madam?
5. Would you rather have/prefer draught or bottled, sir?

Practice 3

Open answers.

Give It a Try

Task 1

Food or Drink Ordered	Conversation 1	Conversation 2	Conversation 3
American breakfast	√		
Coffee		√	√
Healthy breakfast			√
Tomato			

Item				
Grapefruit	✓	✓		
Orange				✓
Danish pastry	✓			
Eggs	✓			
Cheese omelet		✓		
Bacon				
Ham				
Oatmeal				✓
Sausage	✓			
Yoghurt		✓		
Croissant				

Task 2

1. I'll have
2. what kind of
3. would you like with that
4. I prefer boiled
5. Any vegetables
6. Cauliflower
7. I would rather have spinach
8. Any soup or salad
9. Salad
10. What kind of dressing would you like on
11. I'll take
12. what would you like to drink
13. Bottled beer or wine
14. Beer

Task 3

Ordering Western Food

W: What would you like to order, madam?

G: I'd like to take the veal cutlet.

W: I'm sorry, madam. But we are all out of the veal cutlet.

G: Oh, I see. Bring me the fillet of sole then.

W: Very good, madam. Soup or salad?

G: What's today's soup?

W: It is French onion.

G: That sounds good. I'll have the soup.

W: Mashed, boiled, or baked potato?

G: Baked?

W: Any vegetables?

G: I'll have the broccoli.

W: Fine, madam. And what will you have to drink?

G: Nothing right now, thank you.

Key to Exercises

Do Extension Activities

Activity 1

Aperitifs	1	Sherry Vermouth Campari	8	Hors d'oeuvres
Sparkling Wine	2	Champagne	9	Hors d'oeuvres
White Wine	3	Chablis Hock Riesling	10	Fish Chicken
Rosé Wine	4	Rosé d'Anjou	11	Veal Chicken
Red Wine	5	Beaujolais Beaune Burgundy Chianti Rioja	12	Beef Lamb
Dessert Wine	6	Port Madeira	13	Dessert
Liqueurs	7	Liqueur Brandy Cointreau	14	Coffee

Activity 2

Drinks	1	2	3	4	5	6
Bourbon		✓				
Cinzano	✓					
Rye		✓				
Malt		✓				
Martini	✓					
Pernod			✓			
Juice					✓	
Tio Pepe						✓
Sherry			✓			
Louis Bernard				✓		
Mineral water					✓	
Croft Original						✓
Remy Martin				✓		
Martell				✓		
Bristol Cream						✓

Part B

Start You Off

✚ Activity 2
1. c　　2. d　　3. f　　4. a　　5. b　　6. g　　7. e　　8. i　　9. h　　10. k　　11. j

✚ Activity 3
1. Sunny-side Up　　2. Turn Over　　3. Boiled Eggs
4. Poached Eggs　　5. Scrambled Eggs　　6. Omelet

Focus on Language

✚ Language Tips

1. Offering help and ordering room service

✚ Practice 1

1. a bowl of soup　　　　　462
2. two French onion soups　　201
3. 263　　　　　　　　　　send up a Chef's salad
4. This is Room 656　　　　the cold roast beef
5. have a minute steak　　　It's Room 101
6. Room 632 here　　　　　grilled sausages　　　　a veal steak
7. A fried fish　　　　　　It's Room 107
8. Room 44　　　　　　　I'd like you to send up

✚ Practice 2

W=Waiter　　G=Guest

1. **W**: Good evening. Room Service. May I help you?
   G: Good evening. <u>I'd like the tomato soup, followed by the ragout of chicken, please. It's Room 111.</u>
2. **W**: Room Service. May I help you?
   G: <u>Could you send up two consommés, one ragout of chicken and a minute steak to Room 425, please?</u>
3. **W**: Room Service. May I help you?
   G: <u>Yes. This is Room 212. We'd like two cold roast beef salads, please, and one hamburger. And a bottle of red wine, your house wine, to go with it.</u>

Key to Exercises

4. **W**: Room Service. May I help you?

    G: <u>It's Room 808. Something for my children, please. Two fried fish and a veal steak, and also three ice creams.</u>

5. **W**: Room Service. May I help you?

    G: <u>I'd like you to get me a "Cordon Bleu" and a Chef's salad, please, and three veal steaks. We're in Room 108.</u>

6. **W**: Room Service. May I help you?

    G: <u>A bottle of white wine, two Chef's salad, one grilled sausage and an ice cream, please. That's 501, the room number.</u>

Give It a Try

Task 1

1. b   2. a   3. c   4. a   5. c   6. c   7. c   8. c

Task 2

1. Can I help you	2. Good evening	3. like to order
4. salad	5. lettuce salad	6. I'll take
7. dressing	8. salad	9. T-bone steak
10. please	11. thanks	12. name
13. room number	14. lettuce salad	15. Thousand Islands
16. a bottle of	17. calling	18. order

Task 3

W: It's Room Service. May I come in?

G: Yes, come in, please.

W: Thank you, madam. I've brought the salad, a T-bone steak and deserts you just ordered. Where should I put them?

G: On the table, please.

W: All right. Would you please sign the bill?

G: Sure. Here you are.

W: By the way, when could I come back to take away the plates?

G: After 9:00 tomorrow morning.

W: Fine, madam. Please enjoy your food. Just call us when you need more orders. We are always at your service.

G: I will. Thank you.

W: Good bye. Have a good night.

English for Food and Beverages

Do Extension Activities

Activity 1

ROOM SERVICE

Name: ___709___
Room Number: ___John Smith___

Items for Replenishing the Mini-bar

Snacks:
1. ___Mixed nuts___
2. ___Potato chips___

Drinks:
1. ___Three wines___
2. ___Four soda waters___
3. ___Two cokes___

Activity 4

1. Still Wine（静止葡萄酒）including: Red Wine（红葡萄酒）, Rosé Wine（玫瑰红葡萄酒）, White Wine（白葡萄酒）
2. Sparkling Wine（葡萄汽酒）including: Sparkling Wine（加汽葡萄酒）, Champagne（香槟酒）
3. Fortified Wine（强化葡萄酒）including: Sherry（雪利酒）, Port（波特酒）
4. Aromatized Wine（加味葡萄酒）including: Vermouth（味美思）

Unit 5

Part A

Start You Off

Activity 2

pudding   cake   cookie   ice cream
Tang Yuan (Glutinous Rice Ball)
tart   sweet candy   chocolate   haw jelly   pea flour cake
Lüdagunr (Glutinous Rice Roll Stuffed with Red Bean Paste)
pumpkin pie   bean paste cake   glutinous rice sesame balls

Key to Exercises

Focus on Language

✚ Language Tips

2. Asking what the guest would like for dessert

✚ Practice 1

Student A: Would you like some dessert, sir?
Student B: Yes, I'd like some.
Student A: What would you like for your dessert?
Student B: I'd like two raisin cookies and two onion tarts. (It's open to your preference.)

✚ Practice 2

Guest	Dessert ordered
Tom	a lemon pie and a vanilla ice-cream
Mary	two pineapple pies and a coffee ice-cream
Louis	three oatmeal cookies and some fruit puddings
Darth	a black forest cake and a mango ice-cream

3. Asking for and giving dessert menu

✚ Practice

1. Would you like (to have) some dessert?
2. Could I see the dessert menu? /Would you please show me the dessert menu?
3. Sure. Here you are.
4. I'd like to have some mango puddings and a chocolate cake.

4. Asking and telling if anything else is wanted

✚ Practice

Conversation
Waiter: Would you like anything else, sir/madam?
Guest: Yes, I'd like some dessert now.
Waiter: What would you like for your dessert?
Guest: I'd like some fruit puddings and a strawberry ice-cream. (It's open to your preference.)

5. Asking for and giving recommendation

✚ Practice 2

1. satisfaction   2. Would you like anything else   3. I think I will have some dessert now

4. What would you like for your dessert 5. recommend 6. May I recommend
7. tasty 8. marvelous

Give It a Try

Task 1
1. Would you like anything else 2. What would you suggest 3. May I suggest fruit puddings

Task 3
1. How do you like your meal 2. I like it very much
3. really delicious 4. Would you like
5. I would like to try some local ones 6. I wonder if you could recommend some
7. pea flour cakes, haw jellies 8. dessert trolley
9. glutinous rice rolls with sweet bean flour 10. very popular

Do Extension Activities

Activity 2
1. origins 2. traced 3. 4th 4. references 5. mountains 6. fruit toppings
7. creating ice and milk concoctions 8. preferred 9. honey 10. nectars
11. served 12. hints 13. popularity 14. recipes 15. evolved 16. fashionable

Part B

Start You Off

Activity 1
☑ Pastry ☒ Tea ☑ Ice Cream ☒ Coffee ☒ Milk
☑ Milkshake ☑ Toast ☒ Wine ☑ Cheese ☒ Cola
☑ Pudding ☑ Sweet ☑ Chocolate ☑ Cookie ☒ Beer
☑ Apple Pie ☑ Cake ☑ Fruit Jelly ☒ Fruit Juice ☑ Tart

Activity 2
1. The name dessert originates from a French word desservir, which means "to clear the table."
2. Dessert is seveved at the end of a dinner.
3. They are classified as frozen desserts, fruit desserts and some varieties of milkshakes.
4. Desserts are quite popular in the USA, and every occasion is incomplete without a proper dessert being served.
5. Yes, there are several restaurants that specialize in desserts and treat it as a separate meal rather than a course.
6. The most popular desserts are sweet candies, ice creams, puddings and other preparations of chocolates.
7. Yes, desserts are often presented in style with appropriate decorations, in order to enhance the presentation.

Key to Exercises

Focus on Language

Language Tips

1. Telling dessert is out and suggesting something else

Practice 2

e   c   d   b   a

Give It a Try

Task 2

1. He ordered two mango tarts and a coffee ice-cream for his dessert.
2. He ordered some lemon puddings at first.
3. Yes, because lemon puddings were sold out.
4. Then he ordered two raspberry bread puddings for his dessert.
5. No, she didn't order any dessert. She thinks dessert is fattening and she is on a diet.

Do Extension Activities

Activity 2

Part I Spot Dictation

1. dessert	2. sweet, pudding	3. afters	4. pudding
5. consists of fruit	6. colloquial	7. fruits and nuts	8. western meal
9. middle class	10. 19th century	11. sugar industry	12. privilege
13. holiday treat	14. development and popularity		

Part II True or False Questions

1. T   2. F   3. F   4. T

Unit 6

Part A

Start You Off

Activity 2

1. D   2. A   3. H   4. G   5. A   6. B   7. C   8. A   9. F   10. E

Activity 3

1. C   2. B   3. D   4. H   5. G   6. E   7. A   8. I   9. J   10. F

Focus on Language

Language Tips

2. Giving tips and taking or turning down tips politely

Practice 1

1. Waiter!
2. The bill please. / May I have my bill please?
3. Just a second
4. Here is your bill. It comes to one hundred and eight *yuan* altogether.
5. Don't bother with the change. / Keep the change, please.
6. Here is your receipt.

3. Asking the ways of payment and asking and telling if credit card is accepted

Practice 2

1. I'd like to pay/settle the bill, please
2. How would you like to pay/settle your bill, sir
3. May I use credit card?/Will you take credit card?
4. What kind are you holding, sir? /What kind have you got, sir?
5. Could you sign your name here, please
6. Here is your card and your copy

5. Asking and telling if paying separate bills or one bill

Practice 2

1. May I have the bill
2. 258
3. care to have one bill or separate bills
4. It's on me
5. It's my treat
6. Dutch treat
7. It's a good idea
8. Keep the change
9. Don't bother with the change
10. Do come again please

Give It a Try

Task 2

1. No, he didn't.
2. It was 576 *yuan* altogether.
3. He would like to pay the bill by credit card.
4. He was holding Eurocard. No, he could not pay his bill by this card, because the restaurant doesn't accept Eurocard. The restaurant only takes American Express, Master Card and Visa.
5. No, he didn't. Because the restaurant doesn't honor traveller's check as payment either.
6. He paid his bill in cash in the end.
7. No, she didn't. Because a 15% service charge has already been added to the bill.
8. 24 *yuan*.

Key to Exercises

Do Extension Activities

✚ Activity 1

1. May I have the bill
2. How would you like to pay the bill
3. accept
4. Chinese *yuan* for change
5. exchange rate
6. seven hundred eighty five
7. 3% handling charge
8. mind
9. credit card
10. holding
11. Master Card
12. Could you sign your name here, please
13. Certainly
14. Here is your card and your copy

Part B

Start You Off

✚ Activity 1

Discussion

1. ☑ Explain the charge in a patient way.
2. ☑ Ask the cashier to check it up.
   ☑ Make an apology if the guest is overcharged.

✚ Activity 2

| RMB ¥ 217 |

It's two hundred and seventeen *yuan*.

| RMB ¥ 339 |

It's three hundred and thirty nine *yuan*.

| GB £ 451 |

It's four hundred and fifty one pounds.

| GB £ 562 |

It's five hundred and sixty two pounds.

| US$673 |

It's six hundred and seventy three dollars.

| US$985 |

It's nine hundred and eighty five dollars.

Focus on Language

Language Tips

2. Showing disagreement to a bill and explaining a charge

Practice 2

1. Waiter! Bill please.
2. It comes to five hundred and forty *yuan* altogether
3. There seems to be some mistakes on my bill. Shouldn't it be four hundred and fifty *yuan*
4. I'm afraid there is a 10% tax and a 10% service charge added to your bill
5. What is item 6 for
6. This is the charge for 2 bowls of rice
7. May I use credit card? American Express.
8. Yes. That'll be fine

3. Telling you were overcharged and checking the bill for the guest

Practice 2

1. The bill, please
2. comes to two hundred and seventy one
3. seems a little high to me
4. overcharged
5. break the bill down
6. I'd be happy to
7. One hundred and forty
8. Champaign
9. forty six
10. cashier to check it up
11. Excuse me for a moment
12. I'm awfully sorry
13. consumption
14. do apologize for the mistake
15. Two hundred and twenty five

4. Telling there is a wrong change and making an apology for it

Practice 1

1. Excuse me
2. shortchanged
3. It totals ¥310
4. you should have given
5. May I check the bill for you
6. I'm sorry for the mistake
7. apologize
8. change

Give It a Try

Task 1

1. ☑ I'm sorry. May I check the bill for you, please?
2. ☑ I would be happy to.
3. ☑ I'm sorry about that. There is a note at the bottom of the menu explaining our policy. I should have explained that to you.
4. ☑ Oh, yes. Let me explain. We add 5% tax and there is a 10% service charge added to each bill.

5. ☑ Can I check your bill, please? ... Oh, you're absolutely right. I'm so sorry. Here is the rest of your change.

✚ Task 2

1. error   2. overcharged   3. undercharged   4. service charge   5. receipt   6. shortchanged

Do Extension Activities

✚ Activity 1

1. They have to pay 693 *yuan* according to the waitress.
2. No, she doesn't. She thinks that they are overcharged.
3. Yes, there is a mistake. They didn't order coconut juice. But there is a charge for two bottles of coconut juice.
4. It is for the service charge.
5. The food costs 450 *yuan* and the wine costs 160 *yuan*.
6. The service charge should be 61 *yuan*.
7. The bill should amount to 671 *yuan*.
8. They are terribly busy at the hour of the day so they make a mistake and put somebody else's consumption into the bill.
9. The man paid the bill. He paid the bill by credit card.

Unit 7

Part A

Start You Off

✚ Activity 2

1. waiter   2. hostess   3. Bar Manager   4. Head Barman
5. cashier   6. Wine Steward   7. Soda Fountain Captain   8. Bartender

Focus on Language

✚ Language Tips

2. Receiving guests appropriately

✚ Practice 1

1. Welcome   2. reservation   3. name   4. Edward   5. six

Give It a Try

Task 1

Reservation Form

Name of the bar: **Sunflower Bar**
Day taken: **Friday**
Time of reservation: **Around 22:00**
Name of the person making the reservation: **Mr. Jenkins**
Telephone number: **65542849**
Place of the tables: **on the roof**
No. In party: **A party of five**

Task 2

1. Oracle Bar   2. three   3. reservation   4. available   5. by the window

Part B

Focus on Language

Language Tips

2. Ask guests what else they would like to order

Practice 2

1. special   2. Tsingdao Beer   3. take   4. draught or bottled   5. go with   6. enough   7. ready

Give It a Try

Form

Name of the person: **Mr. Landers**
Place of tables: **by the fountain**
No. In party: **3**
Drinks taken: **Beijing Beer   6 bottles**
Food taken: **snacks**
Special requirement: **bottled beer**

Do Extension Activities

Activity 1

☑ Greet your callers warmly and appropriately.
☑ It will be better for the clerks to give the menu to the host/hostess in a large group.

Key to Exercises

☑ You should explain or recommend to the guest some specialty, Today's Specialty or House Specialty.

☑ When taking order, clerks should ask guests about their special requirements.

☑ When having taken order, clerks should confirm what they have ordered.

Unit 8

Part A

Start you off

Activity 1

1. Fruits, counters and bartender.
2. They are about the setting in a bar.
3. A bar.
4. The man is a bartender in the bar.

Activity 2

1. Whisky	2. Tumler	3. Old-fashioned	4. Liqueur	5. Fizz
6. Sherry	7. Wine	8. Cocktail 1	9. Cocktail 2	10. Champagne
11. Stein	12. Sour	13. Brandy	14. Pilsener	

Focus on Language

Language Tips

1. Asking what guests specially require

Practice 1

1. special	2. beer or wine	3. recommendation	4. Brandy, Gin and Sherry
5. strong wines	6. Vermouth	7. Chilled	8. enough

Do Extension Activities

1. A wine glass is a type of glass stemware which is used to drink and taste wine.
2. It is generally composed of three parts: the bowl, stem, and foot.
3. The proper way to drink from the wine glass, when drinking white or otherwise chilled wine is to grasp it by the stem and drink. The purpose of this is so the temperature of the wine is not affected when holding the glass. Also, holding the glass by the bowl will leave fingerprints, which can distort the visual appearance of the wine when examining the clarity and colour of the wine.
4. Glasses for red wine are characterized by their rounder, wider bowl, which gives the wine a chance to breathe.
   White wine glasses are generally narrower, although not as narrow as champagne flutes, with somewhat straight or tulip-shaped sides.

237

A sherry glass is drinkware generally used for serving aromatic alcoholic beverages, such as sherry, port, aperitifs and liqueurs, and layered shooters.

Part B

Focus on Language

Language Tips

2. Telling guests how much is owed

Practice 1

Name of the guest	Bill of the drink	Monetary unit	Ways of paying	Tips
Mr. Brown	70 yuan	US $	In cash	$ 5

Practice 2

1. bill   2. all   3. 98 yuan   4. How much   5. 14 US$ dollars   6. Master Card   7. bill and receipt

Give It a Try

Task 2

1. have the bill   A bill for all   How would you like to settle the bill, sir
   not Diner's Club   sign the bill to your room
2. Yes, sir. Here you are Blush Rose Wine and Liqueur Please sign your name here

Do Extension Activities

Activity 1

No. of guests	Amount	Ways of paying	Accepted cards	Tips
G1	US $ 100	In cash		Change
G2		Credit card	Master Card	

Unit 9

Part A

Start You Off

Activity 2

1 Waiter, there is something in my drink.
2 Waiter, the drink is not what I ordered.

Key to Exercises

3. You are overcharged me with the bill.
4. Your wine has a peculiar smell.
5. Waiter, there is lipstick on my glass.
6. Waiter, the coffee is weak.
7. Waiter, my drink is not cold enough.
8. Waiter, I have kept waiting so long. May I take my order now?

Language Tips

1. Making complaints in a polite way

Practice 1

1. have a word with you
2. I'm sorry to bother you
3. could you tell me what you've ordered

2. Making complaints in a direct way

Practice 2

1. I am fed up with mess!
2. You never let me stay up late!
3. I'm tired and sick of your silly complaints.
4. It's got to stop!

Do Extension Activities

1. In China, people have to boil the water first and then let it cool down to drink.
2. (1) In the United States, people boil water only when they want to make coffee.
   (2) Most Americans have cold drinks when eating regardless of summer or winter.
   (3) In American one's social class is reflected in the choice of alcoholic drinks.
3. Upper class people prefer mixed drinks.
   Working class drinkers prefer straight shots of whiskey or beer.
4. The answer is open.

Part B

Start You Off

Activity 2

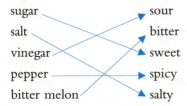

1. I like Sichuan food, which is usually spicy and hot.
2. I like Shanghai food, which is usually sweet and sour.

3 I like Cantonese food, which is usually light and fresh.
4 Peking roasted duck is my favorite. The meat is tender, while the skin is crispy.
5 I like Beijing food, which is a bit heavy, but delicious.

Language Tips

1. Complaining about food

Practice 1

1. Yes   2. steak is too   3. have told   4. well-done   5. so
6. madam   7. wait   8. for   9. longer   10. be done
11. 5   12. you   13. waiting   14. No   15. I want
16. in a

2. Complaining about service

Practice 2

1. ignoring   2. were seated   3. are short of hands   4. half an hour
5. see your order   6. roast duck   7. a drink

Give It a Try

Task 2

1. doing the backstroke   2. can't swim   3. the hot liquid   4. rations   5. extra charge

Unit 10

Part A

Start You Off

Activity 1

People Who Work in a Restaurant

waiter   cook   chef   dishwasher   tip

Meals and the Time of Day

breakfast   lunch   dinner   brunch

Parts of a Meal

appetizer   soup   salad   dessert

Types of Restaurants

fancy   fast-food   buffet   bar   smoking   non-smoking

Activity 2

1 Booking tables   2 Receiving the guest

Key to Exercises

3 Showing the guest to the table
4 Taking order from the guest
5 Serving the food for the guest
6 Recommending the dishes
7 Showing the facilities of the restaurant
8 Checking the bill

Language Tips

1. Making Complaints about Service

Practice 2

1. booked a table 2. this way 3. I ordered 4. by the window 5. promised me one
6. have double booked the table 7. it's occupied 8. see your manager

Part B

Start You Off

Activity 1

1. complaints 2. dissatisfied 3. apology 4. different decision 5. proper service
6. replaced goods 7. person 8. head waiter 9. customer services 10. court

Language Tips

1. How to deal with the complaints properly

Practice 2

1. Yes 2. steak is too 3. have told 4. well-done 5. so 6. madam
7. wait 8. longer 9. be done 5 10. salad 11. No 12. I want
13. in a

2. How to deal with the trouble caused by the guest

Practice 2

6 3 4 5 7 2 1 8

Give It a Try

Task 2

a. I won't let you get into the dinner-dance.

b. No more drink for you, sir.

c. We'll let you out of this lounge, sir.

d. You won't stay here any longer.

e. We'll have to ask you to stop your smoking here, sir, I'm afraid. We have to consider the other guest, you see...

f. I'm sorry sir, but you actually aren't allowed to make too much noise here. Thanks for your concern.

g. I'm sorry, sir. I'm afraid we would be unable to avoid suing you for payment.

h. We'll have to ask you to behave yourself, sir. We have to consider the other guest, you see...

Tapescript

Unit 1

Part A

Focus on Language

  Conversation

Reserving a Table through the Telephone

 Listen to the conversation and read after it. Then try to find the answers to the questions.

C=Clerk   G=Guest

C: Good morning! The Four Seasons Restaurant. May I help you?

G: Yes. What time do you open today?

C: We open at 10 a.m., sir, and we close at 2 p.m.

G: Good. I'd like to reserve a table for lunch.

C: What time would you like to have your table?

G: At 11:30.

C: How many are there in your party?

G: Three.

C: All right. May I have your name, please?

G: Mike Jackson.

C: Would you please give me your telephone number?

G: Sure. My phone number is 64907468.

C: Thank you. A table for three at 11:30 for Mr. Mike Jackson. And where would you like to sit?

G: We'd like to sit by the window as we love a bird's eye view of Beijing city.

C: No problem. We'll arrange it for you. Thank you for calling us. We are looking forward to your coming.

Lauguage Tips

2. Booking a table

  Practice 2

Fill in the blanks with the words that you will hear on the recording.

G=Guest   C=Clerk

C: Four Seasons Restaurant. May I help you?

G: What time do you open this evening?

C: At 6 p.m., madam. And we close at 10 p.m.

G: I'd like to reserve a table, please.

C: Sure. For what time, madam?

G: About 8:00.

C: May I have your name, please?

G: Sara Black.

C: ...

Give It a Try

  Task 1

The clerk is taking a reservation by phone. Listen to the recording and write down the proper information in the telephone reservation form according to the conversation.

C=Clerk　**G**=Guest

C: Rose Restaurant. Can I help you?

G: Yes, I'd like to book a table for dinner this Friday.

C: Certainly, sir. What time would you like your table, sir?

G: I am not sure... perhaps around 7:00 p.m.

C: Good. I'll make a reservation for you at 7:00. And how many in your party?

G: A party of two.

C: And what is it going to be, Chinese food or Western food?

G: Western food, please.

C: What's your name, please, sir?

G: Please book it under the name of Mr. John Smith.

C: So, it's Mr. John Smith, a table for two for this evening. It's Western food and you're coming at 7:00.

G: That's right.

C: Thank you, sir. We are looking forward to your coming.

  Task 2

Listen to the recording and complete the following conversation. Then do the conversation in pairs.

G=Guest　**C**=Clerk

C: Good morning. Flower Garden Restaurant. May I help you?

G: I'd like to reserve a table for the dinner on New Year's Day.

C: Certainly, sir. For how many people, please?

G: Just for two, my girl friend and I.

C: At what time can we expect you, sir?

G: Around 6:00 p.m.

C: Fine. Where would you like to sit, sir, in the main restaurant or in a private room?

G: A private room, please.

C: All right, sir. We'll have Flower Hall reserved for you. May I have your name and phone number, please?

G: Certainly. It's booked under the name of Johnson and my mobile phone number is 13501236688.

C: Mr. Johnson, 13501236688... thank you. By the way, as that is the peak hour, we only can keep your room for half an hour. That means you should come before 6:30.

G: Okay, I see.

C: Thank you for calling. We'll be expecting you this evening, sir. Bye.

Do Extension Activities

 Activity 1

Listen to the banquet reservation and write down the proper information in the reservation form according to the conversation.

C=Clerk   G=Guest

C: Good morning. Flower Garden Restaurant. Banquet Reservations. What can I do for you?

G: Good morning. I'd like to book a banquet in a private room at 7:30 p.m. the day after tomorrow.

C: What kind of cuisine would you like, Chinese, Western, Korean or Japanese?

G: Chinese food, please.

C: For how many people?

G: 10 people.

C: Yes, sir, 10 people. How much for food per person? The minimum charge for a private room is 200 *yuan* per person.

G: 200 *yuan* per person, please.

C: 200 *yuan*. What kind of drinks would you like to have?

G: Are all the drinks on consumption basis?

C: Yes, sir.

G: Just get Martell XO ready and we're going to order other drinks at the dinner time.

C: All right. May I have your name, please?

G: Li Dan.

C: Yes, Mr. Li. And your phone number?

G: My mobile phone number is 13691081196. By the way, could you fax the menu with the name of the banquet room? My fax number is 64901122.

C: Yes, 64901122. We'll be sure to fax you the menu with the name of the banquet room. Is there anything else I can do for you, Mr. Li?

G: No, thanks.

C: So, the reservation is made by Mr. Li, a Chinese banquet for 10 people at 7:30 p.m. the day after tomorrow evening. The price is 200 *yuan* per person excluding drinks. We'll prepare Martell X.O.

G: Fine. Thank you.

C: My pleasure. We look forward to serving you. Thank you for calling us. Good-bye.

Part B

Start You Off

  Activity 2

Listen to the conversation. Tick (√) the names and titles that are correct.

Prof: Hello.

Maya: Hi Professor, it's Maya. I'm calling about those names for the database. Can you read them to me? I'll type them in.

Prof: Sure. I have the names right here. Ready?

Maya: Ready.

Prof: The first person is Maria Cannoli. That's M-A-R-I-A, Maria. Cannoli, C-A-N-N-O-L-I.

Maya: OK. Maria... Cannoli. Is that title Ms. , Mrs. , or Mr.?

Prof: That's Ms. M-S. OK? The second person is James Morrison.

Maya: Uh-huh, that's J-A-M-E-S... Morrison... Is that M-O-R-I-S-O-N?

Prof: No, two R's: M-O-R-R-I-S-O-N. The title's Mr. M-R.

Maya: Got it. What's next?

Prof: Jeanne Hibbard. First name is J-E-A-N-N-E and her last name is H-I-B-B-A-R-D.

Maya: OK, Jeanne Hibbard. Is that Ms. or Mrs.?

Prof: Uh... Mrs. And, the last one is Dave Moore.

Maya: D-A-V-E. And is that Moore with two O's? ... M-O-O-R-E?

Prof: Right. And that's Mr.

Maya: Great. Thanks a lot, Professor. I'll see you tomorrow. Bye.

Prof: Sure, Maya. See you. Bye.

  **Activity 3**

Listen to these people exchanging phone numbers and e-mail addresses. Circle the incorrect information.

1. Joon: I'm very pleased to meet you, Ms. Hodgkinson.

   Lisa: It's nice to meet you, too. Please call me Lisa.

   Joon: Right, Lisa, and here's my card.

   Lisa: Thank you. And let me give you mine. Oh, I have a new e-mail address, let me give it to you. It's L-A-H at zip, that's Z-I-P dot C-O-M dot A-U.

   Joon: OK, that's L-A-H at zip dot C-O-M dot A-U. Great, and my e-mail address is on my card.

   Lisa: Good, thanks. Oh, let me also give you my mobile phone number: it's 61-3-9657-1234.

English for Food and Beverages

Joon: OK. 61-3-9657-1234. Great, thanks.

2. Rick: OK, Junko, can I get some information for our database?

Junko: Sure.

Rick: OK, first, can you spell your full name?

Junko: OK, my first name is J-U-N-K-O and my family name is Kotani, that's K-O-T-A-N-I.

Rick: K-O-T-A-N-I. OK, thanks, and your phone number?

Junko: It's Osaka, area code 06 and then 478-2190.

Rick: That's 478-2190. Good. And do you have an e-mail address?

Junko: Yes, it's Junko at G-O-L dot A-C dot J-P.

Rick: OK, just let me check that. It's Junko at G-O-L dot A-C dot J-P. Well, thanks very much.

3. Angie: This is Angie Stone. I'm not at my desk now. Please leave your voice mail at the sound of the tone.

Sam: Hello, Ms. Stone, this is Sam Lee from Sunrise Book Company. I'm calling about your order. Please phone me. My number is 382-4167. Again, that's 382-4167. You can also e-mail me. It's S-Lee, that's S-L-double-E, at sunrise, that's S-U-N-R-I-S-E, dot com dot S-G. I look forward to hearing from you. Bye.

4. Mari: It's been a nice party, but I have to go or I'll miss my train.

Ken: Mari, before you go, can I have your number? Maybe we can go out sometime.

Mari: Sure. My number's 044-345-7255.

Ken: Wait, that's 044-345-7255. Got it. And do you have an e-mail address?

Mari: Yeah. It's mayo, that's M-A-Y-O, at A-S-U dot E-D-U.

Ken: All right, mayo at A-S-U dot E-D-U. Thanks, I'll call or e-mail you next week.

Focus on Language

  *Conversation*

Would You Mind Changing Your Time

 Listen to the conversation and read after it. Then try to find the answers to the questions.

C=Clerk **G**=Guest

C: Good morning. The Garden Restaurant. May I help you?

G: Yes, I'd like to make a reservation for two for this evening at 8:00.

C: Just a moment, please. Let me check if there is any availability... I'm sorry, sir. There aren't any tables left for 8:00, but we can book one for you at 9:00.

G: Well, I am afraid that's too late.

C: I'm terribly sorry, sir.

G: How about tomorrow evening?

C: We've already received many bookings for tomorrow evening. So we cannot guarantee. I hope you'll understand.

G: I do, but I would appreciate it if you could arrange it.
C: I'll try my best. Would you please leave your name and your phone number?
G: Mr. Rodger William. My phone number is 84632266.
C: I'll call you when there is a free table for tomorrow evening at 8:00.
G: Thank you very much. Bye.
C: Bye.

Give It a Try

  Task 2

Listen to the following conversation and complete the form with the information you will hear.

C=Clerk   **G**=Guest

C: Good morning. Roast Duck Restaurant. May I help you?
G: I want a table in a private room for 6:00 this evening.
C: I am terribly sorry, sir. All the tables in the private rooms have been booked until 7:30.
G: Why is that?
C: Well, there is a big group arriving at 6:00. Would a reservation for 7:30 be too late?
G: Yes, I am afraid so.
C: May I suggest a table in the hall? It is also very quiet there.
G: That will be fine.
C: Would you please give me your name?
G: John Hampton.
C: Could you spell your last name for me, please?
G: It's H-A-M-P-T-O-N.
C: May I have your phone number?
G: 6622-3796.
C: For how many, sir?
G: Just two.
C: A table for two this evening at 6:00 for Mr. Hampton.
G: That's right.
C: Your table number is 16. Thank you, sir.
G: Thank you. Good-bye.

Do Extension Activities

  Activity 2

Listen to the short passage and write down what are needed for taking reservations.

   The reservation desk should be equipped with the items of: a telephone; a pen or pencil; a menu; a wine list; guest checks; dupes; logbook; a telephone number file listing employee and various emergency phone numbers; and perhaps a telephone-answering machine for recording reservation requests when the restaurant is closed.

Unit 2

Part A

Focus on Language

  Conversation

Receiving the Guests with the Reservation

 Listen to the conversation and read after it. Then try to find the answers to the questions.

C=Captain **P**=Mr. Porter

C: Good evening, madam and sir. Do you have the reservation?

P: Yes, we've reserved a table for 2 at 6 o'clock under the name of Mr. Porter.

C: Ah, Mr. Porter (*checking the reservation book*). That's right, a table for 2 at 6 o'clock. Ma'am, sir, your table is ready. Please follow me. Will this table be suitable?

P: Yes. This is nice. Thank you.

C: I'll give you a few minutes to look over the menus. Can I get you anything to drink?

P: I'd like a glass of beer, please. My wife would like ice water.

C: Good. I'll be back with your drinks.

C: (*A moment later*) Here you are: ice water for the lady, and you, sir... and here is your beer. Would you like to hear tonight's specials?

P: Sure.

  Practice 2

Fill in the blanks with the word that you hear on the recording.

G=Guest **C**=Clerk

Dialogue 1

C: Ma'am, sir, your table is ready. Please follow me.

G: Thanks.

C: Will this table be suitable?

G: Yes. This is nice.

Dialogue 2

C: Good evening, Mr. Johnson. We've been expecting you.

G: Good evening. My reserved table is ready.

C: Yes. Would you like to come with me? ... Is this table fine with you?

G: It's OK. But we prefer a table by the window.

C: I'm sorry, but the restaurant is full now. Would you care to have a drink in the lounge while you are waiting?
G: How long a wait?
C: About 15 minutes.
G: Good. Thank you.

Give It a Try

  Task 1

Listen to the recording and complete the following conversation. Then do the conversation in pairs.

G=Guest   C=Clerk

C: Good afternoon, sir. Welcome to the Flower Garden Restaurant. Have you got a reservation?
G: Yes, I reserved a table by phone yesterday morning.
C: Just a moment, please. Let me have a look at our reservation book. Oh, yes. You reserved a table for 12 at 6:30 p.m. under the name of Mr. Charles.
G: That's right, our table is ready now?
C: Yes, Mr. Charles. We've been looking forward to your coming. Where would you like to sit?
G: We prefer a private dining room.
C: Fine. We've had Bamboo Hall reserved for you. Please follow me.
G: Thank you. But the rest of our party...?
C: Don't worry. We'll direct them to the hall if they arrive.
G: Great. Thanks a lot.

Part B

Focus on Language

  Conversation

Receiving the Guests without the Reservation

 Listen to the conversation and read after it. Then try to find the answers to the questions.

C=Captain   H=Mr. Harrison

C: Good evening, sir. How many persons, please?
H: Good evening. Is there a table for 7?
C: Have you made a reservation, sir?
H: No, I'm afraid not.
C: I'm very sorry, sir. All our tables are taken. It's the peak season, you know. But if you'd like to wait, you are more than welcome to do so.
H: How long do you think we'll have to wait?

C: About 15 minutes. Would you mind waiting until it is free? We'll seat your party as soon as possible.

H: Oh... Okay.

C: Would you please tell me your name, sir?

H: Harrison.

(*After 15 minutes*)

C: Mr. Harrison?

H: Yes. Here.

C: I'm sorry to have kept you waiting. Now we have a table for you.

H: Great!

C: Would you please come with me? (*Leading them to a table in the hall*) Is this table fine with you, Mr. Harrison?

H: It's OK. But we prefer a table by the window.

C: All right. Please take your seats. Your waiter will be with you in a minute.

H: Thanks a lot.

1. Receive the guest without the reservation

 Practice 2

The following is a conversation between a guest and a waiter or waitress. Listen carefully and try to fill in the blanks with the word that you hear on the recording.

G=Guest   **W**=Waiter/Waitress

W: Good evening, sir. How many persons, please?

G: Good evening. Is there a table for 3?

W: Have you made a reservation?

G: I'm afraid not. We've just arrived.

W: I'm sorry, sir. It's the hot season. The restaurant is full now. I'm afraid we cannot seat you at the same table. Would you mind sitting separately?

G: No, thanks. We'd rather wait a moment.

3. Seating the guests who have been kept waiting for a while

Practice 1

Listen to the recording and complete the following conversation. Then do the conversation in pairs.

G=Guest   **W**=Waiter/Waitress

...

W: Mr. Black?

G: Yes. Here.

W: We're very sorry for the delay. We can seat your party now.

G: Great!

W: Would you please come with me? ...Would you like to sit on a quiet corner?

G: Nice. We've got something to talk about. Thanks a lot.

Do Extension Activities

Activity 2

The following statements are general rules for receiving the guests without the reservations. Listen carefully once and try to fill in the blanks.

➤ When there is no vacant seats left and the guests have to share a table, it is the restaurant's responsibility to obtain the consent of the two parties.

➤ For those guests who haven't got reservations, the procedure depends on the specific situation. The identity, number and motivation of the guests should also be taken into consideration.

➤ When keeping the guests waiting for free seats, it is necessary to give explanation and apology, and at the same time ensure that he or she will be informed as soon as there is a vacant table.

➤ While seating the guests who have been kept waiting, the host or hostess should also express the apology for having delayed them for a while.

Unit 3

Part A

Start You Off

 Activity 2

Listen to the guests' orders. Then read the answers below. Listen to the question again, and put a tick (√) against the right answer.

Number 1

Guest: Is that room service?

Clerk: Yes, sir, it is.

Guest: I'd like a bottle of white wine, please. It's room 101.

Clerk: Certainly, sir.

Number 2

Guest: Good evening. I'd like a whisky, please with ice.

Clerk: Certainly, sir.

Number 3

Guest: What shall I start with? Well, not the melon. Not the salad. I know. I'll have the soup.

Clerk: Thank you, madam.

Number 4

Guest: Then, let me see. I'm not very hungry, so not the steak. I'll have the fish. I prefer that to an omelet.

Clerk: Thank you, madam.

Number 5

Guest: I'd like an aperitif before dinner. I'll have a gin and tonic, please, with half a bottle of rose wine with the meal. Red wine's too heavy for me.

Clerk: Thank you, sir.

Focus on Language

 Conversation

Listen to the conversation and read after it. Then try to find the answers to the questions.

W=Waiter   G1=Guest 1   G2=Guest 2

W: Would you like an aperitif before you order?

G1: Yes, we'll all have dry martinis.

W: What would you like to start with?

G1: I'd like the smoked salmon.

G2: That sounds good. I'm going to have the caviar.

W: Here's the menu. What would you like for the entrée?

G1: Now let's see... I'll have the beef chasseur.

G2: I don't like beef very much. What is noisettes Milanese exactly?

W: That's lamb cooked with herbs and served with spaghetti.

G2: That sounds interesting. I'll try that.

W: Very good, sir. Any vegetables?

G1: I'll have peas and potatoes.

G2: Just chicory for me, please.

W: Thank you very much. I'll be back in a minute.

1. Asking the guest if having an aperitif or an hors d'oeuvre

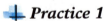 Practice 1

Listen to the recording and you'll hear some guests' requests. Number the sentence which meets the guests' needs.

Number 1

Waiter: What would you like to begin with?

Guest: I want something hot to start with.

Waiter: Would you like the soup, madam?

Number 2

Waiter: What would you like as a starter?

Guest: I like fish as a starter.

Waiter: Would you like the smoked salmon, madam?

Number 3

Waiter: Would you like an aperitif before you order?

Guest: Can you recommend a German white wine?

Waiter: Would you like the Baden dry, sir, or perhaps the Piesporter?

Number 4

Waiter: Would you like an aperitif before you order?

Guest: Can you suggest a French white wine?

Waiter: Would you like the Bordeaux Blanc de Blancs, madam, or perhaps the Chablis?

Number 5

Waiter: What would you start with?

Guest: Have you got a rose wine?

Waiter: Would you like the Anjou Rose, madam?

4. Taking the orders for food or drink

 Practice 1

Listen to the recording and complete the following conversations.

1. A: What would you like to order?

   B: I'll have a glass of white wine, please.

2. A: What would you like to order?

   B: I'll start with the oysters, please, and then the duck.

3. A: What would you like to order?

   B: The mushrooms, followed by the scallops for me.

4. A: What would you like to order?

   B: Soup, please.

5. A: What would you like to order?

   B: A whisky on the rocks for me, please.

6. A: What would you like to order?

   B: I'll have the chicken, with peas, mushrooms and tomatoes.

Give It a Try

  Task 1

Some guests are ordering lunch. Listen to their orders. Then read the answers in your book and make a tick (√) against the right answer.

Number 1

I don't really want any of these aperitifs here. What I'd really like is a nice, cool beer, on a hot day like this.

Number 2

A sherry for me, please. Dry.

Number 3

   Prawns are one of my favorites. I'll have the king prawns.

Number 4

   Now let's see. Something to start with. I'll try the pike mousse, as I haven't had that for years.

Number 5

   Not moussaka today. I had that last night. I'll try the hare, I think.

Number 6

   Chicken is what I'd like. I'll take the chicken chasseur.

Number 7

   Spare ribs, please.

Number 8

   Something filling, but not too filling. I'll have the goulash, thanks.

  Task 2

Look at the menu below. Listen to the guests ordering their meals and write down the orders.

1. I think I'll have the prawn cocktail to start with, please, and then the beef salad.
2. My wife will have the sole, please, and I'll have the lamb cutlets. And we'd also like a bottle of Anjou Rosé.
3. It's one soup, and two smoked salmons. And then one fillet steak, one chicken Kiev and a sole. Also, we'll have a bottle of the Chablis, please.
4. Two Salades Nicoises, one melon and smoked salmon to begin with. And then—what was it? Oh yes, one omelette, one lamb cutlets, one chicken salad and a ham salad. And we'll have a bottle of the Niersteiner Domtal and one of the Cotes du Rhone. That's all, thanks.
5. I'll take the pate to start with, and my husband wants the smoked salmon. He'll have the fillet steak after that, and I'll have the chicken salad. And a bottle of Franken Sylvaner to go with it.
6. Three melons and a pate, followed by one lamb cutlets and three soles. And we'll have the Goldener Oktober to start with, and then the Mouton Cadet to follow. OK? Thanks.

  Task 3

Complete the following conversation according to what you will hear.

C=Clerk   **G**=Guest

C: What would you like to order, sir?

G: My wife will have a Sherry to start with, and I'll have a Gin, please.

C: Certainly, sir. A Sherry and a Gin. And will you be having a starter?

G: Sure. The curried prawns and the clams, please.

C: One curried prawns, one clams.

G: And after that I'll have the hare, and my wife would like the roast duck.

C: And a hare and a roast duck. Thank you, sir.

Tapescript

Do Extension Activities

 Activity 1

Listen to the conversation and make a tick(√) where appropriate.

W: Look. What a good selection of world famous liquors and wines we have here! You see, there are different kinds of whisky on that shelf. They are Bourbon, Scotch, and Rye.

M: Are those whiskies on the right, too?

W: No, they are world famous brandies. We have Remy Martin and Hennessey.

M: What are they made from?

W: You mean brandy? They are made from grapes. But whiskies are distilled from grain.

M: Then, what about wines?

W: We have Bordeaux wines, Burgundy wine and Californian wine. They come from different countries.

M: Are they also made from grapes?

W: Yes, they are. But they are still wines while brandy is distilled.

M: I see.

Part B

Start You Off

 Activity 2

Listen to the description of the four major cuisines in China and match the cuisines in column A with the features in column B.

    There are many regional cuisines in China. There are generally four major cuisines, or say, four styles. They are Shandong style, Guangdong style, Sichuan style and Huaiyang style. What are the main differences? Briefly speaking, Shandong food is heavy while Guangdong food is light and fresh. Huaiyang food is well-known for its cutting technique and original flavor. Most Sichuan dishes are hot and spicy.

Focus on Language

 Conversation

We'd Like to Try Some Chinese Food

   Listen to the conversation and read after it. Then try to find the answers to the questions.

C=Clerk **G**=Guest

C: What would you like to order, sir?

G: I'd like to try some Chinese food.

C: Have you had any Chinese food before?

G: No, I haven't.

C: We serve different styles of Chinese food here. But I'm not sure which style you prefer.

G: I have no idea about it.

C: Well, Cantonese food is rather light, Shandong food is heavy, and Sichuan food is usually spicy and hot.

G: Oh, I see. I'd rather have hot food.

C: If so, I suggest you have a taste of Sichuan dishes. Most Sichuan dishes are spicy and hot. But they taste differently.

G: Really. So what's your recommendation for me?

C: I think Mapo Tofu, Sichuan style and shredded pork with chili sauce are quite special.

G: All right, I'll have them.

C: Would you like to have rice to go with them?

G: Yes, please.

Language Tips

1. Asking if ready to order

Practice 1

Listen to the recording and make a tick (√) according to the conversation.

Number 1

Waiter: Are you ready to order, sir?

Guest: Yes. I'd like to try some Chinese food.

Number 2

Waiter: Have you decided yet, sir?

Guest: Not yet, we're still looking at the menu.

Number 3

Waiter: Would you like to order now?

Guest: Yes. We'd like to try some Guangdong food.

Number 4

Waiter: May I take your order now?

Guest: No, we haven't decided yet.

Number 5

Waiter: Have you chosen what you'd like?

Guest: Not yet. We are not sure what to order.

Tapescript

Give It a Try

 Task 1

Listen to the conversation between the guest and the waiter. Tick (√) the information about what the waiter will recommend and what the guest will take.

Waiter: Good evening, sir. Are you ready to order now?
Guest: Yes. I have a poor appetite. I'd like to take some light food.
Waiter: I see. How about the braised turtle with garlic? It is excellent.
Guest: I had turtle for lunch. Please recommend something else for me.
Waiter: Would you care for the steamed minced pork balls, the Chef's recommendation for today?
Guest: Sounds delicious. I'll take that. I also want to enjoy some soup.
Waiter: How about the bird's nest and shredded chicken soup? It is very nutritious and I believe it will do good to your health.
Guest: Wonderful. I'll have that.
Waiter: Would you like some baked pancakes with your soup? It's marvelous.
Guest: Fine, two pancakes, please.
Waiter: Anything else?
Guest: No more, thanks.

 Task 2

Listen to the following conversation and write down the recommendation made by the waiter.

Waiter: Good evening, madam. May I help you with your order?
Guest: We'll have whatever you recommend.
Waiter: In this weather, I recommend the hot pot, madam. Our hot pot is prepared with unique spices from a recipe passed down from our ancestors. It's marvelous.
Guest: All right. There are four of us, so a medium size will be enough. Could you recommend some meat?
Waiter: We've got a choice of mutton and beef. Which would you prefer?
Guest: Mutton, please. What kind of vegetables do you recommend?
Waiter: Now, it is the season for Chinese cabbage. Would you like some? And I suggest some white gourd as well.
Guest: That's fine. Thank you for your recommendation.
Waiter: You are welcome.

Unit 4

Part A

Focus on Language

 Conversation

How Would You Like Your Steak Cooked

 Listen to the conversation and read after it. Then try to find the answers to the questions.

W=Waiter　G1=Guest 1　G2=Guest 2

W: Are you ready to order, sir?

G1: Yes. I think I'll have the steak.

G2: Steak for me, too, please.

W: How would you like them cooked?

G1: I don't like my steak too underdone. Make mine well done, please.

G2: Rare for me, please.

W: Fine. What would you like to go with your steaks?

G1: Chips and a green salad, please.

G2: I'll have chips. And peas, if you have them.

W: And what would you like to drink? Bottled beer or wine?

G1: We'd like wine better.

W: Would you rather have sweet wine or dry wine?

G1: I prefer sweet wine.

G2: I think dry wine would do nicely.

W: All right, I'll be back soon?

1. Asking and giving special instruction on food

Model 1

A: Is your steak rare **enough**?

B: I'm afraid it's **too** rare. I can't eat it.

Model 2

A: Is your steak **too** well-done?

B: No, it's not well-done **enough**. I like it **very** well-done.

In a similar way, answer the following questions.

1. Is your wine too dry? No, it's not dry enough. I like it very dry.

2. Is your conscons spicy enough? I'm afraid it's too spicy. I can't eat it.

3. Is your coffee strong enough? I'm afraid it's too strong. I can't drink it.

4. Is your martini too weak? No, it's not weak enough. I like them very weak.

2. Asking if having anything to go with food

 Practice 1

Look at the list of vegetables given below. Guests can choose which vegetables they want. Listen to the guests ordering their vegetables and write down the ones they want.

1. Waiter: What would you like with the cold chicken?
   Guest: And with the cold chicken, I'll have lettuce, tomatoes, beans and carrots, please.
2. Waiter: And what would you like with the roast duck, madam?
   Guest: Let me see, er, roast potatoes, I think, spinach and sweet bell pepper. Yes, that'll do fine, thank you.
3. Waiter: What kind of salad would you like, sir?
   Guest: Celery, I love celery, and let's say tomatoes and broad beans. That'll do me nicely.
4. Waiter: And for vegetables, sir?
   Guest: Mushrooms, chips, peas and tomatoes, please.
5. Waiter: Have you decided on your salad, madam?
   Guest: Yes. I'll take the lettuce, cucumber and carrots, please.
6. Waiter: What would you like as vegetables, madam?
   Guest: Let me see. Let's say leeks, boiled potatoes and some cauliflower.
7. Waiter: And as a salad to go with that, madam?
   Guest: Something simple. Just tomatoes and broad beans, please.
8. Waiter: And what vegetables would you like with your roast lamb, sir?
   Guest: Cabbage, chips and, er, what about some broad beans? Oh, and some broccoli. I'm hungry this evening.

3. Asking what the guest prefers for drinks

 Practice 1

Read through the Bar List. Some guests are ordering drinks. Listen to their orders and read the answers in your book. Make a tick (√) against the right order.

Number 1

Guest: I'd like a vermouth, please, a Cinzano.

Number 2

Guest: Now, let's see, what shall I have? I know, a gin, please, regular, with tonic.

Number 3

Guest: I think I'll have a vodka. A Stolichnaya, please.

Number 4

Guest: I rather fancy a whisky, a rye whisky. OK?

Number 5

Guest: I don't want anything alcoholic. I'll take a Perrier water. With ice and lemon.

Number 6

Guest: For me, a brandy. Hm, not the Martell, and not the Remy Martin three star. Make it the Remy Martin VSOP, would you?

Number 7

Guest: A sherry for me, I don't like cream sherry very much, so that leaves a Tio Pepe or a Croft Original. The Tio Pepe, I think.

Number 8

Guest: I take it you have red, rosé and white house wines by the glass?

Barman: Yes, sir.

Guest: Red's too heavy, rosé I don't really go for. The white, please.

Give It a Try

Task 1

Listen to the recording and tick (√) the food or drink ordered by the guests.

Conversation 1

Guest: Good morning. The American breakfast, please.

Waiter: Certainly, madam. Would you prefer tomato, orange or grapefruit juice?

Guest: Oh, I think the grapefruit, please.

Waiter: How would you like your eggs?

Guest: Fried, I think.

Waiter: And would you rather have bacon, ham or sausage, madam?

Guest: Sausage, please. Oh, and tea.

Waiter: Would you like a croissant?

Guest: No, I think the Danish pastry.

Waiter: Thank you, madam.

Conversation 2

Guest: Ah, good.

Waiter: What can I get you, sir?

Guest: I'll have a fresh grapefruit juice.

Waiter: A fresh grapefruit juice, sir, yes.

Guest: Coffee, and a cheese omelette.

Waiter: A cheese omelette. Anything else, sir?

Guest: Er, yes, I'll have a yoghurt, too.

Waiter: And a yoghurt. Thank you, sir.

Conversation 3

Guest: Morning.

Waiter: Good morning, sir.

Guest: The healthy breakfast, I think.

Waiter: Certainly, sir. And would you rather have tomato, orange or grapefruit juice?

Guest: Orange, I think.

Waiter: Oatmeal or yoghurt, sir?

Guest: Oatmeal, please. And coffee.

Waiter: With or without caffeine, sir?

Guest: Without.

Waiter: Thank you, sir.

  Task 2

Listen to the conversation and complete it with the information that you will hear.

G=Guest   W=waiter

W: Would you care to order now, sir?

G: Yes, please. Well, I'll have the baked salmon.

W: Good. And what kind of potatoes would you like with that?

G: I prefer boiled potatoes.

W: Any vegetables?

G: Cauliflower... Oh, no. I think I would rather have spinach.

W: The spinach. Yes, sir. Any soup or salad?

G: Salad, please.

W: What kind of dressing would you like on it: French, Russian or blue cheese?

G: I'll take the French.

W: And what would you like to drink? Bottled beer or wine?

G: Beer, please.

Do Extension Activities

 Activity 2

Listen to the conversation and make a tick (√) against the drinks offered by the bartender.

1. Guest: I'd like a vermouth, please.
   Waiter: Would you like a Cinzano or a Martini?
2. Guest: A whisky, please.
   Waiter: Would you like bourbon, rye or malt, sir?
3. Guest: Some kind of aperitif is what I'd like.
   Waiter: Would you like a Pernod or a sherry, sir?
4. Guest: I could do with a brandy.
   Waiter: Would you like a Louis Bernard, a Martell or a Remy Martin, madam?
5. Guest: I want something soft. What have you got?
   Waiter: Would you like a juice or a mineral water, madam?

6. Guest: A sherry, please.

   Waiter: Would you like a Tio Pepe, a Croft Original or a Bristol Cream, sir?

Part B

Focus on Language

I Would Like Some Breakfast in My Room

 Listen to the conversation and read after it. Then try to find the answers to the questions.

W=Waiter   G=Guest

W: Room Service. Good morning. Can I help you?

G: Good morning. I'd like some breakfast in my room.

W: May I have your room number, please?

G: Room 201.

W: What would you like to have?

G: I'd like some bacon, two boiled eggs, toast, and a cup of black coffee.

W: How would you like your eggs, sir?

G: Lightly done.

W: Is that all?

G: That's it.

W: All right, I'll bring them to your room right away.

   (A few minutes later.)

W: Room Service, may I come in?

G: Come in, please.

W: Mr. Wilson?

G: Yes. Just put them on the table over there.

W: All right. Here are your bacon, boiled eggs, toast and a cup of black coffee. The bacon and toast are 8 *yuan*, the eggs are 3 *yuan* each, and the coffee is 3.50 *yuan*. That comes to 17.50 *yuan*, plus 10% service. So the total is 19.25 *yuan*. Here is the bill.

G: Thank you. Can I have it charged to my account, please?

W: Certainly, sir. Please sign here. Thank you for using room service. Good-bye.

G: Bye.

1. Offering help and ordering room service

Practice 1

Some guests are ordering food. Listen to their orders and then complete the following short conversations.

1. A: Room Service. May I help you?

   B: I'd like a bowl of soup, please, the consommé. In Room 462.

2. A: Room Service. Can I help you?
   B: Could you send two French onion soups to Room 201, please?
3. A: Room Service. May I help you?
   B: This is Room 263. Can you send up a Chef's salad as soon as possible, please? I'm in a hurry.
4. A: Room Service. Can I help you?
   B: This is Room 656. We'd like the cold roast beef, please.
5. A: Room Service. May I help you?
   B: May I have a minute steak, please? It's Room 101.
6. A: Room Service. Can I help you?
   B: Room 632 here. We'd like something to eat for the children, please. The grilled sausages, for one, and a veal steak.
7. A: Room Service. May I help you?
   B: A fried fish for my daughter, please, and a minute steak for me. It's Room 107.
8. A: Room Service. Can I help you?
   B: This is Room 44. I'd like you to send up a tomato soup and a hamburger, please.

Practice 2

Now listen to these guests. They are ordering meals. Write down the orders and the room numbers according to what you will hear.

W=Waiter   **G**=Guest

1. W: Good evening. Room Service. May I help you?
   G: Good evening. I'd like the tomato soup, followed by the ragout of chicken, please. It's Room 111.
2. W: Room Service. May I help you?
   G: Could you send up two consommés, one ragout of chicken and a minute steak to Room 425, please?
3. W: Room Service. May I help you?
   G: Yes. This is Room 212. We'd like two cold roast beef salads, please, and one hamburger. And a bottle of red wine, your house wine, to go with it.
4. W: Room Service. May I help you?
   G: It's Room 808. Something for my children, please. Two fried fish and a veal steak, and also three ice creams.
5. W: Room Service. May I help you?
   G: I'd like you to get me a "Cordon Bleu" and a Chef's salad, please, and three veal steaks. We're in Room 108.
6. W: Room Service. May I help you?
   G: A bottle of white wine, two Chef's salad, one grilled sausage and an ice cream, please. That's 501, the room number.

English for Food and Beverages

Give It a Try

 Task 1

Look at the Breakfast menu. Listen to the recording and put a tick (√) against the right order. Then make conversations of ordering breakfast in pairs.

1. Good morning. I'll have the continental breakfast, please.
2. I'd like the American breakfast. Grapefruit juice, scrambled eggs with ham.
3. The healthy breakfast for me, please. With orange juice. Oh, and yoghurt, and tea.
4. I'll take the orange juice, fresh that is, some coffee and a mushroom omelet, please.
5. I'll have a hot chocolate, and poached eggs, please.
6. The American breakfast for me. Tomato juice, and fried eggs with bacon.
7. I'll have the continental breakfast. Grapefruit juice, croissant and coffee, please.
8. I'd like the healthy breakfast. Let me see, yes, I'll have the tomato juice, oatmeal and caffeine free coffee. That'll do me nicely.

 Task 2

Listen to the conversation and complete it with the appropriate words you will hear.

G=Guest   **W**=Waiter

W: Good evening. Room Service. Can I help you?
G: Good evening. I'd like to order a salad, a T-bone steak and a bottle of red wine. What do you have for salad?
W: We have lettuce salad and Chef's salad today.
G: I'll take the lettuce salad.
W: What kind of dressing on your salad?
G: Thousand Islands, please.
W: All right. And one T-bone steak. What shall I bring you for wine? Sweet or dry?
G: Dry, please.
W: Will there be anything else?
G: No, thanks.
W: May I have your name and room number, please?
G: Catherine Marks. It's Room 1919.
W: Fine. Room 1919, one lettuce salad with Thousand Islands dressing, one T-bone steak, a bottle of dry red wine.
G: That's it.
W: Thank you for calling. I'll send your order up as soon as possible.

Do Extension Activities

 Activity 1

Mr. Robert is staying in a hotel. He finds the mini-bar in his room is nearly empty, so he makes a phone to the Room Service, asking for more replenishment. Listen to the conversation and write down the items for replenishment.

C=Clerk   **G**=Guest

C: Good morning, Room Service. May I help you?

G: Yes. I need more snacks. There isn't any in my mini-bar.

C: We have mixed nuts and potato chips.

G: Very good. Would you please send up some?

C: Sure. May I send some more drinks, sir?

G: Yes, three wines, four soda waters and two cokes, please.

C: No problem. Your name and room number, sir?

G: I'm John Smith in Room 709.

C: OK. Some mixed nuts and potato chips, three wines, four soda waters and two cokes to Room 709.

G: Thank you very much.

Unit 5

Part A

Focus on Language

 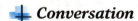

 Ordering Dessert

W=Waiter/Waitress   **G**=Guest

W: Have you found everything satisfactory, madam?

G: Yes, everything is good. Thank you.

W: Would you like some dessert, madam?

G: Yes, I think so. Could I see the dessert menu?

W: Sure, madam. Here you are.

G: What do you recommend? I can't decide.

W: How about apple tarts? They are very popular in our restaurant.

G: Well, thank you. I'd like an apple tart and a strawberry ice cream.

W: Yes, madam. An apple tart and a strawberry ice cream.

English for Food and Beverages

Language Tips

2. Asking what the guest would like for dessert

Practice 2

Tom and his friends are dining in a dessert restaurant. Listen to the conversation and try to find out the dessert they ordered. Fill in the form with what you hear on the recording.

——What would you like for your dessert, Tom?
——I'd like a lemon pie and a vanilla ice-cream.
——What would you like for your dessert, Mary?
——I'd like two pineapple pies and a coffee ice-cream.
——What would you like for your dessert, Louis?
——I'd like three oatmeal cookies and some fruit puddings.
——What would you like for your dessert, Darth?
——I'd like a black forest cake and a mango ice-cream.

5. Asking for and giving recommendation

Practice 2

Complete the following conversation with what you will hear on the recording. Then take turns doing the role-play with your partner.

W: Is everything to your satisfaction, sir?
G: Yes, everything is good.
W: Would you like anything else?
G: Yes. I think I will have some dessert now.
W: What would you like for your dessert, sir?
G: Would you please recommend some?
W: May I recommend haw jellies. They are very tasty.
G: That will be marvelous! I'd like to try some. Thank you.

Give It a Try

 Task 3

Complete the following conversation with what you will hear on the recording, then do the role-play with your partner. One is the waiter, the other is the guest.

G=Guest   **W**=Waiter

W: How do you like your meal, sir?
G: I like it very much, Chinese food is really delicious!
W: Would you like to try something else? Some dessert?
G: Yes, I would like to try some local ones. But I wonder if you could recommend some.

W: Well, there are many traditional desserts in Beijing. They are Lǘdagunr, pea flour cakes, haw jellies etc. I think you can choose from the dessert trolley. May I bring it over for you, sir?
G: Yes, thank you. That's very kind of you. (1 minute later)
G: What is this?
W: It's called Lǘdagunr, that is the glutinous rice rolls with sweet bean flour.
G: Is it the local dessert in Beijing?
W: Yes, it is. It's very popular among the local people in Beijing.
G: Oh, really? Then I'd like to try some.
W: Yes, sir. I'm sure you will enjoy it.

Do Extension Activities

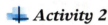 *Activity 2*

Fill in the blanks in the following passage with the information you will hear on the recording.

The origins of ice cream can be traced back to at least the 4th century B.C. Early references include the Roman emperor Nero (A.D. 37—68) who ordered ice to be brought from the mountains and combined with fruit toppings, and King Tang (A.D. 618—907) of Shang, China who had a method of creating ice and milk concoctions. It is also said that Alexander the Great preferred ice flavored with honey and nectars after his meals. This was also served to his guests after their meals. This hints the popularity of desserts even in those days. Over time, recipes for ices, sherbets, and milk ices evolved and served in the fashionable Italian and French royal courts.

Part B

Focus on Language

  *Conversation*

Ordering Dessert

W=Waiter/Waitress   G=Guest

W: How was the food, madam?
G: Very delicious. Thank you.
W: Would you like anything else?
G: Yes, I'd like to try some dessert. Could you please show me the dessert menu?
W: Yes, madam.
G: I'd like to have some apple tarts and one vanilla ice-cream.
W: Sorry, madam, there are not any apple tarts left. But there are many other desserts you can choose from the menu. Would you please try something else?
G: Well, then make it one chocolate pie.
W: Yes, madam. One chocolate pie and one vanilla ice-cream.

Give It a Try

  Task 2

Listen to the conversation and answer the following questions.

W=Waiter   **G1**=Guest 1   **G2**=Guest 2   **G3**=Guest 3

W: Is everything all right with your meal, madam and sirs?
G1: Yes, everything is fine and we would like to have some dessert now.
W: What would you like, sir?
G1: I'd like to have two mango tarts and a coffee ice-cream.
W: Yes, sir. Two mango tarts and a coffee ice-cream. And for you, sir?
G2: I'd like to have some lemon puddings.
W: I'm sorry, sir. I'm afraid there are not any lemon puddings left. Would you like to try something else?
G2: Well, what would you recommend?
W: May I recommend raspberry bread puddings? They are very popular.
G2: Ok, then bring me two raspberry bread puddings.
W: How about you, madam? What would you like for your dessert?
G3: I don't think I would have any dessert. They are fattening and I'm on a diet. Thank you.

Do Extension Activities

  Activity 2

Part I. Spot Dictation

Fill in the blanks in the following passage with the information you will hear on the recording.

　　The word dessert is most commonly used for this course in U.S., Canada, Australia, and Ireland, while sweet, pudding or afters would be more typical terms in the UK and some other Common Wealth countries. According to Debrett, pudding is the proper term, dessert is only to be used if the course consists of fruit, and sweet is colloquial.

　　Although the custom of eating fruits and nuts after a meal may be very old, dessert as a standard part of a western meal is a relatively recent development. Before the rise of the middle class in the 19th century, and the mechanization of the sugar industry, sweets were a privilege of the aristocracy, or a rare holiday treat. As sugar became cheaper and more readily available, the development and popularity of dessert spread accordingly.

Unit 6

Part A

Focus on Language

  **Conversation**

Paying in Cash

W=Waiter/Waitress   **G**=Guest

G: Waiter! The bill, please.
W: Yes, sir, Just a moment, please. (Two minutes later) Here is your bill, sir. It comes to one hundred and sixty eight *yuan* (RMB 168) altogether.
G: Here you are.
W: Thank you. Please wait for a moment, I'll be right back with your change and receipt. (5 minutes later)
W: Here is your change of thirty two *yuan* and your receipt.
G: Thanks.
W: Have a nice evening.

4. Asking and telling if traveller's check is accepted

  **Practice 1**

Paying by Traveller's Checks

W=Waiter/Waitress   **G**=Guest

G: Waitress! May I have the bill, please?
W: Yes, sir.
G: Do you accept traveller's cheques?
W: Yes, if you can give us your address and some identification.
G: Will my driver's license be all right?
W: That's quite all right.
G: Should I put my name and address on the back of the cheque?
W: Yes, please write your name in printed words.
G: Okay, thank you.

5. Asking and telling if paying separate bills or one bill

Practice 2

Fill in the blanks in the following passage with the information you will hear on the recording.

W=Waiter/Waitress   G1=Guest 1   G2=Guest 2

G1: Waiter! May I have the bill, please?
W: Sure. It comes to 258 dollars altogether. Would you care to have one bill or separate bills?
G1: It's on me this time.
G2: Oh, no. It's my treat, I insist.
G1: Well, we'd better make it a Dutch treat.
G2: It's a good idea.
G1: Here is 130 dollars. Keep the change, please.
G2: Here is 130 dollars. Don't bother with the change.
W: Thank you, sir. Do come again please.

Give It a Try

  Task 2

Listen to the conversation and answer the following questions.

W=Waitress   G=Guest

W: Would you like anything else, sir?
G: No, thank you. I'll take the bill now.
W: Just a second, sir. Your bill comes to 576 *yuan* altogether.
G: May I use credit card?
W: What kind have you got?
G: Eurocard.
W: I'm sorry, sir. We don't accept that card. We only take American Express, Master Card and Visa.
G: May I use traveller's cheques.
W: I'm sorry, sir. I'm afraid we don't honor traveller's cheques either. Will you please pay in cash?
G: Well, okay. Here you are. Keep the change, please.
W: It's very kind of you, sir. But we don't accept tips. A 15% service charge has already been added to your bill. Thank you all the same.
   (5 minutes later)
W: Here is your change of 24 *yuan* and your receipt.
G: Thanks.
W: Thank you for coming.

Tapescript

Do Extension Activities

 Activity 1

Fill in the blanks with what you will hear on the recording.

In a Chinese Restaurant

G=Guest　　　　　W=Waiter

G: Waiter! May I have the bill, please?

W: Yes, madam. How would you like to pay the bill?

G: Do you accept U.S. dollars?

W: Yes, we do. But we only have Chinese *yuan* for change. The exchange rate is one hundred U.S. Dollar to seven hundred eighty five Chinese *yuan*. Besides, there's 3% handling charge for paying U.S. dollars in cash. Do you mind that?

G: Well, may I use my credit card?

W: What kind are you holding, madam?

G: Master Card. Do you honor it?

W: Yes, madam.

G: That'll be fine. I'll pay the bill by my credit card. Here you are.

W: Thank you. I'll be right back.

　　(2 minutes later)

W: Could you sign your name here, please?

G: Certainly.

W: Thank you, madam. Here is your card and your copy.

Part B

Focus on Language

  Conversation

Explaining the Charge

Listen to the conversation and read after it. Then do the following conversation in pairs and try to find answers to the questions above.

W=Waiter/Waitress　　　　　G=Guest

G: Waitress.

W: Yes, Madam.

G: There seems to be some mistakes on my bill. What is this extra $ 2 for?

W: May I have a look at your bill, Madam?

　　(The guest shows the bill to the waitress.)

W: This is the charge for the cold towels.

G: The towels?
W: Yes, the cold towels. (Pointing to the towels on the table.)
G: Oh, I see.

Language Tips

2. Showing disagreement to a bill and explaining a charge

Practice 1

Listen to the conversation and read after it. Then do the role-play in pairs.

G: Excuse me.
W: Yes, Madam.
G: I have a question about the bill. I think it should come to 480 *yuan* altogether, but the bill here is for 552 *yuan*.
W: Oh, yes. Let me explain that for you, Madam. We add 5% tax and there's a 10% service charge added to each bill.
G: Well, I wasn't aware of that.
W: I'm sorry about that. There's a note at the bottom of the menu explaining our policy. I should have explained it to you.
G: I am afraid I haven't enough cash on me. Do you honor credit card?
W: What kind are you holding, Madam?
G: Master Card.
W: That'll be fine.
G: Here you are.
W: Thank you, Madam. Just a moment, please.
   (2 minutes later)
W: Could you sign your name here, please?
G: Certainly.
W: Thank you. Here is your card and your copy.

3. Telling you were overcharged and checking the bill for the guest

 ## Practice 2

Fill in the blanks with what you will hear on the recording. Then do the conversation in pairs.

W=Waitress   G=Guest

G: Waitress. The bill, please.
W: Yes, sir. Here it is. Your bill comes to two hundred and seventy one dollars altogether.
G: The bill seems a little high to me. I think I was overcharged. Can you kindly break the bill down for me?
W: I'd be happy to. One hundred and forty dollars for the food, eighty five dollars for the Champaign and forty six dollars for the beer. Is that right, sir?

G: I'm afraid not. I didn't order any beer.

W: I am sorry, sir. I'll ask the cashier to check it up. Excuse me for a moment.

W: I'm awfully sorry, sir. We put somebody else's consumption into your bill. We do apologize for the mistake.

G: That's all right.(5 minutes later.)

W: Here is your bill. Two hundred and twenty five dollars.

4. Telling there is a wrong change and making an apology for it

 Practice 1

Fill in the blanks with what you will hear on the recording. Then do the conversation in pairs.

W=Waitress   **G**=Guest

G: Excuse me, waitress.

W: Yes, sir.

G: I'm afraid you shortchanged me. How much is the total of the bill?

W: It totals ￥310.

G: I gave you ￥350. I think you should have given me ￥40 for the change. But you gave me ￥20 only. You shortchanged me ￥20.

W: I'm sorry, sir. May I check the bill for you, please? ... Oh, you are right. I'm sorry for the mistake.I do apologize. Here is the rest of the change.

Do Extension Activities

 Activity 1

Listen to the conversation and answer the questions.

Man: Waitress, the bill, please.

Waitress: Yes, sir, just a moment. (2 minutes later)
　　　　　　May I know who is paying, please?

Man: Give it to me, please.

Waitress: Here is your bill, sir. Your bill totals 693 *yuan*.

Woman: This costs more than we have expected. I think we were overcharged. Can you kindly break it down for us?

Waitress: Sure. 450 *yuan* for food, 160 *yuan* for the red wine, and 20 *yuan* for two bottles of coconut juice.

Woman: Would you stop here, please? We didn't order coconut juice.

Waitress: I am sorry, Madam. I will ask the cashier to check it up.

Woman: Wait a moment.What this figure for? (Pointing to an item on the bill)The 63 *yuan*?

Waitress: Oh, this figure is for the service charge. I am afraid there is a 10% service charge.

Woman: Oh, I see.

English for Food and Beverages

(5 minutes later, the waiter comes back to the guest.)

Waitress: We are terribly sorry, sir and madam. We made a mistake, we put somebody else's consumption into your bill. We are terribly busy at this hour of this particular day, you know. We do apologize for the mistake.

Man: That's all right.

Waitress: Here is your bill.

Man: Do you accept Visa Card?

Waitress: Yes, sir.

Man: Here you are.

Waitress: Thank you.

Unit 7

Part A

Focus on Language

  Conversation

Booking a Table at the Bar on the Telephone

 Listen to the conversation and read after it. Then try to find the answers to the questions.

C=Reservation Clerk   **G**=Guest

C: Good morning. Sunny Day Bar. May I help you?

G: I'd like to reserve a table for a party on Valentine's Day, please.

C: Certainly, sir. For how many people, please?

G: Ten. My old friends are coming to see me then.

C: At what time can we expect you and your friends?

G: Around 20:30.

C: I see. Would you like a table in the lounge or in a private room?

G: A private room is preferred.

C: Certainly sir. We'll have Sunflower Hall reserved for you. Will that be fine? May I have your name and telephone number, please?

G: Sure, it's Larry. My mobile phone number is 13901390139.

C: Mr. Larry, 13901390139... thank you. By the way, we can only keep your room till 10:00 pm.

G: OK. I see.

C: Thank you. We look forward to serving you.

Tapescript

2. Receiving guests appropriately

 Practice 1

Listen to the conversation and fill in the blanks with the words that you will hear on the recording.

G=Guest   **C**=Clerk

C: Good evening, sir. <u>Welcome to</u> Beach Resort Bar. Do you have a <u>reservation</u>?

G: Yes. I've reserved a table last Sunday.

C: May I have your <u>name</u>, please?

G: <u>Edward</u>.

C: How many persons, please?

G: A table for <u>six</u>.

C: This way, please. A waiter will come soon to take your order.

G: Thank you.

C: My pleasure.

3. Showing guests to their seats

  Practice

Go over the model expressions above. Listen to the conversation and do it in pairs.

G=Guest   **C**=Clerk

C: Good evening, sir. Welcome to Shining-Star Bar. Have you made a reservation, please?

G: Yes, I've booked a table for six.

C: May I have your name, please?

G: MacBeth.

C: Where would you like to sit?

G: We prefer a table on the roof, where we can enjoy the moonlight.

C: I'm afraid the table is not available now. How about one near the pool?

G: OK. It's fine.

C: This way, please. A waitress will come soon to take your order.

G: Thank you.

C: You're welcome.

4. Asking what guests want to drink

  *Practice*

Listen to the conversation and try to answer the questions given below.

1. What does the clerk recommend to the guest?
2. What does the guest order?
3. What kind of salad does the guest order?
4. What is House Specialty?

C=Clerk   **G**=Guest

C: May I take your order now, sir?

G: Ur... I don't know much about the drinks here. Can you recommend something to us?

C: Certainly. How about Yanjing Beer. It's not too strong and quite popular in Beijing.

G: I'll take it. What goes with the beer?

C: Some snack or salad will okay. Would you like to have some salad with it?

G: Fine. I'll take the light one.

C: Would you like to try our House Specialty?

G: No, thanks. It's enough for us two.

C: OK. Thank you.

Give It a Try

  Task 1

The clerk is taking a reservation by phone. Listen to the recording and fill in the form according to the conversation.

C=Clerk   **G**=Guest

C: Good afternoon. Sunflower Bar. May I help you?

G: I'd like to reserve a table for Christmas Eve, please.

C: For how many people, sir?

G: Five, my colleagues and I.

C: When can we expect you, sir?

G: About 10:00 pm, Friday evening.

C: I see. Where would you prefer to have your table?

G: On the roof, please.

C: OK. May I have your name, sir?

G: Mr. Jenkins. And my phone number is 65542849.

C: Mr. Jenkins, phone number is 65542849. A table on the roof for five. Around 10:00 pm. Is that correct?

G: Exactly, thank you.

C: We look forward to serving you. Thanks for calling.

 Task 2

Listen to the recording and complete the following conversation.

G=Guest   **C**=Clerk

C: Good evening, sir. Welcome to <u>Oracle Bar</u>. How many persons, please?

G: A table for <u>three</u>, please?

C: Do you have a <u>reservation</u>?

G: No, we don't.

C: Could you please wait a moment? I'll go and see if tables are <u>available</u> or not.

How about this table <u>by the window</u>, sir?

G: Fine. Thanks.

C: This way, please.

Part B

Focus on Language

  Conversation

Taking Orders at the Bar

Listen to the conversation and read after it. Then try to find the answers to the questions.

Clerk: What may I offer you, ladies and gentlemen?
Bill: I don't know what I want. I'm not really a drinker.
Clerk: An aperitif or some white wine?
Bill: Um... a Sunrise Beer.
Clerk: I don't believe we know that one. How about our special cocktail?
Bill: That sounds good. How about you, Sally?
Sally: I don't drink at all. Do you serve soft drinks?
Clerk: Of course, ma'am. But how about a non-alcoholic cocktail?
Sally: It sounds interesting. I'll take that.
Clerk: What would you like to drink, gentleman?
Tom: Well, none of that stuff they're drinking, eh John?
John: No, Tom. We'll have the usual beer, I suppose?
Tom: Yes, I'm very thirsty.
Clerk: Any special brand, sir?
John: What about your local brew? I hear it's good.
Clerk: It is Five Star Beer. Bottled or draught?
Bill: Let's try the draught.
Clerk: Fine. One special cocktail and one non-alcoholic cocktail for the ladies and two draught Five Star Beer.
John: Could we have some snacks?
Clerk: Certainly, I'll get a fresh supply.

 Language Tips

1. Ask if guests have finished their order

  Practice 1

Listen to the conversation and try to answer the questions given below.

Bartender: Good evening, sir! What can I make for you tonight?

Guest: I'll have a Scotch.

Bartender: We have Chivas Regal, Old Par, Johny Walker Black and Red Labels, Cutty Sark, Queen Ann. Which would you like?

Guest: Give me a Chivas Regal.

Bartender: Royal Salute or 12 years?

Guest: Royal Salute.

Bartender: One Chivas Regal Royal Salute. And How would you like your Scotch, straight or on the rock?

Guest: With iced water.

Bartender: Here you are, sir. Scotch with iced water.

2. Ask guests what else they would like to order

  *Practice 1*

Listen to the conversation and read the bill to see what the guest has ordered. Then work in pairs to make conversations with the information given below.

Guests	Drinks	Snacks/foods
1. Mr. Brown	cognac	salad
2. Ms. Cleric	martini	shrimp
3. Mr. Howard	bottled beer	vegetable
4. Ms. Sanders	iced water	nuts
5. Mr. Ricardo	Chinese red wine	seafood

Practice 2

Fill in the blanks with the words that you will hear on the recording.

G=Guest   C=Clerk

C: Can I take your order now?

G: What special do you have for this evening?

C: Our specialty today is iced Tsingdao Beer.

G: I'll take it, please.

C: Sure. Would you like to have beer draught or bottled?

G: Draught, please.

C: Would you want to try some seafood?

G: No, thanks.

C: Is there anything you want to have to go with beer?

G: No, it's enough for me.

C: OK, your wine will be ready soon.

Give It a Try

 Task 1

The clerk is taking an order. Listen to the recording and write down the proper information in the form.

C=Clerk　　**G**=Guest

C: Good evening, sir. May I have your name, please?

G: Landers. I've made a reservation, a table for three by the fountain.

C: This way, please.

　　...

C: Excuse me, Mr. Landers. May I take your order now?

G: Yes... but I've no idea what to drink. Can you give us any recommendation, please?

C: Would you like to try some local beer in Beijing? How about Tsingdao or Beijing Beer?

G: Since we are in Beijing, we'd like to have Beijing Beer.

C: Bottled or draught?

G: Bottled. Six, please.

C: OK, sir. Would you like to have anything to go with your beer?

G: Could we have some snacks here?

C: Certainly. Anything else?

G: No, thanks.

C: You will be served soon.

Unit 8

Part A

Focus on Language

 Conversation

Reserving a Table through the Telephone

 Listen to the conversation and read after it. Then try to find answers to the questions.

B=Bartender　　**G**=Guest

B: Good evening, sir. What can I make for you tonight?

G: I'll have a Scotch.

B: We have Chivas Regal, Old Par, Johny Walker Black and Red Labels, Cutty Sark, Queen Ann. Which would you like?

G: Give me a Chivas Regal.

B: Royal Salute or 12 years?

G: 12 years.

B: One Chivas Regal 12 years. And how would you like your Scotch, straight or on the rock?

G: Staight.

B: Here you are, sir. Straight Scotch.

G: Thank you.

1. Asking what guests specially require

 Practice 1

Listen to the conversation and fill the blanks with the words you will hear. Then check it in pairs.

G=Guest   **C**=Clerk

C: Good evening, sir. Can I help you?

G: Yes, I'd like to try something special here.

C: What would you like to have, beer or wine?

G: Wine, please. Could you give me any recommendation?

C: Sure. We have Brandy, Gin and Sherry. We also have some strong wines.

G: How about Vermouth?

C: Yes. How do you like it?

G: Chilled, but not too much.

C: OK. Anything else would you like to have?

G: No, thanks. It's enough for me.

C: Thank you. Your wine will be ready soon.

3. Serving guests

 Practice

Listen to the conversation and try to answer the questions given below.

1. What does the sommelier do in a bar?
2. What does the guest order?
3. How does the sommelier serve the guest?
4. What does he say to the guest when he serves him?

G=Guest   **S**=Sommelier

S: Your Muscatel, sir. May I serve it now?

G: Sure, go ahead.

S: How is it, sir?

G: Very good.

S: May I decant it now to allow it to breathe?

G: Yes, please.

S: (Pouring the wine) Please tell me when it is enough.

G: OK, that's enough.

S: Thank you. Please enjoy.

4. Serving during the drink

 Practice

Listen and read the conversation, and try to tell dos and do nots during the service.

G=Guest   **C**=Clerk

C: Your Champagne, sir. Please enjoy.

G: Thank you.

C: Excuse me, may I take your glass?

G: Sure, go ahead.

C: Would you like to have anything else?

G: Please give the menu. I'd like to try some snacks.

C: Here you are.

G: I'd like to have a chocolate pudding.

C: OK. Your pudding will be ready soon.

Part B

Focus on Language

 Conversation

Asking the Guests to Pay the Bill

 Listen to the conversation and read after it. Then try to find the answers to the questions.

B=Bartender   **G**=Guest

B: OK. One Chivas Regal Royal Salute. And how would you like your Scotch?

G: With iced water.

B: Here you are, sir. Scotch with iced water.

G: Thank you. Now how much do I owe you?

B: The Chivas Regal Royal Salute is 40 *yuan* plus 10% service charge. So the total is 44 *yuan*. You can hold the payment of the bill until you decide to leave if you like.

G: Really? In American bars you pay drink by drink as you get it.

B: But isn't that too much of trouble?

G: Well, yes, it is. But then it is much safer. You see, American bars can be very crowded and it is very hard to keep an eye on everyone. Besides you can never know what may happen when people drink too much.

B: I see. But we've never met with any experience of a guest sneaking out on us without paying his bill or a situation where the guest is unable to pay his bill or refuses to pay his bill.

G: Well, you've been pushing your luck and you've been lucky so far. That's all. OK, here is 45 *yuan* and you can keep the change.

B: That's very kind of you, sir. But there is no tipping in China. And here is the change.

1. Asking guests if they have finished

 Practice 1

Listen and read the conversation. Then work in pairs to practise it by turn.

G=Guest   **C**=Clerk

G: Hi, waiter.

C: Yes, sir. Can I help you?

G: Please give me the menu. I'd like to try something special here.

C: Sure. Here you are.

G: Local brew, Beijing Beer, two bottles, please.

C: OK. You will be served soon.

...

C: Excuse me, sir. How is Beijing Beer?

G: Very good. I like it very much. Can I have the bill please?

C: Yes, a moment, please.

2. Telling guests how much is owed

 Practice 1

Listen to the conversation and fill in the blanks.

G=Guest   **C**=Clerk

G: Could I have the bill, please?

C: Yes, Mr. Brown. Here it is.

G: How much do I owe you?

C: That amounts to 70 *yuan*.

G: Can I pay that in US dollars?

C: Yes, you can. Let me see. It is 10 US dollars at today's exchange rate.

G: I see. Here you are. 15 dollars. You can keep the change.

C: Thank you. Here are your bill and receipt.

G: Thank you.

 Practice 2

Fill in the blanks with the words that you will hear on the recording.

G=Guest   **C**=Clerk

G: Could I have the <u>bill</u>, please?

C: Yes, sir. A bill for each or a check for all?

G: A bill for <u>all</u>.

C: Here it is, sir.

G: How much?

C: That amounts to 98 *yuan*.

G: How much is that in US dollars?

C: Let me see. It is 14 US dollars.

G: I see. Can I pay by Master Card?

C: Certainly, sir.

G: Here you are.

C: Thank you. Here are your bill and receipt, sir. Have a nice day.

G: Thank you.

3. Asking guests to pay the bill

 **Practice 1**

Listen to the conversation and try to answer the questions.

G=Guest　　　**C**=Clerk

G: Give me the bill, please.

C: Yes, sir. Just a moment, please. (He unfolds the folder and the guest goes over it.)

G: What's this for?

C: It's for the Semi-Dry Wine and Whisky…

G: I see. And what's this for?

C: That's for the Tsingdao Beer.

G: OK. Here is 100 *yuan*. Give me the receipt, please.

C: Yes, sir. I will. Here're the change and the receipt.

G: Thank you.

C: We look forward to your coming back again.

G: We will.

Give It a Try

  Task 2

Listen and complete the following conversations:

W=Waiter　　　**G**=Guest

1. **W**: Would you like any salad?

   G: No, we're full. I'd like to have the bill now.

   W: A bill for each or a bill for all?

   G: A bill for all. It's my treat.

   W: How would you like to settle the bill, sir?

   G: By credit card. Here's it.

   W: I'm sorry. But not Diner's Club. We only accept Visa, American Express and Master.

English for Food and Beverages

    G: Well, I don't have them about me.

    W: Are you staying in the hotel?

    G: Yes, my room number is 2305.

    W: In that case, you can <u>sign the bill to your room</u>.

    G: OK, thanks.

2. G: Waiter, the bill please.

    W: <u>Yes, sir. Here you are.</u>

    G: What's this for?

    W: <u>Blush Rose Wine and Liqueur.</u>

    G: I see.

    W: <u>Please sign your name here.</u>

    G: I'll sign the bill.

    W: Please put your room number here.

    G: OK. Thank you.

Do Extension Activities

 Activity 1

Listen to the conversation and write down the proper information in the form according to the conversation.

C=Clerk   **G1**=Guest 1   **G2**=Guest 2

G1: Hello, waiter!

C: Yes, sir. May I help you?

G1: The bill, please.

C: One bill or separate bills?

G1: Two separate bills.

C: Yes, sir. How would you like to settle the bill?

G1: I'll sign my bill in cash. Here is US $100.

G2: Can I pay by credit card?

C: Yes, of course.

G2: Do you accept Master Card?

C: Yes, sir.

G2: Here you are.

C: Thank you.

    ...

C: Excuse me, sir. Here're your card and the receipt.

G1: Thank you.

Unit 9

Part A

Focus on Language

  Conversation

Complaining about Drinks

 Listen to the conversation 1 and read it aloud.

W=Waiter **G**=Guest

G: Excuse me, waiter.

W: Yes, ma'am. What can I do for you?

G: I'm sorry to bother you, but I wanted a bottled mineral water, not bottled beer.

W: Sorry, Madam. Let me check the order.

G: Ok, go ahead.

W: I'm terribly sorry about that. It's my fault. Your bottled mineral water will be ready soon.

1. Making complaints in a polite way

 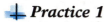 Practice 1

Listen and complete the following conversation.

(A guest is making a complaint to the headwaiter in a restaurant.)

G=Guest　　**H**=Headwaiter

G: Excuse me, are you the headwaiter? I want to have a word with you.

H: Yes, sir. What can I do for you?

G: I'm sorry to bother you, but my friend and I have been waiting 20 minutes for our drinks.

H: I'm very sorry, sir. Our staff are very busy this evening. could you tell me what you've ordered?

G: One Gin and one Sherry.

H: Don't worry. I will attend to it at once.

2. Making complaints in a direct way

  Practice 1

Listen to the conversation and read after it.

W=Waiter　　**M**=Madam

M: Jack, look what that waiter's done! Spilt drink all over my new dress!

285

W: I'm terribly sorry, madam. Perhaps if I could sponge it with a little warm water...

M: Leave it alone, man. You'll only make it worse.

W: So, what can I do for you now?

M: I want to speak to the manager! You got a big trouble.

3. Making apologies

 Practice 1

Listen to the conversation and read it after it.

M=Man   **H**=Headwaiter

M: Headwaiter, I want to have a word with you.

H: Yes, sir. Is there something wrong, sir?

M: Something wrong? I should think there is something wrong. My wife and I have been kept here waiting nearly an hour for our meal!

H: I'm terribly sorry about that, sir. Our staff has been kept unusually busy this evening. I'll see to it personally myself. Now, if you wouldn't mind just telling me what you ordered.

 Practice 3

Listen to the recording. Try to find out what the customer is complaining about and how the waiter responds. Then fill out the table below.

D1: Woman: Look at these glasses, this one's even got lipstick on it.

  Waiter: I'm very sorry, madam. I'll bring you clean ones right away.

D2: Woman: This coffee is practically cold.

  Waiter: I am sorry, madam. I'll bring you a fresh pot straight away.

D3: Woman: Waiter, this just won't do. This wine's got a most peculiar flavor.

  Waiter: Sorry, sir. I'll take it back. Perhaps you would like to choose another wine instead, sir?

D4: Man: Three gin and tonics, please.

  Waiter: I'm sorry, sir. But we're not allowed to serve drinks before 12 o'clock midday. Would you like me to bring you something else? Some coffee?

D5: Woman: Waiter, this table-cloth is a disgrace. It's covered with soup stains.

  Waiter: Oh, I'm so sorry, madam. It should have been changed before. If you'll just wait one moment.

Part B

Focus on Language

 Conversation

Complaining about Meat and Food

Listen to the conversation and read after it. Then do the following conversation in pairs and try to find the answers to the questions above.

W=Waiter   **G**=Guest

G: Waiter! This meal is like old leather! It's enough to break every tooth in your head.

W: Perhaps you'd like to change your order, sir. The steak is very tender.

G: Ok, man. I think I'll have the steak.

W: How would you like your steak cooked?

G: Rare for me, please.

Language Tips

1. Complaining about food

 Practice 2

Listen to the conversation and answer the following questions.

G=Guest   **H**=Headwaiter

G: Waiter.

H: Yes, madam?

G: This coffee is too weak.

H: I'm sorry, madam. I'll get you another one. Is everything all right?

G: No, this meat was recommended, but it is not fresh.

H: Oh! Sorry to hear that. This is quite unusual as we have fresh meat from the market every day.

G: So what? It is not fresh and I am not happy about it.

H: I'm terribly sorry, madam. I'll look into the matter. I can give you something else, if you'd like a change. That would be on us, of course.

G: No. Thanks. I don't want to find it is not fresh again! This is very annoying.

H: I see, madam. Just give us another chance. I'm sure everything will be all right again the next time you come.

G: all right. I'll come again.

H: Thank you very much, madam.

2. Complaining about service

Practice 2

Listen to the conversation carefully and try to fill in the blanks with the missing words.

G=Guest **W**=Waiter

G: Waitress.

W: Yes, madam.

G: You've been ignoring us since we were seated.

W: I'm terribly sorry. We are short of hands.

G: You've kept us waiting for almost half an hour. How long are we going to wait for our dinner?

W: Let me see your order. I'm afraid roast duck takes quite a while to prepare. Would you like a drink while you're waiting?

G: No, thanks.

Give It a Try

 Task 2

Listen to the restaurant jokes and complete the answers given by the waiter.

1. Waiter, there's a fly in my soup.
   I think it's doing the backstroke, sir.
2. Waiter, there's a fly in my soup.
   That's impossible. A dead fly can't swim.
3. Waiter, there's a fly in my soup.
   Yes, sir. It's the hot liquid that killed them.
4. Waiter, there's a fly in my soup.
   Yes, sir. We give extra rations on Fridays.
5. Waiter, there's a fly in my soup.
   Don't worry, sir. There is no extra charge.

Unit 10

Part A

Focus on Language

 Conversation

Complaining about Service

Listen to the conversation and read after it. Then do the conversation in pairs and try to find the answers to the questions above.

H=Hostess **G**=Guest

H: Good evening, madam.

G: Good evening. My name is Fiona. I have booked a table for two for 7:00.

H: Ah, Ms Fiona. That's right, a table for two. Would you come this way, please? Here is your table.

G: Oh, no. It's not the right table I ordered. I have told you I would like a table by the window. And you promised me one when I made the reservation. Please, check it out.

H: I am sorry, madam. We will check the reservation soon.

G: Ok.

H: I am terribly sorry, madam. It's our fault. We have double booked the table you wanted. And now, it's occupied. Would you like to change a table or wait for the table you booked?

G: Oh, it's ridiculous. I want to see your manager...

Language Tips

1. Making complaints about service

Practice 2

Listen to the conversation carefully, then try to fill out the blanks in the conversation.

H=Hostess **G**=Guest

H: Good evening, madam.

G: Good evening. My name is Fiona. I have <u>booked a table</u> for two for 7:00.

H: Ah, Ms Fiona. That's right, a table for two. Would you come <u>this way</u>, please? Here is your table.

G: Oh, no. It's not the right table I ordered. I have told you I'd like a table <u>by the window</u>. And you <u>promised me one</u> when I made the reservation. Please, check it out.

H: I am sorry, madam. We will check the reservation soon.

G: Ok.

H: I am terribly sorry, madam. It's our fault. We <u>have double booked the table</u> you wanted. And now, <u>it's occupied</u>. Would you like to change a table or wait for the table you booked?

G: Oh, it's ridiculous. I want to <u>see your manager</u>...

2. Saying "No" politely when you cannot do any help

Practice 1

Listen to the conversation carefully and answer the questions below.

M=Manager   **G**=Guest

M: Excuse me, madam. I am the manager of the restaurant. I have heard what happened to you. I am sorry to hear that.

G: What happened to me? I was badly treated. I must complain about the service here.

M: Okay, madam. Would you mind coming with me to my office and telling me what exactly happened there?

G: By all means, I just want to get my table back now...

M: Sit down, please. I sincerely apologize for the inconvenience. However, I have checked your

289

reservation. It says you booked the table for 7 p.m. But it was 7:35 when you arrived here this evening. So...

G: So what? My car broke down on the way here.

M: We only keep the reservation half an hour at dinner time. That is the policy in our restaurant. The receptionist must have told this when you booked the table by phone.

G: Just five minutes late? It is unfair.

M: That is the rule. I am sorry for that. You can take another table and a free drink. Otherwise, I can't do any further.

Part B

Start You Off

  Activity 1

Listen to the following text about how to complain in a restaurant or a bar three times and try to fill in the blanks with the exact words you have just heard.

 Being a customer, you have the right to make complaints and ask for the compensation, if you are dissatisfied with the food, drink or service in a restaurant or a bar. However, before you do so, just calm down and be clear in your own mind what you want to happen as a result of making a complaint. Do you want an apology? Do you want a different decision? Do you want the proper service that should have been provided in the first place? Do you want replaced goods? You should mention this to the right person or department you are complaining to and ask for prompt action, for instance, the waiter, (or the waitress) the head waiter, the duty manager, even customer services department. Finally, if none of them can help you, court or arbitration services maybe the final choice.

Focus on Language

 Conversation

Complaining about Meat and Food

 Listen to the conversation and read after it. Then do the conversation in pairs and try to find the answers to the questions above.

W=Waiter   **G**=Guest

G: Waiter.

W: Yes, madam?

G: This coffee is too weak.

W: I'm sorry, madam. I'll get you another one. Is everything all right?

G: No, this fish was recommended, but it is not fresh.

W: Oh! Sorry to hear that. This is quite unusual as we have fresh fish from the market every day.

G: Who knows? It is not fresh and I am not happy about it.

W: I'm terribly sorry, madam. I'll look into the matter. I can give you something replaced, if you'd like a change. That would be our treat, of course.

G: It is very kind of you, but I suffered too much here. All that I need is fresh and healthy food. I don't want to trouble anyone. No more, thanks.

W: Just feel ease, madam. Please give us another chance. I'm sure everything will be all right again the next time you come.

G: I hope so.

W: Thank you very much, madam.

Language Tips

1. How to deal with the complaints properly

Practice 2

Listen to the following conversation and complete it according to the context.

D: Waiter.

W: Yes, madam?

D: This steak is too raw. I have told you I want it well-done.

W: I'm so sorry, madam. Would you wait it for a little longer?

D: How long will that be done?

W: Just 5 minutes. Would you like a salad, while you're waiting?

D: No, thanks, but I want them in a hurry.

W: Yes, madam.

2. How to deal with the trouble caused by the guest

Practice 1

Listen to the conversation and answer the quertions below.

M=Manager   **G**=Guest

M: Good evening, sir. I'm the manager of the restaurant.

G: Ah, good evening.

M: I'm afraid we've had a complaint about the noise from your neighbors around your table. They are trying to get a nice and quiet dinner in this restaurant. I'm sure you understand.

G: Oh, I see. We are having birthday party. We are singing "Happy Birthday" to the birthday boy and cutting the cake.

M: Could we ask you and your friends to keep the noise down a little? We do like to give our guests a chance of getting a perfect meal here.

G: Oh, I'm sorry. I suppose we were talking rather loudly. We were having a bit of celebration.

M: I'm pleased to hear it. I still have another word with you.

G: Ok, go ahead.

M: I had a report from my staff that one of your friends was drunk, and he broke a vase in the lounge.

G: Yeah, he is a bit drunk. Well, just a few little things. I don't think you will expect us to pay for that, manager.

M: I'm sorry, sir. As the restaurant policy, I'm afraid that you have to pay for the damage.

G: You don't have right to do so. My friend didn't mean to do that. It's an accident.

M: Sorry, if you think so, we'll call the police to handle this.

G: Oh, come on. Don't do that. We'll pay for the damage.

附录

酒的名称

白兰地（Brandy）

人头马 V.S.O.P. Remy Martin V.S.O.P. 法国
人头马 X.O. Remy Martin XO. 法国
人头马路易十三 Remy Martin Louis 13 法国
人头马拿破仑 Remy Martin Napoleon 法国
人头马特级 Club De Remy Martin 法国
轩尼诗 XO. Hennessy X.O. Cognac 法国
轩尼诗 V.S.O.P. Hennessy V.SO.P. 法国
长颈 F.O.V. Cognac 法国
御鹿 V.S.O.P., Hine V.S:O.P. 法国
御鹿 XO. Hine XO. 法国
万事好 V.SO.P. Raynal V.SO.P. 法国
万事好 XO. Raynal XO. 法国
金牌马爹利 Martell Medaillon 法国
蓝带马爹利 Martell Corden blue 法国
马爹利 XO. Martell XO. 法国
奥吉尔 V.S.O.P. Augier V.S.O.P. 法国
奥吉尔 XO. Augier XO. 法国
麦迪沙五星 Metexerbrandy 5-star 法国
雪里玉 V.S.O.P. Salignac Cognee V.S.O.P. 法国
登喜路 V.S.O.P. Dunhill V.S.O.P. 法国
拿破仑 XO. Courvoisier XO. 法国
豪达 V.S.O.P. Otard V.S.O.P. 法国
金花 V.S.O.P. Camus XO. 法国
百事吉 V.SO.P. Bisquit V.S.O.P. 法国

威士忌类（Whisky）

占边 Jim Beam Bourbon Whiskey 美国
威雀 Famous Grouse Whisky 苏格兰
龙津十二年 Long John 12 years Whisky 苏格兰
白马 White Horse Whisky 苏格兰
红方 Joannie Walker Red lable 苏格兰
黑方 Johnnie Walker Black lable 苏格兰
老伯 Old Parr Whisky 苏格兰
金铃 Bell's Extra Special 苏格兰
天宝十五年 Dimple 15 years 苏格兰
芝华士十二年 Chivas Regal 12 years 苏格兰
护照 Passport Scotch Whisky 苏格兰
安尼皇后 Queen Anne Scotch Whisky 苏格兰
皇家礼炮 12 年 Royal Salute 12 years 苏格兰
兰利 Glenlivet Scotch Whisky 苏格兰
施格兰 V.O. Seagrartis V.O. Whisky 加拿大
四玫瑰 Four Roses Bourbon Whiskey 美国
皇冠 Crown Royal 加拿大
七冠 Seven Crown Whiskey 美国
格兰 Grant's Blended 苏格兰
格兰 12 年 Grant's 12 years Deluxe 苏格兰
格兰菲迪 Glenfiddich 爱尔兰
珍宝 J&B 苏格兰
顺风 Cutty Sark 苏格兰
登喜路 Dunhill 苏格兰
百龄坛 Ballantine's 苏格兰
加拿大俱乐部 Canadian Club 加拿大
杰克·丹尼尔斯 Jack Daniel's 美国
三得利皇冠 Suntory Royal 日本

金酒类（Gin）

建尼路金 Greenall's 英国	钻石金 Gilbey's 英国
哥顿金 Gordon's 英国	水晶宫金 Crystal Palace 英国
伯纳特金 Burnett's 英国	必富达金 Befeater 英国
布多恩金 Boodle's 英国	莱利金 Lariors 英国

朗姆酒类（Rum）

百家地 Bacardi Rum 巴西
奇峰 Mount Gry Rum 英国

伏特加酒（Vodka）

芬兰伏特加 Finlandia 芬兰	绿牌伏特加 Moskovskaya 俄罗斯
红牌伏特加 Stolichnaya 俄罗斯	皇冠伏特加 Smirnoff 俄罗斯

特基拉酒（Tequila）

凯尔弗 Jose Cuervo White Tequila 墨西哥	白金武士 Conquistador 墨西哥
金快活 Cuervo Special Gold Tequila 墨西哥	

利口酒（Liqueur）

佳连露 Galliano Liqueur 意大利	薄荷蜜 27 Get 27 Peppermint（G/W）法国
芳津杏仁 Amaretto 法国	皮特樱桃甜酒 Peter Hearing 丹麦
君度 Cointreau 法国	金巴利 Campari 意大利
飘仙 1 号 Pimm's NO.1 英国	苦精 Bitters 西班牙
咖啡利口 Coffee Liqueur 荷兰	苹果白兰地 Calvados 法国
棕可可甜酒 Creme de Cacao Brown 荷兰	椰子酒 Malibu Liqueur 牙买加
杏仁白兰地 Apricot Brandy 荷兰	百利甜酒 Bailey's 爱尔兰
白可可甜酒 Creme de Cacao White 荷兰	安德卜格 Underberg 德国
橙味甜酒 Triple Sec 荷兰	咖啡蜜酒 Kahlua 墨西哥
蜜瓜酒 Melon Liqueur 荷兰	蓝橙酒 Blue Curacao 美国
樱桃酒 Kirchwasser 荷兰	蛋黄酒 Advocaat 荷兰
香草酒 Marschino 荷兰	天万利 Tia Maria 牙买加
黑加仑酒 Black Cassis 荷兰	金万利 Grand Mania 牙买加
石榴糖浆 Grenadine Syrup 荷兰	杜本那 Dubonnet Red 法国
杜林标 Drambuie 英国	当姆香草利口酒 Benedictinea 法国
潘诺茵香酒 Penoal 英国	

开胃酒 (Aperitif)

哈维斯些厘 Harvey's Sherry 西班牙
干仙山 99 Cizano Vermouth Dry 意大利
红仙山露. Cizano Vermouth Sweet 意大利
马天尼(红)Martini Rosso 意大利
马天尼(干)Martini Dry 意大利
马天尼(半干)Martini Bianco 意大利

参 考 文 献

[1] Andrew E, Bennett （美）*English for Restaurant Workers*，北京：外语教学与研究出版社，2007年3月

[2] Andrew E, Bennett （美）*English for Hotel Workers*，北京：外语教学与研究出版社，2006年10月

[3] Edward G. Seidensticker，*Modern American Colloquialism*，北京：外语教学与研究出版社，1990年12月

[4] Grahame T. Bilbow, John Sutton.《郎文现代酒店业英语》，北京：外语教学与研究出版社，2005

[5] Keane L. *International Restaurant English*. Cambridge: Prentice Hall International (UK) Ltd., 1990

[6] 艾丽丽，《宾馆餐饮英语急用话题124个》，北京：中国宇航出版社，2007年9月

[7] 蔡寒松，《酒楼餐厅英语》，广州：广东旅游出版社，2001年9月

[8] 郭兆康等，《宾馆英语》，北京：高等教育出版社，2003年7月

[9] 浩瀚等，《敢说酒店宾馆英语》，北京：中国水利出版社，2008年1月

[10] 金惠康、罗向阳，《酒楼服务英语》，广州：广东旅游出版社，2006年1月

[11] 李秀斌主编，《现代餐饮英语实务教程》，广州：世界图书出版公司，2007年9月

[12] 李佳主编，《饭店英语》，北京：化学工业出版社，2007年1月

[13] 李秀斌，《现代餐饮英语实务教程》，北京：世界图书出版社，2006年6月

[14] 李广荣，《宾馆服务英语》，广州：广东旅游出版社，2006年3月

[15] 罗伯特·马杰尔，《餐饮英语》，北京：旅游教育出版社，2003年8月

[16] 潘素玲、赵丽，《旅游涉外饭店实用英语（听说部分）》，中央编译出版社，2002年9月

[17] 盛丽生等，《英语习语大辞典》，北京：商务印书馆，2003年3月

[18] 孙冰，《餐饮管理英语入门》，北京：清华大学出版社、北京交通大学出版社，2007年11月

[19] 唐莉主编，《饭店情景英语》，北京：中国人民大学出版社，2007年11月

[20] 邢怡主编，《餐饮英语》，北京：高等教育出版社，2006年5月

[21] 肖璇，《现代酒店英语实务教程》，广州：世界图书出版公司，2007年9月

[22] 杨淑惠，《旅游英语》，天津：天津科技翻译出版社、天津外语音像出版社，2007年10月